Bringing Knowledge Back In

'This book tackles some of the most important educational questions of the day. It is rare to find a book on education which is theoretically sophisticated and practically relevant: this book is' (from the Foreword by Professor Hugh Lauder).

What is it in the twenty-first century that we want young people, and adults returning to study, to know? What is it about the kind of knowledge that people can acquire at school, college or university that distinguishes it from the knowledge that people acquire in their everyday lives, at work, and in their families?

Bringing Knowledge Back In draws on recent developments in the sociology of knowledge to propose answers to these key, but often overlooked, educational questions. Michael Young traces the changes in his own thinking about the question of knowledge in education, since his first book *Knowledge and Control*, published in 1971, and *The Curriculum of the Future* (Falmer Press 1998). This rethinking partly reflects his own experience as a policy analyst and advisor in the UK, South Africa and a number of other countries. He argues for the continuing relevance of the writings of Durkheim and Vygotsky and the unique importance of Basil Bernstein's often under-appreciated work. He illustrates the importance of questions about knowledge by investigating the dilemmas faced by researchers and policy makers in a range of fields; these include the integration of academic and vocational learning, the role of qualifications in educational reform, professional and vocational education, curriculum theory, and the assessment of experiential learning. He also considers the broader issue of the role of sociologists in relation to educational policy in the context of increasingly interventionist governments. The book:

- provides conceptual tools for people to think and debate about knowledge and education in new ways;
- provides clear expositions of difficult ideas at the interface of epistemology and the sociology of knowledge;
- makes explicit links between theoretical issues and practical/policy questions;
- offers a clear focus for the future development of the sociology of education as a key field within educational studies.

This compelling and provocative book will be essential reading for anyone involved in research and debates about the curriculum as well as those with a specific interest in the sociology of education.

Michael F.D. Young is Professor of Education at the Institute of Education, University of London, and in the Department of Education at the University of Bath, UK.

Bringing Knowledge Back In

From social constructivism to social
realism in the sociology of education

Michael F.D. Young

Routledge
Taylor & Francis Group

LONDON AND NEW YORK

First published 2008
by Routledge
2 Park Square, Milton Park, Abingdon, Oxon OX14 4RN

Simultaneously published in the USA and Canada
by Taylor & Francis Inc
711 Third Avenue, New York, NY 10017

Routledge is an imprint of the Taylor & Francis Group, an informa business

© 2008 Michael F.D. Young

Typeset in Times by
GreenGate Publishing Services, Tonbridge, Kent

Every effort has been made to ensure that the advice and information in this book
is true and accurate at the time of going to press. However, neither the publisher
nor the authors can accept any legal responsibility or liability for any errors or
omissions that may be made. In the case of drug administration, any medical
procedure or the use of technical equipment mentioned within this book, you are
strongly advised to consult the manufacturer's guidelines.

British Library Cataloguing in Publication Data
A catalogue record for this book is available from the British Library

Library of Congress Cataloguing in Publication Data
Young, Michael F.D.
  Bringing knowledge back in : from social constructivism to social
realism in the sociology of education / Michael F. D. Young.
     p. cm.
  Includes bibliographical references.
  1. Educational sociology. 2. Education–Curricula. 3.
  Constructivism (Education) I. Title.
  LC191.Y568 2007
   306.43–dc22
2007017238

ISBN-10: 0–415–32120–4 (hbk)
ISBN-10: 0–415–32121–2 (pbk)
ISBN-10: 0–203–07366–5 (ebk)

ISBN-13: 978–0–415–32120–4 (hbk)
ISBN-13: 978–0–415–32121–1 (pbk)
ISBN-13: 978–0–203–07366–7 (ebk)

**For my daughters
Alice and Elinor**

'WHAT *is Truth?*' said jesting Pilate; and would not stay for an answer...

... Truth, which only doth judge itself, teacheth that the Inquiry of truth, which is the love-making or wooing of it, the knowledge of truth, which is the presence of it, and the belief of truth, which is the enjoying of it, is the sovereign good of human nature.

(Francis Bacon (1597) *Essays*)

Contents

Foreword

Ever since the publication of *Knowledge and Control* in 1971, Michael Young has played a major role in debates within the sociology of education. His writing, both theoretical and applied, has crossed the borders between epistemology and social theory. In this book he tackles some of the most important educational questions of the day: the academic vocational divide that has so troubled educationists and policy makers, the legitimacy of qualifications frameworks, the nature of professional educational knowledge, the status and legitimacy of policies in relation to the recognition of prior learning, and most importantly of all the role of knowledge and curriculum in today's test-driven competency-based approaches to education. At times he links topics such as the nature of professional knowledge with the critique of test- and market-driven education in a novel account of what he calls 'the nationalization' of education. This book also gains from the comparative dimension he is able to bring from his study of educational developments in South Africa. He has been a keen observer and participant in South African educational policy and the themes that are developed in the book are brought into sharp relief by his experience there.

This discussion, by a writer of Michael Young's stature, will ensure that the book is widely read but it is a far more ambitious work than it first appears because there is a common framework underlying the issues he tackles. While, in his earlier years, he could be interpreted as a relativist in that he viewed knowledge and the curriculum as a manifestation of power rather than having secure grounds in a defensible view of knowledge, he has now moved on. His project is to recognize that knowledge is socially produced but that it also requires warrant independent of social interests and the related dynamics of power. To this end he develops what he calls a social realist account of knowledge: social because it recognizes the role of human agents in the production of knowledge and realist because he wishes to stress the context independence of knowledge and, crucially for his views on the curriculum, the discontinuities between knowledge and common sense.

In order to mark out this social realist account of knowledge, he needs to address a series of tensions: the first is that between the 'social' and the 'realist'. Since the social world is subject to change, it follows that conceptions of what constitutes knowledge rather than opinion are also subject to change; this raises problems about the criteria by which knowledge is determined. At the same time, the idea that there is context-independent knowledge (realism, in Young's terms) suggests that there is some skilful negotiation necessary through the waters of an empiricist foundationalism on the one hand and the relativism that he now rejects on the other. At root this comes down to a tension between stability and change. Empiricist accounts of knowledge were stable because the foundations of knowledge were rooted in a naive view of observation and the truth-preserving qualities of induction and later deduction. Once such foundations are considered untenable the crucial epistemological question turns on the judgements we make between competing knowledge claims, or more precisely, theories.

This is Michael Young's domain and he returns to some of the great social theorists and philosophers – Durkheim, Vygotsky, Cassirer and Bernstein – to transcend the tensions in the position that he seeks to develop and defend. His chapters on Durkheim, Vygotsky and the nature of knowledge are exemplars in the use of theories developed in the early twentieth century to address twenty-first-century questions. Not only does he make original use of their work in the service of his position but he reminds a younger generation that the issues with which he is struggling have a history that extends beyond the latest fashionable theorists in the sociology of education.

Indeed, the chapter that sets the tenor of the book, 'Curriculum studies and the problem of knowledge', is subtitled 'updating the Enlightenment?', and it is in this subtitle that Michael Young nails his colours to the mast. In opposition to the nihilism associated with much of the relativism of postmodern thought and his own acute awareness of the role of powerful interests in the way knowledge and the curriculum can be shaped, he is attempting to preserve the notion of progress in education and particularly in relation to knowledge. Theoretically he is concerned with the way knowledge progresses and why some areas of enquiry, e.g. the natural sciences, appear to progress in ways that the social sciences do not. Practically he applies these concerns to a critique of curricula that endorse 'common sense' and deprive students, especially those from less powerful social groups, of the systematic structures of thought that distinguish knowledge and enable a critical understanding of the natural and social world.

It is rare to find a book in education which is theoretically sophisticated and practically relevant: this book is. It should be valued because while Young raises as many questions as he answers he does not shirk from the difficulty of the task he has set himself, thereby inviting a necessary conversation with past theorists and the present generation of academics, policy makers and teachers. There never has been a more important time to return to the basic questions that underlie education.

Hugh Lauder
Professor of Education and Political Economy,
University of Bath

Acknowledgements

Most of the work that led to this book has been undertaken while I have been Emeritus Professor of Education at the Institute of Education, University of London. My first thanks therefore are to the Institute, and in particular to its Director, Geoff Whitty, whom I have been fortunate to know as a professional colleague and a friend for almost 40 years, to my Head of School, Sue Hallam, and to Richard Noss, Director of the London Knowledge Laboratory, for their support. I have been most fortunate in my close colleagues at the Institute of Education; especially David Guile, Norman Lucas, Jan Derry, Lorna Unwin, Judy Harris and Michael Barnett. Many others, in particular Zoe Fearnley, Bob Cowen, Ingrid Lunt, Elaine Unterhalter, Frank Coffield, Alex Moore, John Hardcastle, Paddy Walsh and Gerald Grace, have been no less supportive in different ways.

Since September 2006 I have also held a part-time post at the University of Bath, and have been equally fortunate in my colleagues there – in particular, Hugh Lauder, Ian Jamieson, Harry Daniels, Rajani Naidoo and Maria Ballerin. They have made me most welcome as a new colleague. I am especially grateful to Hugh Lauder both for the initial invitation to work at Bath and for agreeing to write the foreword to this book.

Like most intellectual communities, the ones in which I have worked, which cut across a number of policy and disciplinary boundaries, are far from limited to one institution or one country. In the UK, the colleagues from whom I have learned most are Ian Hextall, Phil Hodkinson, Richard Winter, David Raffe, Harry Daniels, Peter Medway, John Beck, Rob Moore, John West, Ron Tuck and Keith Brooker. In other countries, I would like to mention those in South Africa (Joe Muller, Peter Kallaway, Jeanne Gamble, Andre Kraak, Stephanie Allais and Peliwe Lolwana), Australia (Jack Keating), Norway (Karen Jensen), Finland (Ari Antikainen) and Brazil (Antonio Flavio).

My special thanks also go to Anna Clarkson (RoutledgeFalmer) for her patience in waiting for a much delayed manuscript, to her colleague Amy Crowle for getting the manuscript turned into a book so efficiently and to Lizzie Andrew at the London Knowledge Laboratory for her remarkably calm and efficient work on my text. I am most grateful to my friend Jack Mallinson, not only for the quote from Francis Bacon but for constantly reminding me that though sociologists of education may need to develop new concepts, this is no excuse for being obscure.

Thanks too to Charmian and Cyril Cannon for continuing to ask me (but not too often!) when this book would be finished.

Chapter 2 is a revised version of a paper that I originally wrote jointly with Rob Moore (University of Cambridge) (Moore and Young 2001). Chapter 10 draws on material that I also used in a paper jointly written with John Beck (University of Cambridge) (Beck and Young 2005). Chapter 15 was written jointly with Johan Muller (University of Capetown) (Young and Muller 2007); it appears in this book unchanged. I am most grateful to all three colleagues to whom I owe far more than is expressed in our jointly published work. I hope they feel that this book makes a contribution to a project in which we all share.

Introduction

This book is about the importance of knowledge in education. It is written from the perspective of a sociologist who works in the field of curriculum studies and education more generally. However, the argument of the book is that questions such as 'what is worthwhile knowledge?' and 'what should we teach?' are important for all involved or interested in education. With the increased focus by governments on access to and participation in education on one hand, and on targets defined by qualifications on the other, the question of knowledge, or what it is that it is important that students learn, has, as a result, been neglected both by educational policy makers and by those working in educational studies. The book aims to be a contribution to overcoming that neglect.

Bringing Knowledge Back In follows *The Curriculum of the Future* (Young 1998) in charting a further stage in an intellectual journey that began in 1971 with *Knowledge and Control* (Young 1971). However, since the end of the 1990s this journey has taken a rather different course from what Geoff Whitty aptly referred to as the 'possibilitarianism' of the 'new sociology of education' of the 1970s (Whitty 1985) and the more 'policy-oriented' optimism of the 1990s that was reflected in *The Curriculum of the Future*. In contrast to *The Curriculum of the Future* and reflecting both the changing times and, I hope, a growth in my understanding, this book is more sceptical about the progressive consequences of current social and economic changes and what they might mean for education at least in the short term. As a consequence, it gives more importance to the spaces that are still available for scholarship and research in educational studies that are not directly related to particular policies and practices. As I argue in Chapter 5, although our role as sociologists of education and as members of the wider educational research community is always, in the broadest sense, political, it needs to involve less position-taking and policy advocacy, and more scholarship and rigorous analysis.

The period in which the papers that formed the basis of the chapters of this book were originally written (1999–2007) began when I read and decided to respond to Moore and Muller's critique of 'the new sociology of education' (Moore and Muller 1999). Their critique was directed, at least in part, to my own and others' work in the 1970s. Chapter 1 is a revised version of my response to their critique (Young 2000). However, in endorsing many of Moore and Muller's arguments, I am aware that I may do less than justice to the positive achievements of the 'new sociology of education'. Hindsight is too easy, and not always a reliable source of insight. Progress in developing a social realist theory of knowledge of the kind that this book makes claims for would not have been possible without the emancipatory vision of the 'new sociology of education' of the 1970s and its success in calling into question the idea of knowledge itself and its role in education. The problem, I have increasingly come to realize, and which this book tries to express, is to recognize that if an emancipatory vision of education and, it follows, the sociology of education is not to be vacuous, it must include rather than try to wish away the centrality of epistemological constraints and the inescapable reality that acquiring and producing new knowledge is never easy.

The approach to knowledge that I develop in this book is very different from the one that inspired *Knowledge and Control* and the 'new sociology of education'; hence the subtitle of the book – From social constructivism to social realism in the sociology of education. I want therefore to begin by offering a brief outline of the approach that I take in this book; the argument is developed more fully in Chapter 15.

Thinking about knowledge in education (and more generally) has to begin, I suggest, not with knowledge itself or questioning what we know and how, but with our relationship to the world of which we are a part and the symbols that we develop to perceive and make sense of it (Cassirer 2000). It is the symbolic nature of our relationship to the world that is the basis of our knowledge, and it is that relationship that distinguishes us as human beings, who create and acquire knowledge, from animals. As Aby Warburg, Cassirer's contemporary, put it: 'The conscious creation of distance between oneself and the external world may be called the fundamental act of civilization' (cited in Habermas 2001: 7). This symbolic relationship necessarily constrains the range of social and educational possibilities open to us at any particular time, in ways that I at one time thought could be 'constructed away' by political or pedagogic action. However, these constraints are not merely barriers to be overcome in the struggle for a better world or even for better understanding. They are the basis of any kind of progress in education, science, politics or personal life and therefore of any kind of knowledge. It has been coming to recognize the dual role of these fundamental constraints that has led me to change my ideas about how the question of knowledge in education should be approached – towards what this book refers to as a form of 'social realism'. Why this change is important and exploring what it might mean for the question 'what do we teach?' in a variety of contexts is what this book is about.

In bringing these papers together as a book I have found that the question of knowledge in education is more difficult than I first thought. Why might this be so? First, questions about knowledge always take us back to some of our most basic assumptions about what it is to be educated or to educate someone; they are, in the broadest sense, philosophical and political questions about who we are and what we value. This means that in this book I have set myself the almost impossible task of holding together, sometimes in the same chapter and sometimes across different chapters, issues and questions that conventionally are discussed in quite distinct specialist literatures (for example, epistemology and the sociology of knowledge, and educational policy and practice) that traditionally have had few if any connections. Inevitably this means that I do not fully grasp the complexity and detail of either set of specialist literatures, and as a result am likely frustrate a variety of readers at different points and in different chapters. My response is first that I see my primary readership as those teaching, studying and researching in educational studies, many of who are grappling with similar issues, and second, that I believe these are risks worth taking. Thinking about and debating educational issues has to be both conceptual and practical if we are going to progress, for all the pitfalls that this lays one open to. The best that I can aim for is to try and be clear about what I am attempting to do and why, and hope to stimulate debate about educational questions that are important and too often not asked. A less immediate aim is to hope that those working in fields such as the sociology of knowledge and epistemology will, like Emile Durkheim, see the importance of giving greater recognition to the value of educational issues.

In focusing on the question of knowledge one is reminded of the limits of one's own knowledge. What authority can I, as a sociologist, claim in writing about knowledge, given that, historically, ideas about knowledge in general (as opposed to the knowledge associated with different specialist disciplines) have been the specialist province of philosophers? I offer two comments on this question. The first is that sociology can also claim a tradition (the sociology of knowledge) within which asking questions about the roots of knowledge have been central. It was initiated by Emile Durkheim and Karl Mannheim, among others, almost a century ago. Furthermore, the fact that Durkheim was Professor of Education as well as Professor of Sociology at the Sorbonne is not irrelevant to the theme of this book. Of even more significance is that his lectures on the sociology of knowledge published as *Pragmatism and Sociology* (Durkheim 1983) were initially given to students attending the equivalent of a Post Graduate Certificate in Education course. He certainly was in no doubt that it was important that future teachers should think about epistemological questions. It is worth reflecting that if he lived today, it is unlikely that he would be an adviser to the Teacher Development Agency on standards!

The example of Durkheim is not to deny that more often than not the sociology of knowledge has led to the intellectual cul-de-sac of relativism. However, the fundamental importance of recognizing the social basis of knowledge remains, nearly a century after he died, and is most recently exemplified in Randall Collins's majesterial *The Sociology of Philosophies* (Collins 1998) and, in relation to education, in Basil Bernstein's last book *Pedagogy, Symbolic Control and Identity* (Bernstein 2000). My second comment is that on the issue of the fundamental sociality of human beings (and therefore of knowledge), sociology and philosophy are increasingly coming together (Cassirer 2000; Bakhurst 1995).

In making the argument that a social theory of knowledge is integral to any adequate educational theory, sociologists face two particular difficulties. The first is a tendency to slip into a form of reductionism. Reductionist social theories of knowledge are superficially attractive, especially to many on the Left. Knowledge is reduced to interests, standpoints or just knowers and all kinds of emancipatory possibilities are implied. Furthermore, such theories grasp at least a partial truth. However, sociological reductionism can too easily mean that questions about the curriculum lose their specificity and are reduced to politics. A tendency to lose what is specific to education was the trap that the 'new sociology of education' often fell into.

The alternative to reductionism which is argued for in this book follows from Durkheim's assertion that a social theory grounds the very possibility of us having objective knowledge about the world. However, such a position also has its dangers. It can easily slip from providing grounds for the authority of knowledge to being a licence for authoritarianism and losing its claims to be critical (Ballarin 2007). These are not easy dilemmas to resolve, as will be apparent in the chapters that follow.

I have found that Bernard Williams, in his book *Truth and Truthfulness* (Williams 2002), expresses these difficult issues as well as anyone. How, Williams asks, does a necessary scepticism towards truth claims avoid either arrogantly claiming to know more about specialist fields than the specialists themselves, or degenerating into the nihilist irony of those like Richard Rorty who he refers to as the 'truth deniers'? Williams's answer is that serious sceptics must set limits to their own scepticism; in other words it must be a scepticism that implies a notion of truth. As he puts it: 'you do the best you can to acquire true beliefs, and what you say reveals what you believe' (Williams 2002: 11). For Williams this is the basis for the authority of all scholarship. It is also the basis for the authority of teachers; how can one teach history, he asked in a seminar about his book at the British Academy, if one rejects the possibility of historical truth? It is a tough guide, but I have not come across a better one.

The title of this book, *Bringing Knowledge Back In*, began as the title of a paper I wrote on the neglect of the curriculum in lifelong learning policies (Young 2000). The title, but certainly not the content, owes a debt to the American sociologist George Homans, and his paper 'Bringing men back in' (Homans 1964). The subtitle, *From Social Constructivism to Social Realism*, expresses the change in my own thinking that began with the paper (Young 2000), which appears in revised form as Chapter 1.

The book is divided into two main parts: 'Theoretical issues' and 'Applied studies'. However, as will be apparent, the distinction is far from clear-cut. Although Chapters 1, 2 and 8 were written several years before the others, the chapters in each section appear only loosely in the sequence in which they were originally written. Readers will no doubt turn to them in different orders.

The chapters in Part 1 are concerned with the issue of knowledge in the sociology of education and in educational studies generally. Chapter 1, as I have already mentioned, was written as a response to the paper by Moore and Muller (1999) and begins to distinguish between different social theories of knowledge. Chapter 2 is a revised version of a paper originally written jointly with Rob Moore (Moore and Young 2001). It argues the case for a social realist approach to knowledge in the sociology of education and its implications for the curriculum. Chapters 3 and 4 arose out of being introduced to the work of Lev Vygotsky by my colleague, Harry Daniels. Chapter 3 draws on the parallels that I saw between Vygotsky's ideas and those of his near contemporary, Emile Durkheim, in addressing the role of knowledge in the curriculum and the form it should take. The chapters follow two themes. The first is to explore how far Vygotsky's dialectical approach can be the basis for overcoming the tendency for social realist theories like Durkheim's to be static and unable to deal adequately with historical change. The second theme is to explore why the activity theory research traditions which have such strong roots in Vygotsky's ideas have neglected the question of knowledge and in particular the theory implicit in his key distinction between theoretical and everyday concepts. Chapter 5 began as a contribution to a series of seminars at the Institute of Education on the theme 'Rethinking Curriculum Studies'. It begins to explore the implications for curriculum studies of the approach to knowledge developed in Chapter 3. Chapter 6 takes a rather different approach. It sets out to bring together the issues raised by two strands within the sociology of education which have had few links in the past. I am referring to the strand concerned with privatization and the role of the state, and that concerned with knowledge and the curriculum. The chapter argues that recent trends in educational policy can usefully be seen as a form of the 'nationalization of educational knowledge'. Chapter 7 concludes Part 1 by reflecting on my experience of trying to influence educational policy in England and South Africa, and the wider issues that this raises about the political role of the sociology of education.

The chapters in Part 2 relate the more general questions about knowledge discussed in Part 1 to specific curricular issues, largely but not solely in the field of post-compulsory education. Chapter 8 is only indirectly concerned with the question of knowledge in education. However, in its focus on the ways that governments are increasingly using qualifications to drive educational reform, it sets the policy context for the later chapters. Chapter 9 on vocational knowledge was originally presented at an Economic and Social Research Council (ESRC) workshop on Workplace Learning. It starts with the dual purposes of modern vocational education and draws on the debate between social theories of knowledge to argue for a reconceptualization of the vocational curriculum. Chapter 10 draws on some of Basil Bernstein's less well known ideas to consider the extent to which the knowledge base of professionals is increasingly being undermined by current trends for greater regulation and marketization. Chapter 11 focuses on the issue of academic/vocational divisions in the post-compulsory curriculum and presents a critical reassessment of the case for unification that I and others argued for in the 1990s. Chapters 12–14 arise out my work in South Africa (Kraak and Young 2001; Young and Gamble 2006) and pick up some issues raised in Chapter 7. They have a more specific policy focus; at the same time they seek to maintain the knowledge/education link developed in earlier chapters. Chapter 12 is concerned with the knowledge base of vocational teachers in FET (further education and training) colleges in South Africa, and draws some parallels with the situation in the UK. Chapter 13 addresses the question of RPL (recognition of prior learning), which is a particular concern in the South African context, but has much wider implications. An underlying theme of the chapter is how far adults who were denied formal education under apartheid can be compensated by equating their experience with formal qualifications. Chapter 14 raises more general issues within educational debates in South Africa. It argues for the relevance of the book's overall thesis on knowledge and education regarding the challenges facing educational policy makers and practitioners in South Africa. Part 3 includes only one chapter – a recent paper written jointly with Joe Muller (University of Capetown). It begins with some of the lessons that can be learned from reflecting on the experience of the 'new sociology of education' of the 1970s and traces the lineage of an alternative approach to knowledge from Durkheim to Bernstein and starts to explore the possibilities of drawing on Ernst Cassirer's ideas about forms of symbolization.

Basil Bernstein played a very important role in my academic career, both as a teacher and as a senior colleague. In recent years, my research and writing has been much influenced by a re-engagement with some of his ideas. I felt therefore that it was appropriate that the short piece which I originally wrote for the tribute to him, published by the Institute of Education in 2001, should be included in this book as an Endword.

The majority of the chapters in this book are based on papers that have been previously published in academic journals or edited books since 1999. Some chapters have undergone more revision than others. In bringing together papers that were originally written for different audiences, there is inevitably some overlap and repetition of arguments. In particular, there is overlap in the discussions of Durkheim and Vygotsky's ideas in Chapters 3 and 4, and some repetition in other chapters of arguments about social constructivist and social realist theories of knowledge. I hope that the advantages of maintaining the coherence of the chapters outweigh the disadvantages of the overlap and repetition.

Part 1

Theoretical issues

1 Rescuing the sociology of educational knowledge from the extremes of voice discourse

Introduction

This chapter is based on my response to a widely cited paper by Moore and Muller (Moore and Muller 1999). They argued that both the early sociology of knowledge which drew on ideas from Max Weber and the symbolic interactionists and informed the new sociology of education (Young 1971) and the later post-structuralist variants influenced by writers such as Foucault and Lyotard were both forms of 'voice discourse' which reduce knowledge to knowers, their standpoints and interests. Reading their paper was a formative experience for me as it challenged the basic assumptions of my earlier work. It forced me to ask what exactly I meant by the claim that knowledge is 'social'. Does it, as Moore and Muller appeared to argue in that paper, inevitably lead to relativism and therefore have no implications for the decisions that are made about the selection of knowledge in curricula? The chapter begins to develop an alternative social theory that does not reduce knowledge to the practice of knowers. It represented my first attempt to articulate a social realist view of knowledge and to work out some of its implications. Later chapters of this book take this argument much further by drawing on the much neglected social theory of knowledge first proposed by the great French sociologist, Emile Durkheim, and later developed in the second half of the twentieth century by Basil Bernstein.

In their paper in the *British Journal of Sociology of Education*, Moore and Muller (1999) mount a powerful attack on those strands in the sociology of education that have rejected any epistemological grounding of knowledge or truth claims in favour of a sociological approach that treats such claims as no more than the standpoints or perspectives of particular (invariably dominant) social groups. Their argument is important, and much of their critique is justified. However, whether intentionally or not, what begins as a critique of the extremes of what they refer to as 'voice discourse' becomes, in effect, a rejection of the claims of any sociological account of knowledge that sees it as more than a 'field positioning strategy'. The result, though I am sure not their intention, is to limit the sociology of education to the problems and approaches that it was concerned with until the late 1960s, when it was little more than an extension of studies of social mobility, stratification and the distribution of life chances.

In responding to their paper and, I hope, building on it, I seek to accomplish a number of things. First, I summarize their argument against voice discourses. I then go on to point to a number of problems in their argument, and suggest that they arise from their over-polemical stance, and are not intrinsic to the case against voice discourses that they want to make. Finally, I shall build on some points that are hinted at in their paper, to suggest the kind of positive contribution that a sociological approach to knowledge could make to the sociology of education, and to the study of the curriculum in particular.

Moore and Muller's arguments against 'voice discourses'

In their paper, Moore and Muller trace what they refer to as the debunking of epistemology in the sociology of education from its early expression in the 1970s, with its theoretical basis in the phenomenology and pragmatism of Alfred Schutz and C. Wright Mills, to its more recent postmodernist forms which draw on the writings of Foucault and Lyotard (Usher and Edwards 1994). They rightly point to the links between this sociological approach to knowledge and various traditions of radical politics that I and others endorsed and which in the 1970s were largely socialist and populist (Young and Whitty 1977; Whitty and Young 1976).

More recently, the sociological critique of epistemology has taken two paths: one largely eschews any specific politics at all (Usher and Edwards 1994) and the other has been taken up by feminist and postcolonial writers, who use it as a basis for de-legitimizing what they see as the unjustified dominance of western, white, male knowledge and expertise (e.g. Lather 1991). Moore and Muller argue that these approaches, which they refer to collectively as 'voice discourses', are based on a number of untenable assumptions. The first is the claim that there can be no epistemology or theory of knowledge because fundamentally, it is only experience, not knowledge, science or expertise that we can ultimately rely on in judging whether something is true. Second, Moore and Muller argue that 'voice discourse' approaches misuse the writings of historians of science such as Kuhn (1970) in claiming that they have shown that scientific truths are no more than what scientists at the time say is true. Third, they argue that those such as Usher and Edwards (1994) who adopt a postmodernist position misunderstand science in equating its claims with the widely discredited philosophy of positivism. As Moore and Muller point out, such writers appear ignorant of the recent work of philosophers of science (Papineau 1996; Toulmin 1996) who are well aware of the issues raised by postmodernists, but reject their relativist conclusions.

Moore and Muller argue that the result of these errors is that proponents of 'voice discourses' find themselves in two related kinds of contradiction, one theoretical and one practical, both of which have profoundly negative consequences for research in the sociology of education, and its possible influence on educational policy and practice. They point out that the theoretical implication of 'voice discourse' approaches is a relativism that leads to the rejection of all epistemologies; at the same time, these approaches are far from relativist about their own position, which denies the possibility of any objective knowledge at all. The practical and political implications of such a rejection of all knowledge claims is that voice discourses are self-defeating. They deny to the subordinate groups, with whom they claim to identify, the possibility of any knowledge that could be a resource for overcoming their subordination. There is no *knowledge* for voice discourses, only the power of some groups to assert that their experiences should count as knowledge.

Why then do these ideas persist if, as Moore and Muller argue, their flaws are so obvious and have long been known to be so, and in practice they offer so little to the groups that they claim to identify with? Moore and Muller suggest that the debunking of epistemology does not find support because it has any intellectual or political merit; for them it self-evidently does not. The reason it is supported, they claim, is sociological. Their general argument is really about ideology – that essentially flawed ideas persist because they have powerful social functions in society. Any ideas, however flawed, may, like fascism and racism, have a function for certain groups in society. Equally, in the narrower context of education, ideas and methodologies can persist because they reflect the professional interests of members of particular intellectual fields. Debunking dominant knowledge claims is one way for members of the younger generation in an intellectual field to assert themselves, and even to displace existing leaders. Moore and Muller point out that the weak intellectual basis of sociology of education, together with its relative insulation from intellectually stronger sub-fields within sociology, has made it particularly vulnerable to this type of positioning strategy.

There is no doubt that, as Moore and Muller argue, this kind of sociological account of knowledge did play an important positioning role in the sociology of education in the 1970s, and that it was related to the location of the emerging generation of sociologists of education in colleges and university departments of education with their responsibility for training teachers (Young 1971; Young 1998). The sociological approach to knowledge that came to be associated with what became known as the 'new sociology of education' not only challenged the old sociology of education and its association with the political arithmetic tradition of policy-oriented educational research; it also challenged the knowledge base of the liberal academic curriculum that had long dominated the grammar and public schools and the universities. The radicalism of this sociological approach to knowledge was well expressed in its interpretation of the continuing school failure of large numbers of pupils from working-class backgrounds. As was argued at the time, it was not working-class pupils who were failing in terms of the academic curriculum, as was maintained by mainstream researchers; from the perspective of the sociology of knowledge, it was the academic curriculum, historically constructed to preserve the status quo of a class society, that systematically ensured that the majority of working-class pupils were failures.

I have commented elsewhere (Young 1998) on the oversimplification of such conspiracy theories and the misguided nature of arguments that equate the legitimacy of knowledge solely with the social position of those who produce it. Moore and Muller offer a valuable extension of this argument by pointing to the episodic character of the debunking of epistemology. Such sociological critiques of knowledge, they point out, have recurred regularly over the past decades, appearing at different times and using quite different and often opposing theories. They cite the case of how postmodernism in the 1980s and 1990s served a similar social function as the Marxism and phenomenology of the 1970s; at the same time, each tradition mounted a devastating critique of the other. Moore and Muller draw on the work of Usher and Edwards (1994) in adult education as an example of a sociological approach to knowledge which has quite different intellectual roots and political concerns from the earlier 'new sociology of education' of the 1970s. Indeed, from Moore and Muller's position, by claiming no particular political commitment or policy implications for their position, Usher and Edwards adopt a position that is more logically consistent than that of the 'new' sociologists of education of the 1970s, who saw their attacks on epistemology as having, at least in principle, a politically emancipatory role. As Ward (1996) points out, some postmodernists such as Baudrillard take the position of Usher and Edwards on knowledge even further, and argue that there is no point in any social science or philosophy; one might as well write novels or poetry. However, what such positions never seem to account for is both the practical efficacy of scientific knowledge (and even, in a more limited sense, of knowledge in the social sciences) which makes it materially different from knowledge based solely on experience, and that writing good novels or poetry is difficult, and arguably more difficult than writing postmodernist critiques. In other words, postmodernism provides no escape from the familiar dilemma of any relativist position. Regardless of the relativist arguments, people in all societies make judgements about good and bad literature as well as about different explanations of natural phenomena, and debate the criteria for making such judgements. This, of course, is also what scientists and social scientists do, though their judgements and criteria are not of the same kind.

Moore and Muller's critique of voice discourse approaches, and how they tend to reduce knowledge to varieties of experience, has a compelling power and a basic common-sense appeal. Many examples would serve to illustrate the force of their main argument that some kinds of knowledge are, without question, more powerful than others and that asserting that all knowledge claims are no more than an expression of the claimant's experience is absurd. Here are two such examples:

1   Try designing a domestic lighting system without relying at least implicitly on Ohm's Law, or designing an aeroplane without knowing the laws of fluid dynamics. All the experience in the world will not help you, unless it is guided by rules that are not generated by experience alone.

2   How do we account for the problem of the two scientists who, some years ago, claimed that they had discovered how to create energy by the 'cold fusion' of hydrogen in a test tube? Their results could not be replicated when the experiments that they claimed to have carried out were repeated, and they were exposed as either fraudulent or bad scientists. We have to treat their claims in some sense as false, like that of the alchemists before them, and the existing scientific view that cold fusion of hydrogen, however desirable, is, for good reasons, impossible, as knowledge.

Moore and Muller are correct to point out the flaws in the postmodernist arguments. They show how writers such as Usher and Edwards construct a 'straw man' account of science; this they label as positivist and as representing the pinnacle of claims to objectivity, in order to show its untenabilty. The fact that science does not operate and indeed could not operate in the way positivists claim it does in no way detracts from the explanatory power of scientific concepts. Postmodernist attacks on positivist concepts of science say little about science. They say more about the attackers themselves. At best, they offer objections to those types of social science which take over the mathematical form of the natural sciences, but lack its conceptual basis; hardly a new thought.

The other powerful argument that Moore and Muller make is against the way that voice discourses invoke experience as the foundation of all knowledge, and therefore the basis for claiming that all knowledge or truth claims are equivalent – whether they derive from common sense, folk tradition, laboratory-based scientific research or systematic, disciplinary knowledge. One does not need to denigrate the knowledge that people gain from experience, or even to deny that there is an experiential element in all knowledge, however abstract, to recognize that experience is often an extremely unreliable basis for deciding whether something is true.

Moore and Muller's argument, that voice discourse approaches, whether wrapped in the obscure jargon of postmodernism or in a political correctness that identifies uncritically with the experience of subordinate groups, have been a cul-de-sac for the sociology of education, is important. However, in providing a constructive basis for a way ahead for the sociology of education, their paper does not take us very far. In the next section of this chapter I want to try and explain why this is so, and then to develop an alternative approach that begins to rescue the sociology of knowledge from both the relativist excesses of voice discourses and the limitations of the kind of a-social epistemological realism which Moore and Muller seem to slip into. I shall develop this alternative by commenting on three issues that arise from their paper. These are (i) the role of the sociology of knowledge as a 'field positioning strategy',[1] (ii) the implications of the relative insulation of the sociology of education from other 'stronger' fields of academic study, and (iii) the question of theory and practice in educational studies.

Beyond the extremes of 'voice discourses' and a-social realism

The first issue relates to the sociological argument that they draw from Bernstein (1971, 2000). This seeks to explain the persistence of what they refer to as the sociology of knowledge approach in the sociology of education, in terms of its role as a 'field positioning strategy' in a weak intellectual field that is highly insulated from other bodies of related and more reliable knowledge. Of course they have a point; first, it is true that sociology of education, like educational studies generally, is and has long been a weak intellectual field with what Bernstein (2000) calls a 'weak grammar' or set of rules for describing the phenomena that it seeks to explain. Furthermore, at least in the 1970s, when a sociological critique of epistemology was first applied to the curriculum, the sociology of education, based largely in university schools of education, was relatively insulated from mainstream sociology and the other social sciences. It is also true, as Bernstein also pointed out, that in the 1970s there were elements of a generation struggle in the debates between the 'new' and 'old' sociologies of education in the UK. No doubt a similar point can be made about feminist, postcolonial and postmodernist attempts to set experience against knowledge in the 1990s. However, this sociological point is not the end of the matter. The critiques of the possibility of grounding truth claims in epistemology have gained plausibility in many fields far closer to what might be defined as the intellectual mainstream than the sociology of education, and this has been going on since Nietzsche's writings became influential from the turn of the twentieth century.

What Moore and Muller refer to as the debunking of knowledge has had a significant influence in philosophy. Toulmin (1996) refers to the crisis in epistemology, literary and cultural studies that are far from being intellectually or socially insulated. It follows that the insulation argument essentially fails, in as much as it cannot explain the pervasiveness of the same ideas in other intellectual fields with few of the characteristics of the sociology of education. If the insulation argument is rejected, we have a bigger question about knowledge for both sociology and philosophy which Moore and Muller do not address but which continues to haunt intellectuals such as Ward (1996) in his excellent book, and which Toulmin (1996), in his brief but characteristically elegant article, describes so well.

Ward and Toulmin both state that the argument for an epistemological grounding of knowledge, at least in its strong form, no longer has any intellectual credibility. In his paper 'Knowledge as shared procedures' (1996), Toulmin argues that the crisis in epistemology is as old as the twentieth century. Philosophers from Husserl to Rorty, Toulmin states, 'have destroyed the programme for finding the unshakable foundations for human knowledge dreamed up by Descartes and his successors from 1630 onwards' (Toulmin 1996).

Toulmin's point is that earlier epistemological arguments were flawed because of their obsessive concern with how individuals can arrive at any certain knowledge about the world, as if this is *the* knowledge problem. The rationality of scientific (or, equally, of judicial) procedures is not, he argues, a matter of clarity and distinctness or logical coherence alone, and therefore just a question of epistemology. It depends on the way in which these procedures are developed in the historical evolution of any given discipline; in other words, it is also a sociological question. Moore and Muller appear to grasp Toulmin's point at a latter stage of their paper, when they refer to 'post empiricist epistemology'. However, they do not, I think, grasp its implications, and in particular the importance of distinguishing between three distinct arguments. They equate the first and second and do not consider the third. The arguments are:

The postmodernist argument that there are only at best pragmatic grounds for distinguishing knowledge from experience; hence knowledge, in the sense that the word is normally used in being linked to something that is true, is impossible.

The voice discourse argument that knowledge claims are always the political claims of dominant groups. The voice discourse position follows from the post-modernist argument. It does not distinguish between knowledge and experience and gives equal validity to the perspectives of all groups, whether expert or not, on the grounds that claims that knowledge can in some objective sense be independent of the social position of the knower are untenable.

The multi-dimensional argument. This asserts that the objectivity of truth claims always depends on (i) their external validity – that they explain something in a convincing way, (ii) their internal consistency – that they are coherent, and (iii) their ability to invoke support from a particular community of experts and with a wider legitimacy.

In the case of the example of the cold fusion of hydrogen mentioned earlier, the claims of the two scientists failed in relation to the multi-dimensional argument on at least criteria (i) and (iii). In many cases, especially in the social and educational sciences, the issues will be less clear-cut. There may be disagreements within particular communities, or the legitimacy of a community may be challenged, as in the case of increasing numbers of environmental and health issues.

The multi-dimensional argument, which is the one adopted in this chapter, is not relativist. However, it allows and indeed requires sociological and historical research into the development and application of knowledge in different contexts, into changes in knowledge communities, whether of experts or non-experts, specialists associated with disciplines or those who transcend disciplines, and how they construct, challenge and modify knowledge, and how they are challenged from within their communities and from without.[2] In the process, we can reconstruct the origins and histories of subjects, disciplines and curricula without claiming that subjects and disciplines are totally constructed by the ideas and practices of specialist communities, whether their specialism is history, geography, chemistry or even literature. A 'totalizing' social constructionism is as flawed as Lysenko's environmentalist view of biology (Lecourt 1977). By claiming that nature was endlessly modifiable, he not only ended up being able to say nothing useful or new about nature, but laid his work open to abuse by Stalin, who thought that nothing was beyond the control of the Party, even nature!

Moore and Muller raise another important issue but do not develop it very far in their paper. This concerns the relations between theory and practice. At least in the short term, and certainly from a practical or policy point of view, whether philosophy or literary or cultural studies adopt a postmodernist perspective that rejects all claims to truth and knowledge may not matter much. However, there could be serious consequences if, during their training, intending teachers learn not only that all curriculum knowledge is socially constructed but that it inevitably reflects the values and interests of the dominant class. For example, it could appear to follow that the same claims could be made for the everyday mathematics of the street market as are made for the mathematics of the textbook. From a postmodernist perspective, the only difference between the two types of mathematics would be that the latter reflects the dominant perspective shared by professional teachers and mathematicians. The limited scope of 'street' or what is sometimes known as 'ethno-mathematics', at least beyond a very specific set of contexts, is neatly forgotten. This kind of sociological approach to mathematics can easily lend support to those seeking to undermine the curriculum rationale for teaching formal mathematics at all (Bramall 2000). The issue is of course much broader than mathematics; it applies to all curriculum subjects. If in literary or media studies students learn that there are no criteria for claiming the literary superiority of the novels of Jane Austen over the TV programmes such as *Big Brother* or *Holby City*, then the only basis for selection of texts for the English literature curriculum is the white middle-class biases and prejudices of teachers or curriculum policy makers on the one hand or 'what students want' – a kind of consumer approach – on the other. It is this issue, (the possible link between theories and practice), and the fact that such a sociological view of knowledge might actually influence the ways that teachers think about their role, that makes the knowledge question so much more problematic in the sociology of education than in intellectual fields such as cultural and literary studies, that are far more insulated from any practice external to themselves. This possible link between a sociological view of knowledge and practice is, however, only a problem if it is based on the relativistic view of knowledge that I referred to earlier. I shall argue later in this chapter that this link between the sociology of knowledge and relativism is more complex than Moore and Muller recognize, and can be understood in a way that enables it to be a constructive element in a more enhanced view of the teacher as a professional in an increasingly knowledge-based economy.

One problem with Moore and Muller's paper is that whereas at some points they appear to challenge the sociological approach itself, as reducing knowledge to relationships or processes, at other times they take a far subtler and more nuanced position. They expose the flaws in Usher and Edwards' postmodernist arguments, in order to argue against crude versions of sociology that polarize social and epistemological positions on knowledge; however, the overall thrust of their argument seems to imply that all sociological accounts tend towards the extremes of voice discourse approaches. As they put it, voice discourses do not allow science to claim less than absolute truth. From the perspective of voice discourse, if science and rationality cannot be absolute then they cannot be objective at all. I will suggest that a middle way that combines the sociology of knowledge and epistemology in making truth claims can be developed as a defensible position. However, it would imply that there is far more common ground between Moore and Muller and a non-postmodern, non-voice-discourse sociological approach to knowledge than would be apparent from the sharpness of their attack. My argument therefore is that Moore and Muller, in not making clear distinctions between what we might call 'voice' and 'non-voice' sociologies of knowledge, are in danger of laying themselves open to the same criticism that they make of those they attack, such as Usher and Edwards. As Moore and Muller rightly claim, Usher and Edwards fail to distinguish between science as practised by scientists and theorized by philosophers of science, and the 'straw man' account of science that they criticize. What Moore and Muller do is to choose an extreme and naive sociological approach to knowledge (Usher and Edwards 1994), point out its flaws and link these flaws to a whole theoretical tradition in sociology of knowledge as it has been applied in educational research. In a parallel way, they equate the voice discourse approaches of certain feminist, post-feminist and postcolonial views of knowledge with all attempts to explore the practical or political implications of social theories of knowledge and in what ways different concepts of knowledge may be related to social interests. The outcome is that they leave us with a distinctly impoverished view of the sociology of education and in particular of the sociology of the curriculum. Moore and Muller are right to worry that structural level concerns with inequalities are neglected in much recent educational research. However, this is as likely to be the result of the current obsession by government and research funders with a peculiarly narrow view that the role of research is to provide evidence for policy, than of the continuing influence of the sociology of knowledge. At least implicitly, Moore and Muller's programme for the sociology of education seems to hark back to the 1960s, when sociologists knew their place in the academic division of labour, and when their role was to map the unequal distribution of educational opportunities. Explaining why this continued to be so despite decades of educational reform was, like fundamental questions of the purpose of formal education, left to philosophers and politicians.

Let me summarize my argument so far. Moore and Muller are correct to criticize the excesses of voice discourses, and in particular the dangers of invoking experience against the knowledge claims of expertise, science or other bodies of specialist knowledge. Despite the fact that in practice there has been a slippage between sociological approaches to knowledge and what Moore and Muller describe as voice discourses, and that this has happened in the peculiar episodic way that they describe, I shall argue that this is not an inevitable process. Furthermore, it does not follow from their argument that sociological analysis cannot be applied to questions of knowledge and truth, or have implications for the curriculum and educational policy more generally.

The sociology of knowledge reminds us that history and experience inevitably enter into all forms of knowledge, whether or not it is produced by specialists within particular disciplinary traditions. The fact that the inescapable role of experience in the production of new knowledge is often denied is itself a problem for both sociology and epistemology, and may or may not have practical implications. However, it is quite another matter to use an argument about the role of experience in even the most abstract forms of knowledge as a way of dismissing the degree and form of objectivity that such knowledge can provide; this is what voice discourses do. In relation to education, it follows from the more general claim of the sociology of knowledge that we have to accept the hypothesis that social class, gender and race inequalities, as well as a variety of professional interests, are embedded to varying degrees in the organization of the school curriculum as well as in the academic disciplines and other structures within which new knowledge is acquired and produced. However, we also have to recognize that how this embedding takes place in particular cases, and with what consequences, is far from clear.

Furthermore, such conclusions from the sociology of knowledge give no necessary grounds for rejecting a particular form of knowledge organization. Arguments about the embeddedness of social interests in different forms of knowledge organization are at best hypotheses to be explored; they are never, on their own, grounds for supporting (or opposing) particular curriculum proposals.

It is philosophy rather than sociology,[3] and in particular the idea in Wittgenstein's later argument that knowledge obtains its meaning collectively through forms of life, that in the 1970s and 1980s began to take the sociology of knowledge beyond the rather narrow constraints imposed on it by Karl Mannheim[4] and put an end to epistemology in its traditional sense. However, despite a number of novel ethnographies (Knorr-Cetina 1999) and well argued position statements (Bloor 1991), Wittgenstein-inspired sociology of knowledge has been able to say little about the nature of those collectivities or forms of life that underpin disciplines, fields or school subjects. Nor can it say anything about the practical implications for teachers of accepting the idea of that curriculum subjects are not given but themselves shaped by society and, therefore, a product of the practice of subject specialists themselves.[5]

Sociologists, especially those who want their sociology to have a direct political role in overcoming social inequalities, have been too quick to jump from Wittgenstein's philosophical principle to drawing concrete conclusions about particular forms of life. They have been slow to recognize that Wittgenstein's ideas can be no more than a premise for the sociology of knowledge (or the curriculum); they are not a substitute for a sociological approach to the curriculum itself. Even if we accept that knowledge takes its meaning from the forms of life within which it is located, it does not follow that any specific form of life – a group of specialists, a social class, a gender category, a group defined by its ethnicity or a disability – is a form of life for giving particular meanings to knowledge in the sense Wittgenstein meant. The process of embedding or giving meaning to knowledge is much more subtle and complex; analyses have to start from specific cases of actual 'communities', but also take account of the wider social and historical contexts which shape particular communities. Sociologists who have argued for an ethnographic approach to knowledge are therefore at least partly correct, and are supported by Toulmin as a philosopher. His argument is that if we accept that knowledge is in some sense the shared procedures of particular professional or other communities, it is the particular processes of knowledge production in such communities that we need to describe, and which will form the basis for any broader or more universalistic statements about truth and objectivity, whether about the natural or social world. Toulmin warns against the tendency in the social sciences to 'move on to theory' too soon, when we would be better focusing on 'the humbler task of giving accurate descriptions of human activities [which might help us to judge when] formal theories can do us any good' (Toulmin 1996). What he does not take on in making such a recommendation is that 'giving accurate descriptions' is nothing like as simple as he supposes; neither the ethnographer nor his/her subjects inhabit laboratories in which history and the wider context can, at least for research purposes, be excluded.

Towards an alternative

The recognition that knowledge and truth claims are always in some sense rooted in social activities, forms of life or practices has a number of implications for research in the sociology of education. I shall discuss each briefly, as a way of concluding this chapter and my response to Moore and Muller. First, it suggests that, contrary to the arguments of Karabel and Halsey (1977) and others that the location of the sociology of education in institutions dominated by the practical activity of training teachers was a weakness, it is or could be a strength. Following Toulmin's argument, referred to earlier, it is a mistake to imagine that there is something called 'theory' or research in the social sciences which is best developed independently of the exigencies of policy and practice.[6] If sensitive and accurate descriptions of practice form at least part of the bedrock of our knowledge of human activities such as learning and teaching, then educational researchers such as sociologists of education have to, as Toulmin puts it, 'get their hands dirty and work with and alongside the (educational) professionals whose enterprises they study'. Second, the social theory of knowledge that is implicit in Wittgenstein's propositions involves two interdependent steps. As Toulmin puts it, 'all meanings are created in the public domain in the context of collective situations and activities'. Furthermore, he states, these meanings are internalized by individuals 'in the learning processes by which we master everyday language and *subsequently* the conceptual content of more sophisticated enterprises [such as science, poetry or management]' (my italics and addition in brackets). The key issue for the sociology of education is the relationship between these two types of learning process. Essentially, they parallel the distinction between the tacit knowledge that is embedded in every practice (and of course in the language of the community into which one is born), and the codified knowledge that is abstracted from practice for different purposes, such as the subject knowledge of the school curriculum. It follows that just as the sociology of knowledge is inseparable from the sociology of learning, so the study of the curriculum is inseparable from the study of learning and pedagogy.

In raising a third issue, I part company from Toulmin and agree with Moore and Muller's argument – though not with the precise implications that they draw. Moore and Muller argue that the misplaced invoking of experience by 'voice discourse' theorists has led them to reduce sociological research to ethnographic description, thus avoiding the major structural issues of inequality that dominate mass education systems as much today as when they were first established in the nineteenth century. In contrast, the logic of Toulmin's argument that understanding human activity must eschew generalizations and theory and concentrate on the careful description of practice would preclude a focus on such 'structural' issues. The outcome of Toulmin's recommendation, therefore, is essentially the same as that from the voice discourse theorists, whose political goal is to claim that all knowledge can be reduced to experience – the contexts which shape different kinds of practice disappear, and we are left with descriptions of practice as if they had no context. Toulmin is right in my view to warn of the dangers of premature moves to theory and the absurdity of trying to achieve the kind of abstract theoretical structures in the social sciences that characterized Newtonian physics. Despite their postmodernist rejection of science, in applying their dominant/subordinate group distinction to undermine the legitimacy of science or other forms of expertise, voice discourse approaches imply a very similar 'structural' model.

Where Toulmin takes his argument too far, at least from the sociological perspective developed here, is in rejecting attempts to develop concepts for making sense of the contexts that shape practices and the 'forms of life' in which they are embedded. We must be cautious about giving such concepts an objectivity that they do not warrant. However, it is equally mistaken to deny that concepts such as social class, alienation, ideology and bureaucracy, as well as Durkheim's two types of the division of labour, do not have a conceptual power that enables us to use them to go beyond common sense and beyond the contexts in which they arose.

In making clear the difference between Toulmin's approach and the one I am arguing for here, I suggest that it is useful to distinguish between two senses, that are separate but related, in which knowledge can be understood as being social. I shall call them *anthropological* (in the broader sense of referring to human activities rather than referring to the specialist discipline) and *sociological*. The former anthropological meaning of a social theory of knowledge refers to the view adopted by philosophers such as Toulmin that now complements or some would say has replaced traditional epistemological concerns. It is the position staked out clearly by Wittgenstein in his later writings, but also has something in common with Durkheim's early writings, in which he argued that even the most basic categories of thought such as cause and time are social in origin. Such a view of knowledge is a conceptual statement about its social nature; it is not a statement about how different social realities shape the structure and content of knowledge. It is social in the sense that it asserts that any claim to knowledge is premised on some idea of society. The second *sociological* meaning of a social theory of knowledge depends on the former; however, because it has different purposes, it is both more ambitious and more modest. It is more ambitious in that it goes beyond the general principle that knowledge is social in origin, and argues that it is important to identify the particular ways in which social interests shape the structuring of knowledge. The continuing task of sociologists is to explore to what extent, in particular cases, whether concerned with the environment, health, electronics or the curriculum, social relations of power and interest are expressed in the organization of knowledge. On the other hand, a sociological approach to knowledge, in the sense used here, is (or should be) more modest in recognizing not only that what is defined as knowledge at a particular time is invariably more than a reflection of the distribution of power and social interests, but also that the question of in what ways and to what extent social interests of different kinds shape knowledge has to be explored in specific cases. We can make no claims to a general or universal law of the sociology of knowledge beyond what I have referred to as its anthropological basis.

Implications

In my own work on the sociology of the curriculum in the 1990s (Young 1998), I focused on the changing form of specialization, both in relation to the production of knowledge and the division of labour generally, and as one of the ways in which wider contexts shape the organization of educational knowledge. I suggested that changing *forms of specialization* are among the ways in which the wider context shapes the production of knowledge (Gibbons *et al.* 1994) and the organization of the curriculum. I argued that a distinction between *insular* and *connective* specialization captures some of the underlying tensions and contradictions in contemporary curriculum debates, and can provide a way of linking these debates with wider changes in the division of labour. However, this is not to propose either that 'connective specialization' is some kind of grand theory that can be imposed mechanically to interpret current changes in the curriculum, or that it is a curriculum principle that teachers can or should be applying in their practice. It has a number of more modest purposes. First, the distinction between two forms of specialization offers a way of making sense of current curriculum debates, especially, but not only, in the post-16 phase of education. Second, in the specific case of the English post-16 curriculum, it provides the basis for a critical analysis of the continuing debate over the future of A-levels (see Young 1998). Whereas it is difficult to dispute that insular specialization is an accurate description of the traditional A-level curriculum and its basis in groups of separate subjects, connective specialization does not propose the abolition of subjects, but a redefinition of their role in relation to the purposes of the curriculum as a whole.

I suggested (Young 1998) that the distinction between insular and connective specialization can be applied to a number of aspects of the curriculum. For example:

- the relationship between the everyday common-sense knowledge that learners bring to the curriculum, and the organization of the curriculum itself;
- the relationship between tacit knowledge that learners acquire in any context (including schools) and the conceptual or codified knowledge associated with the curriculum;
- the relationship between the component elements of the curriculum (subjects or vocational fields of study) and the curriculum as a whole;
- the relationship between school knowledge and the workplace knowledge that students acquire through work experience, part-time jobs or placements (Griffiths and Guile 2001).

In the case of each relationship, it is possible to trace a tension in the history of mass education between the trend to greater (and more insular) specialization in the curriculum (and in work and knowledge generally), and the recent attempts to connect different types of knowledge and learning.[7]

Conclusions

In responding to Moore and Muller's paper, I have, first, argued that in the soci-ology of education, we need to take seriously their criticism of certain trends that have been devoted to debunking knowledge and epistemology. Second, I have suggested that while their criticisms are well merited, they are weakened by broadening their attack beyond where it can claim validity. Third, I have attempted to rescue a social theory of knowledge from the extremes to which it was taken by the relativism of voice discourses and postmodernism. Fourth, I built on the limitations of Toulmin's Wittgensteinian arguments for a social the-ory of knowledge, and suggested that it is useful to make a distinction between anthropological and sociological meanings of the social basis of knowledge. Last, I have indicated how a research programme in the sociology of education that focuses on the issue of knowledge specialization and its relationship with the distribution of power and the role of institutions might complement the rather limited ethnographic role for sociology suggested by Toulmin.

Finally, it is legitimate to ask whether this somewhat esoteric discussion about knowledge matters, when inner city schools are failing and good head teachers are resigning in exhaustion. Are the real issues not the perennial ones of govern-ments being reluctant to spend the necessary money to improve the curriculum? Who bothers any more about knowledge issues, when everyone is chasing after grants to do more research on the literacy hour, and other examples of what claim to be evidence-based policies?

I originally wrote the paper on which this chapter is based because I thought that the issues raised by Moore and Muller do matter, not only for sociologists but for anyone interested in education, even when I disagree with them. Seven years later, I still hold this view for a number of reasons, hence the rationale for includ-ing a version of the original paper as the first chapter of this book. First, the intellectual dishonesty of the voice discourse theorists and the potential damage that may be caused for those in the most vulnerable situations needs to be pointed out loud and clear – and Moore and Muller do that. Voice discourse theorists are clever, and in appearing to be democratic and even populist both in their defer-ence to experience and in their critique of expertise, they are also seductive, especially to those most frustrated with the continuing failures of the existing sys-tem. In rejecting the claims for any kind of objective knowledge, the logic of their position is at best nihilist. It leads either to the cynicism of social scientists who do not believe that there are any grounds for their own practice or, as in the case of those such as Baudrillard, to giving up social science altogether. If taken seri-ously, as vitalist philosophers such as Heidegger did in Germany (Loft 2000; Cassirer 2000: Introduction), the rejection of knowledge can lead to something far worse – the view that the only question is who has the power. It is disturbing that such arguments can be found among those identifying most closely with the real subordination of minorities or excluded groups. Second, Moore and Muller's critique of social theories of knowledge itself needs to be challenged; it removes from sociologists some of the tools they need, both in exposing the hypocrisies and contradictions in official policies, and in suggesting realistic criteria for alternatives. A social theory of knowledge is important in exposing the rhetoric of standards, targets and quality assurance (all good principles of course, but easily misused), and how they become ends in themselves, rather than the means to achieving wider purposes.

This is not to argue that sociology of education should just be a critique of whatever policies are proposed by government, and therefore that it is always in opposition; far from it. It is rather to argue that if sociologists of education and other educational researchers are to have a productive role in relation to educational policy, they need to start from a position that many of the givens that are unquestioned in policy should not be taken as such. The lessons from the past 30 years of the sociology of education are not that the starting assumptions of the sociology of knowledge are wrong. It is rather that they were one-sided, and often applied crudely. Their assumptions need re-examination, and their sociological theory of knowledge needs to take more account of the realities and constraints of educational policy and practice.

The sociology of knowledge cannot avoid being radical in the theoretical challenges that it poses. However, this does not excuse it from taking account of epistemological constraints or from the fact that one of its tasks is to identify the boundaries which cannot be blurred if learners are to acquire real knowledge. Educational policies and practices are like all human products, developed consciously, and sometimes unconsciously, for particular purposes. The sociology of knowledge is an important set of conceptual tools for preventing us from becoming immersed in the minutiae of specific policies, and for reminding us that the big questions about how promoting greater equality is not separate from the structuring of knowledge and the conditions for its acquisition still need to be asked. However, as Moore and Muller show clearly in their paper, the sociology of knowledge is a set of ideas that can easily be used rhetorically and irresponsibly. My argument has been that these possibilities are not intrinsic to the sociology of knowledge; they are a reflection of how it has been used in the sociology of education, and how, at different times, many of us have seen our role. An over-politicized view of theory that has characterized voice discourse approaches and some early versions of the 'new sociology of education' was one outcome, and a denial of responsibility for the consequences of one's theory is sometimes another. Both can be found in the writings of educational theorists in recent decades, and both have had negative consequences for the position and achievements of the sociology of education. Neither possibility is a reason for rejecting the necessary role of the sociology of knowledge in any serious educational research, however uncomfortable this may be for government, and whatever the intellectual and moral difficulties that are involved for researchers. The remaining chapters of this book seek, not always successfully, to hold together two sets of debates. One debate is between different approaches to the idea that knowledge has a social basis, and the other concerns the implications of these debates for a range of decisions about curriculum and pedagogy.

2 Knowledge and the curriculum in the sociology of education

Introduction

Politicians tell us that we are (or soon will be) in a 'knowledge society', and that more and more jobs require people to be 'knowledge workers'. At the same time, government policy documents have been remarkably silent about what this knowledge is (Department for Education and Employment 1998, 1999). Is it more of the old disciplinary knowledge, or is it a new kind of trans-disciplinary knowledge that is more transient and local (Gibbons *et al.* 1994; Muller 2000)? Answers to such questions should lie at the heart of the sociology of education, but have until recently been strangely absent there as well (Moore and Muller 1999; Muller 2000; Moore 2004) This chapter has two aims: the first is to clarify the nature of the problem and the second is to build on Chapter 1 and propose the theoretical basis for a way ahead for the sociology of education. In developing the argument, the chapter will examine the problem of knowledge in the curriculum, but also raise some concerns about how the sociology of education has tended to treat the issue of knowledge more generally. It will argue that contemporary trends in the sociology of education make it peculiarly ill equipped to meet the curriculum challenge posed by debates about the implications of globalization (Castells 1998) and the massification of post-compulsory education (Scott 2000) of the past decade.

The chapter begins by describing and contrasting the two dominant (and contending) sets of assumptions about knowledge and the curriculum that are reflected in contemporary curriculum policy: 'neo-conservative traditionalism' and 'technical-instrumentalism'. It then goes on to examine the postmodernist critique of these assumptions that has been developed within the sociology of education (Hartley 1997; Moore 2000). Despite the critical stance of postmodernism, the chapter argues that the two themes underlying government policy and the postmodernist critiques exhibit some fundamental similarities. Each, in its own way, precludes a debate about knowledge as a category in its own right.[1] It follows that what is lacking from current debates about the curriculum is precisely any theory of knowledge. It is here that the issue becomes most acute for the sociology of education. It is fair to say that postmodernist perspectives have become firmly entrenched, although not hegemonic, within the sociology of education (Hartley 1997) and, in addition, that their proponents adopt a critical position vis-à-vis neo-conservatism and instrumentalism (Griffith 2000). In this respect, postmodernists hold in a contemporary guise the place formerly held, within the sociology of education, by progressivism and certain kinds of Marxist critiques. Although on theoretical grounds postmodernists reject both the essentialist model of the child held by progressive educationalists, and the economic determinism of Marxism, they continue to emphasize the 'experiential' basis of knowledge associated with progressivism and the view of academic knowledge as elitist and ideological that is found in many Marxist critiques. Furthermore, postmodernists have developed the relativism that is immanent in both Marxist and phenomenological theories of knowledge into a point of principle. Despite the fact that in ideological terms postmodernism is critical of both neo-conservative and technical-instrumental views of the curriculum, it can be argued that in relation to their assumptions about knowledge, it is the similarities of the three approaches that are more significant than their differences. Moreover, for reasons developed in this chapter, the relativizing of knowledge claims associated with postmodernist critiques vitiates both their critiques and their ability to mount any effective advocacy of realistic curriculum alternatives.

The implication of this argument is that there is a potential fourth position (the one developed in this chapter) that brings knowledge itself back into the debate about the curriculum without denying its fundamentally social and historical basis. However, such a position requires the sociology of education to develop a theory of knowledge that, while accepting that knowledge is always a social and historical product, avoids the slide into relativism and perspectivism with which this insight is associated in postmodernist writings (for example, Usher and Edwards 1994).

The chapter has three main parts. First, it argues that there are important developments in related academic fields (especially in the sociology and philosophy of science) that can be drawn on in developing the alternative referred to earlier. Second, although what counts as school knowledge will always be a contested issue, it is important that this should be seen as something more than a power play between contending social interests. Account needs to be taken of how knowledge is developed (and acquired) within particular epistemic communities or 'cultures' (Hoskyns 1993; Collins 1998; Knorr-Cetina 1999). Third, the chapter argues that the outcomes of disputes about knowledge are not mere academic issues. They directly affect learning opportunities for pupils in schools and have wider consequences through the principles by which knowledge is distributed in society.

The policy debate

Recent curriculum policy has been driven by two competing imperatives or ideologies – one largely covert but embedded in the leading educational institutions themselves, and the other more overt and increasingly dominant in government rhetoric. The first can be described as 'neo-conservative traditionalism'. The idea of the curriculum as a given body of knowledge that it is the responsibility of the schools to transmit is as old as the institution of schooling itself. It is only articulated (for example, Woodhead 2001) when it is felt that the traditional body of knowledge is being challenged. A good example is the response on the part of successive governments over the past 20 years to proposals for the reform or even the replacement of A-levels.[2] For neo-conservatives (the most recent example is the Labour Government (DfES 2005)!), A-levels represent a 'gold standard' against which all other curricula must be evaluated. For them, real learning is still essentially a contemplative process that has its roots in the monastic tradition. The role of the curriculum and its attendant examinations is to engender respect for whatever are the canonical texts. It is therefore not just the specific texts (for example, particular authors in the case of English literature) that are held to be of enduring value by neo-conservatives, but the relationship of deference to a given body of knowledge. In other words, what is important is the experience of submitting to the discipline of a subject and becoming the kind of person it is supposed to make you. In terms of the conventional knowledge-centred/child-centred and traditional/progressive dichotomies that have organized curriculum debates for so long, it must be stressed that neo-conservatism is not motivated primarily by 'epistemological' concerns. Rather, it is inspired by the view that the traditional discipline of learning promotes proper respect for authority and protects traditional values (for a clear example of this argument, see Scruton 1991).

The disregard by neo-conservatives of the importance of specific knowledge is associated with a peculiarly English form of anti-intellectualism (Wellens 1970) and a cult of amateurism and scepticism about expertise that still shapes the world view of the higher grades of the civil service and the top echelons of parts of industry and commerce (Wilkinson 1970). The typically pragmatic endorsement of the idea of the 'civilized generalist', which is expressed in the English sixth form curriculum that has traditionally allowed students to choose which collection of subjects to study, has allowed an increasing range of 'modern' subjects to be included. English literature, modern (sic) foreign languages, geography and science were included in the nineteenth century, and the social sciences later in the twentieth century (Young 1998). However, this diversification of the content of the sixth form curriculum bears little relation to the transformations that have taken place in society or the actual development of knowledge itself. In the period of over 50 years since A-levels were launched their basic structure has remained largely unchanged, while whole new fields of knowledge have been created and the economy and society as a whole has changed out of all recognition. Furthermore, the numbers of students taking A-levels has expanded tenfold as most jobs for 16-year-olds disappeared by the 1980s, and the numbers continuing as full-time students after the age of 16 doubled by the mid-1990s.[3]

Those who Raymond Williams (1961) referred to as the 'industrial trainers', but who are referred to here by the broader term 'technical-instrumentalists', have consistently challenged the neo-conservative view of education, and in policy terms are now the dominant group. For them, the curriculum imperative is not educational in the traditional sense, but directed towards what they see as the needs of the economy. In the late 1990s this was expressed in terms of preparing for the global and more competitive knowledge-based economy of the future (Department for Education and Employment 1998, 1999). There is a strong continuity between such arguments and the recent Foster Report (2005) on further education and the Leitch Report (2006) on skills. From this perspective, education, the curriculum and even knowledge itself become a means to an end, not ends in themselves. It is the curriculum's role in making a particular form of society that is stressed. Only secondarily is it seen as a maker of persons, and even then only to the extent that they exhibit the qualities of trainability and flexibility that it is assumed will be needed in the future 'knowledge society'.

What has changed, even as recently as in the past ten years, and as indicated by the recent White Paper on Higher Education (DFES 2003), is the scope of these instrumentalist views of the curriculum and knowledge. Prior to the 1970s, they were largely confined to vocational education and training (hence Williams's term 'industrial trainers'), although they were also reflected in the assumption that 20 per cent of each cohort who left school without any qualifications needed a more practically oriented, work-related curriculum. However, in the past decade and a half, and particularly since the two Dearing reports (on 16–19 Qualifications (Dearing 1996) and on Higher Education (National Committee of Inquiry into Higher Education 1997)) instrumentalism, under the guise of promoting the employability of all students, has been extended to the academic curriculum for 16–19-year-olds, and even to the apex of academic learning – the universities. All students are now encouraged to combine academic and vocational subjects, and all subjects taught at university, from fine art to pure mathematics, are expected to incorporate key skills and show their students how to apply their knowledge (Bridges 2000). Subject specialists are required to make explicit not only how their subject links with other subjects, but also how it facilitates such generic employment-related skills as teamwork, communications or number skills. Technical-instrumentalism also imposes on educational institutions a style of managerial regulation that is integrated with the broader apparatus of performance indicators, target setting and league tables (Beck 1998). While the formalities of academic freedom in deciding the university curriculum are retained, cash-starved institutions are unavoidably influenced by the incentives of funds linked to such government objectives as widening participation and promoting employability.

The tension between the two models has influenced the development of the curriculum for more than a century. However, it is particularly in the past decade that technical-instrumentalism has provided the dominant rhetoric for change as well as influencing substantive reforms. Both models operate 'diagnostically', by identifying deficiencies in existing educational arrangements. The traditionalists assert that the substantial expansion of post-compulsory education has only been possible by allowing the standards of excellence that were established in the past (the 'golden age') to fall. In contrast, the instumentalists claim that the uneasy compromise between pressures to expand participation and maintain standards has resulted in a curriculum that fails to satisfy the skill and knowledge demands of the emerging economy. In both models, a view of the curriculum is related to a particular historical narrative of social change (Moore 2000).

With governments unable to resolve the tension between these two imperatives, it is not surprising that curriculum policy and its implementation is, at best, confused. Some schools and colleges are making a heroic effort to articulate a vision of a broader curriculum of the future, while others adapt as best they can to the vagaries of student choice and the idiosyncrasies of higher education admissions tutors. Nor is it surprising that new divisions are emerging, In the most successful institutions (such as many sixth form colleges and private schools), students are encouraged to take four or even five A-level subjects, at least in the first year of their post-16 studies, and degree programmes are being enhanced in the leading universities. In contrast, students with lower achievements at the age of 16 (and even at the age of 14) and who are assumed to be 'non-academic', are directed to the new diplomas which are employer led but, it is claimed, not vocational.

Neither the neo-conservative nor the instrumentalist views have gone unchallenged by social theorists. However, my argument is that, in failing to provide a way of discussing what must be central to any serious curriculum debate – the question of knowledge – the critiques from social theory fall into the same trap as the views they oppose. This is not as straightforward a point as it sounds because the critiques, increasingly from a postmodernist perspective, present themselves as treating the question of knowledge as central. They focus largely on the academic curriculum and claim that it relies on essentially arbitrary assumptions about knowledge and culture generally (see Hartley (1997) for one of the most balanced and sensitive accounts). It follows, from their perspective, that in asserting the givenness of what they claim to have demonstrated is arbitrary, the curriculum is responsible for the perpetuation of social inequalities.

Starting from the assumption that all knowledge is embedded in the interests of particular groups of 'knowers', postmodernist critiques appear to provide powerful support for the cultural demands of subordinate groups, whether these are ethnic, gender or (although increasingly less frequently) social class based. However, by arguing that knowledge is inseparable from how it is constructed, they cannot avoid the conclusion that all knowledge, whether based on professional expertise, research, or the experience of particular groups, is of equal value. It follows that, when the standpoint and interests of those producing the knowledge have been identified, all that needs to be said has, in essence, been said. Debates between postmodernists and those they critique become little more than arguments about whose experience should underpin the curriculum, and the purpose of social theory becomes the critical deconstruction of the dominant forms of knowledge associated with subjects and disciplines. If all standards and criteria are reducible to perspectives and standpoints, no grounds can be offered for teaching any one thing rather than any other (or, ultimately, for teaching anything at all!). It is not surprising that such theories, whatever their appeal to intellectuals, have made little contribution to curriculum policy. Worse than that, they have effectively marginalized the role of sociology in providing a theory for how we might think about knowledge in a 'knowledge society', and what the curriculum implications of such a theory might be.

Postmodernist ideas about knowledge have not only been the basis of critiques of traditionalist views of the curriculum; they have also been used to challenge the prevailing instrumentalism of current government policy and its rhetoric of performativity (Usher and Edwards 1994). However, because they have no theory of knowledge as such, they can do little more than expose the way that curriculum policies always mask power relations. Furthermore, by depending on an irreducible notion of experience, they neglect the uneven distribution of the experiences that the curriculum needs to take account of if students from diverse backgrounds are to have opportunities to acquire knowledge that takes them beyond their experience.

The problems with postmodernist critiques of knowledge

Why do postmodernist accounts of knowledge and the curriculum neglect the very problem that they set out to address? One reason is that in their critique of neo-conservatism and instrumentalism, they polarize the alternatives, as if each position that they critique did not have within it a kernel of truth. The neo-conservative position may be flawed, but it is not false. It reminds us that (i) education needs to be seen as an end in itself and not just as a means to an end (the instrumentalist position), and that (ii) tradition, though capable of preserving vested interests, is also crucial in ensuring the maintenance and development of standards of learning in schools, as well as being a condition for innovation and creating new knowledge. More generally, neo-conservatives remind us that the curriculum must, in Matthew Arnold's words, strive to make 'the best that has been thought and known in the world current everywhere' (Arnold 1960: 70).

There are good reasons why we still want young people to read Jane Austen's novels, which are not weakened by the narrow community that she wrote about. Her novels are situated in time and context, but they are also timeless in the moral and relationship issues that they explore. One can make a slightly different kind of argument for keeping Newton's laws of motion and Mendeleev's periodic table on science syllabuses; both are examples of knowledge that remains powerful and transcends its origins in a particular social context.[4]

The problem with the neo-conservative position is that, like Arnold, it treats 'the best' as given and not the outcome, at any time, of wider social changes as well as internal debates within disciplines. Because neo-conservatives play down the social and historical nature of knowledge, they see no need for a theory about what should (and should not) be in the curriculum, whether it is particular novels or new subjects. For them, the canon of English literature and the traditional school subjects are, self-evidently, just there; they define what a curriculum is. The consequence of neo-conservatism having been the dominant view, at least until recently, is that actual curriculum changes have invariably been ad hoc and pragmatic.

In opposition to neo-conservatism, instrumentalism reminds us that the curriculum has always been, albeit selectively, related to economic changes and the future employability of students, despite claims to the contrary by liberal educators. It was not by chance that the numbers taking physics and chemistry grew substantially after the Second World War. It also reminds us that schools and colleges are never as insulated from the rest of society as they are portrayed to be in the subject-based curriculum. The issue that instrumentalism does not address is the conditions that are necessary if knowledge is to be produced or acquired, and why economic realities can never be the only criteria for the curriculum. In contrast, social theories of knowledge, whether humanist, Marxist, or more recently postmodernist, all make explicit the social and historical character of knowledge, and that knowledge is always, at least in part, 'some people's' knowledge. However, in making such features of knowledge explicit, these theories all too easily end up in claiming that knowledge is only some people's knowledge – no more and no less.

The second problem with postmodernist theories is that they imply that social theories of knowledge inevitably lead to relativism and the denial of any possibility that knowledge can be objective. Arguments about relativism have dominated and distorted research in the sociology of education since the 1970s (Moore and Muller 1999), in ways that have seriously impeded the development of a theory that might address the many urgent curriculum issues. Most social theories of knowledge have remained at too high a level of abstraction to have any clear curriculum implications, and if not, as in the case of some forms of Marxism and feminism, they have made unsupportable claims about the links between knowledge and particular social interests. In this chapter, a 'social realist' view of knowledge, derived from Durkheim (1995) and developed more recently by Collins (1998), Alexander (1995) and Bernstein (1996, 2000) is proposed. In contrast to postmodernist theories, these writers argue that it is the social nature of knowledge that in part provides the grounds for its objectivity and its claims to truth. In the final section of the chapter, the implications for curriculum debates of such a social realist approach to knowledge are discussed, and how it might take us beyond both prevailing orthodoxies of neo-conservatism and instrumentalism and their postmodernist critics.

The epistemological dilemma

In developing an alternative to relativism, it is worth noting the peculiarity that anyone should hold such a position in the first place. In the academic community, objections to relativism are long established and widely known (Gellner 1974, 1992; Fay 1996; Harre and Krausz 1996). Furthermore, at a common-sense level, it is inconceivable that advocates of relativism could actually live their personal lives as relativists. They may celebrate the uniqueness of individual standpoints 'in theory' but, at the same time, in their everyday lives they cannot avoid making assumptions that transcend the uniqueness of particular standpoints. The question remains – why, particularly in the sociology of education, has the appeal of relativism persisted?

Relativism has taken different forms in the sociology of education. As a methodology, it refers to the critical questioning that is a feature of the beginning of any enquiry. What distinguishes its use in the sociology of education is its role in questioning the form and content of the curriculum, the taken-for-granted assumptions that it makes about what counts as knowledge and, therefore, about the society that supports those assumptions. However, relativism is never just a methodological strategy. Invariably, theoretical claims are made about the social basis of knowledge, as well as political claims about the consequences of particular theories of knowledge in terms of wider questions of power and inequality. By arguing that all knowledge derives from partial and potentially self-interested standpoints, relativism can be seen as a superficially powerful basis for challenging what are assumed to be the repressive and dominant knowledge forms of the existing curriculum. Relativists attack the claims to objectivity of dominant forms of knowledge and, by implication, defend the 'voices' that are denied or hidden. It is this combination of the methodology and politics of relativism that goes some way to accounting for its appeal and the opposition that it generated in the 1970s (Gould 1977). However, its critics seem to have been almost as paranoid as some of its proponents were naive. The actual political and educational significance of relativism outside the teaching of sociology of education in universities was minimal. This is best accounted for by its *theoretical* weakness, especially in its most recent postmodernist form; as a theory it does not in the end explain anything. By polarizing dominant knowledge forms against 'silenced' others, postmodernism achieves its radical objective of not having to refer to any established traditions of academic debate; all academic theories, by definition, exclude 'silent' others. However, in dismissing other theories rather than entering into a dialogue with them, postmodernism precludes the possibility of an alternative theory of knowledge, except one that reduces all knowledge to experience or statements about knowers (Maton 2000). Debates about knowledge for postmodernists become forms of attack and defence between oppressors and oppressed (or rather those claiming to defend their interests). At the same time, by privileging the exclusiveness of particular experiences, they deny to oppressed communities the possibility of knowledge that goes beyond their experience and might play a part in enabling them to overcome their oppression.

This tendency to over-dichotomize has a deeper basis in what is sometimes referred to as the 'linguistic turn' in social theory. Language is treated not as an aspect of social order or as a useful metaphor for characterizing aspects of social relations, but as the only way we have of representing social relations (Gellner 1992). From such a dichotomizing perspective, knowledge identified as dominant (such as that inscribed in the curriculum) requires the exclusion of the knowledge of the non-dominant or subordinate. It follows that the only task of social analysis is to 'name' the producers of the dominant knowledge (Moore 2000).

A number of commentators have noted that, in their critique of knowledge, postmodernists invariably characterize it as 'positivist' (Alexander 1995: Chapter 3). The typical version of positivism that is attacked is one that locates truth outside society and presents it as accessible through a 'neutral' language that is a direct representation of the external world. The postmodernist view of the inseparability of knowledge and knowers is then used to challenge the claims of the natural sciences that they can provide access to a truth that is in some sense outside society and history. The implication of this polarization between postmodernism and a positivist view of science is termed by Alexander 'the epistemological dilemma', which he summarizes as follows:

> Either knowledge ... is unrelated to the social position and intellectual inter-
> ests of the knower, in which case general theory and universal knowledge are
> viable, or knowledge is affected by its relation to the knower, in which case
> relativistic and particularistic knowledge can be the only result. This is a true
> dilemma, because it presents a choice between two equally unpalatable alter-
> natives. [However, the] alternative to positivist theory is not resigned
> relativism and the alternative to relativism is not positivist theory. Theoretical
> knowledge can never be anything other than the socially rooted efforts of his-
> torical agents. But this social character does not negate the possibility of
> developing either generalized categories or increasingly disciplined, imper-
> sonal and critical modes of evaluation.
>
> (Alexander 1995: 91)

An alternative to this polarization so well articulated by Alexander will be
explored in some detail later in this chapter. Postmodernism as a critical social
theory has other problems – in particular, its concept of knowledge.

Postmodernism reduces knowledge to a simple monolithic form that is then
held to be hegemonic. However, as Collins (1998) argues in his *The Sociology of
Philosophies*, it is only rarely and under exceptional conditions that a single certainty about what is true is hegemonic in any intellectual field.[5] He shows that
intellectual fields are typically structured by competing traditions and positions,
and that the dominance of one is only ever partial and transient. Indeed, for
Collins, the reality of competing traditions is one of the conditions for the objectivity of knowledge. In contrast, postmodernism polarizes present and absent
meanings, leading to an inevitably schematic and partial view of knowledge. The
manner in which postmodernists typically equate science with positivism, despite
the fact that, at least in its cruder forms, positivism has never been widely
accepted as a theory of science, is an example of this. Philosophers such as
Toulmin (as discussed in Chapter 1), as well as some sociologists, have, since the
1970s, shown that locating knowledge socially need not lead to the abandonment
of truth and objectivity. It is these developments that provide a way out of
Alexander's 'epistemological dilemma'.

The argument of this chapter so far has been that in reducing knowledge to
particular standpoints, postmodernism follows a reductive logic that polarizes
dominant knowledge against absent or silent voices that it excludes. It then goes
on to treat this exclusion as mirroring the inequalities of power in the wider society. However, this reduction of knowledge to standpoints has a number of
implications for the ability of sociology to contribute meaningfully to curriculum
debates. Four such implications are worth discussing.

- *The genetic fallacy*: if knowledge is reduced to the conditions of its production, it is denied any intrinsic autonomy either as a social institution in its
  own right or in terms of the application of independent truth criteria that
  might be applied to curriculum debates.

- *Oversimplifying the nature of intellectual fields*: if knowledge is reduced to the standpoint of a social group, the complexity of positions within any field at any point in time is neglected. Dominance and exclusion are at best very partial categories for explaining the dynamics of an intellectual field (Bourdieu 1975). Applied to curriculum analysis, such polarization is unable to question why any knowledge is or is not included.
- *Reducing knowledge to experience*: standpoint analysis reduces knowledge to what is known by different groups, the power relations between them and their different experiences. Thus, all we are left with is a sociology of knowers, which can say little about knowledge or the curriculum itself.
- *Denying the possibility of categories that transcend experience*: equating knowledge with the experience of knowers means that research can lead only to non-generalizeable findings and curricula can only be different forms of 'localism'.

It is not difficult to see the problems that are left for sociology as a basis for a critical theory if the logic of the postmodernist argument is accepted. It can be critical only in the limited sense of identifying possible interests behind claims to disinterestedness. The possibility remains that claims to knowledge and objectivity may be linked to social interests (the history of educational testing is but one well known example). The problems arise when knowledge is taken to be 'always' and 'only' identical with 'interest'. If this is accepted, there are only different interests, and no good grounds for preferring one interest to another. It is a form of 'criticism in the head' or 'in the armchair' – a kind of academic radicalism of no consequence to anyone else. No wonder there have been suggestions, however misguided, to transfer resources for educational research away from academics. If all knowledge is from a standpoint and there are no standpoint-independent criteria for making judgements, appeals in terms of 'social justice' or the 'common good' become no more than other standpoints. Similarly, peer reviews for preserving objectivity and standards become no more than a form of professional hegemony. In contrast, the view taken here is that while peer reviews are inevitably fallible (and sometimes get it wrong), their claims to objectivity have an objective basis in the codes, traditions and debates of different intellectual fields that give them a degree of autonomy beyond the personal and professional interests of any particular group of academic peers. Postmodernism, as we have argued earlier, is trapped in its insistence that objectivity can only be supported by the untenable and a-social claims of positivism.

The educational dilemma

The problem faced by the sociology of education is twofold. First, at least in the past decades, most attempts to address the knowledge question have been by postmodernists, with the consequences already described. Second, attempts to develop a sociology of education that gives knowledge its central place in the curriculum easily slip back into the discredited neo-conservative traditionalist position that was discussed earlier in this chapter. This is what can be termed the 'educational dilemma' – either the curriculum is a given or it is entirely the result of power struggles between groups with competing claims for including and legitimizing their knowledge and excluding that of others. This can be seen as a more specific example of the 'epistemological dilemma' (Alexander 1995) which was referred to earlier. It is in pointing to a way of resolving both dilemmas that the next section of this chapter introduces a 'social realist' approach to knowledge.

Towards a social realist approach to knowledge

The argument so far can be summarized in the following four points.

- Relativism does not necessarily follow from a 'social' theory of knowledge. On the contrary, a social theory can be the basis for claims to truth and objectivity by identifying the distinctive 'codes and practices' through which they are produced.
- A social theory must recognize that some knowledge is objective in ways that transcend the historical conditions of its production (e.g. Euclid's geometry and Newton's physics).
- A social theory that seeks to link knowledge to social interests has to distinguish between two types of interest. These are (i) the 'external' or contextual interests, which may reflect wider divisions in society, and (ii) the 'internal' cognitive interests that are concerned with the conditions for the production and acquisition of knowledge itself. Plagued by the assumption that it is always dealing with 'external' interests and their basis in the wider society, the sociology of knowledge has, until recently, given little attention to forms of 'internal' cognitive interest; this point is developed later.
- In contrast to postmodernist theories, with their tendency to use dichotomous categories such as dominance and exclusion, a more adequate social theory must treat knowledge as 'rarely if ever' monolithic. This points to the value of detailed historical and ethnographic studies that can make explicit the contested character of intellectual fields (e.g. Shapin's account of the emergence of seventeenth-century physics (Shapin 1994)).

The political thrust of much recent social theory has assumed that (i) the social interests underpinning knowledge can be equated with wider inequalities of social class, and, more recently, of gender and race, and that (ii) social interests are typically distorting, and involve the introduction of bias in directions that need to be opposed. The argument in this chapter does not deny the possibility of social interests introducing bias and contributing to unequally distributed advantages and disadvantages. However, it does not assume that this is inevitable in either the production or the acquisition of knowledge, or that such 'external' interests are the sole or even the dominant definers of what counts as knowledge in a particular intellectual field. With these provisos in mind, the next section of the chapter will describe the elements of a social realist theory of knowledge and the manner in which it might resolve the epistemological and educational dilemmas already outlined. In the final section, an indication of possible implications of the theory for current debates about the curriculum will be suggested. In particular, an alternative is needed to the reductionism and ultimately inconsequential social critiques of postmodernism. Essentially, this means developing a knowledge-based model of the curriculum that is an alternative to neo-conservatism. Such a model would need to interrogate the knowledge structures and contents of the curriculum in a way that acknowledges their social and historical origins and their capacity (or lack of capacity) to transcend them.

In their various forms, reductionist sociologies of knowledge produce critiques of knowledge by describing it in terms of interests and perspectives. Walter Schmaus has pointed out that this assumes that cognitive goals do not enter into the explanation of actions and beliefs. 'Interest theories', he argues, 'are unable to recognize intellectual desires and motivations as being on a par with desires for power, prestige, money or sex ...' (Schmaus 1994: 262). He goes on to question the view that subscribing to a cognitive goal can always be reduced to belonging to a particular social group. He argues that knowledge relies on its own forms of collective social formation that are not just a reflection of some other social relations of power (Schmaus 1994). The crucial point is not necessarily to give cognitive interests primacy, but to recognize that they are also social in character, and have their own constitutive principles of autonomy from other social interests. As Schmaus says in relation to science (although the implications of his point are much wider):

> like any other social institution, [science] is defined in terms of the norms and values that govern it. To the extent that science aims at the growth of knowledge, it is characterized by cognitive norms and values. Cognitive values specify the aims of science, while cognitive norms specify the means to achieve these goals. Both cognitive values and norms range widely. Cognitive values may include everything from a scientist's position regarding the ontological status of unobservable entities to the desire to solve a specific set of problems or to explain a particular set of facts. Cognitive norms may range from rules governing the forms of persuasive argument that can be brought in defence of one's theory in a journal article to procedures for manipulating 'inscription devices' in the laboratory. To say that such cognitive factors should play a role in the sociology of scientific knowledge is not to say that all scientific activity must be explained exclusively in terms of cognitive factors. There is no question that scientists can and have been influenced by many non-cognitive interests. However, it does not follow from this fact that cognitive goals must always be reduced to non-cognitive goals and interests.
>
> (Schmaus 1994: 263)

As Schmaus goes on to stress, he is not implying that there is only one social form that these cognitive values and norms can adopt; scientific communities can adopt a wide variety of forms. His crucial points are (i) that it is arbitrary to exclude cognitive interests by adopting a reductive view of interests associated with power or prestige, and (ii) that cognitive interests are embedded within specific forms of social life or collectivities with their own distinctive 'associational codes' (Ward 1996). To assert that all knowledge is socially produced and historically located, as is agreed by virtually all traditions of the sociology of knowledge, does not provide adequate demarcation criteria for identifying what is 'social' or what is knowledge. Only positivists and their postmodernist critics insist that for knowledge to be knowledge it must be outside history, although of course they then draw precisely opposite conclusions as to whether this is, in reality, possible.

The exclusion of cognitive interests by standpoint and interest theories involves their 'replacement' (Mills 1998: 402) by other interests that the theories are prepared to acknowledge, e.g. the sectional interests of power and domination. This replacement renders invisible the social form of the 'knowledge producing' or 'knowledge transmitting' communities as distinctive specialist collectivities; they are seen simply as homologues of some other social relationship (such as those between ruling and ruled classes, men and women, black and white, etc.). This reduction masks the possibility of an asymmetry between cognitive and other interests, whereby the social construction of knowledge is collectively realized through certain necessary practices and social relations that transcend other interests with values, norms and procedures of their own. However, from a social realist point of view, epistemological demarcation criteria are not concerned with distinguishing the social from the non-social in knowledge claims. They are concerned with investigating the distinctive forms of social organization whereby powerful codes and procedures for the production and acquisition of knowledge have been developed that are increasingly global in scope (Ziman 2000).

The codes and procedures associated with the production of knowledge are reflected in research traditions and curricula, but also inherit and are shaped by a legacy of wider social divisions and inequalities that are becoming more acute, especially on a global scale. They exhibit an inertia and resistance to change, which are only partly cognitive in origin. However, they can in no meaningful sense be reducible to the interests of any particular social class, gender, nationality or ethnic group. It is precisely the relationship between these collective codes of knowledge production (research), knowledge acquisition (teaching and learning) and the wider social changes in the societies in which they are located that should form a major focus of study for the sociology of education.[6]

A social realist approach to knowledge can avoid Alexander's 'epistemological dilemma' by arguing (in contrast to positivism and postmodernism) that the social character of knowledge is an indispensable basis for its objectivity, rather than the condition that makes this objectivity impossible (Shapin 1994; Collins 1998). More generally, the social realist view of knowledge has implications for our understanding of the idea of a 'knowledge society'. It was argued earlier in this chapter that neither neo-conservative traditionalism, technical-instrumentalism nor their postmodernist critics have, in any proper sense of the term, a theory of knowledge. Consequently, knowledge is precisely the central category that is missing from debates about the knowledge society and its educational implications. In contrast, this chapter has stressed (i) the intrinsically social and collective character of knowledge production, (ii) the complexity of intellectual fields and the processes of knowledge production and transmission, and (iii) the asymmetry between cognitive and other interests that are involved in knowledge acquisition and production. Together, these issues bring the question of knowledge into focus in such a way that it becomes central to the future of knowledge societies and the relationship between the social organization of knowledge and social formations more generally (Young 1998; Moore 2000). This in no way denies that the production and transmission of knowledge is always entangled with a complex set of contending social interests and power relations. However, broad social trends that encompass both the emergence of what Castells (1998) calls a 'networked society', and the persistence, and in some ways the extension, of structured inequalities, always have to be seen in interaction with the social configurations of knowledge production itself (Ward 1996). It is only when the cognitive interests involved in the production of knowledge and the pedagogic interests involved in its transmission are given the importance they warrant that a social theory of knowledge can avoid an all too often facile reductionism. The two complementary goals of a social realist theory are (i) to properly reveal the manner in which external power relations might be affecting knowledge both in research and in the curriculum and how, and (ii) to explore how the forms of social organization that arise from 'cognitive' interests may themselves shape the organization of society itself.

The curriculum implications of a social realist approach to knowledge

Drawing on writers such as Ward (1996, 1997), Shapin (1994), Collins (1998) and Alexander (1995), the argument has been made that the objectivity of knowledge is in part located in the social networks, institutions and codes of practice built up by knowledge producers over time. It is these networks of social relations that, in crucial ways, guarantee truth claims, and give the knowledge that has produced its emergent powers. The structure of these networks has changed in increasingly complex ways as part of the overall transformation of societies during the past two centuries, and any attempt to depict these changes is in danger of oversimplification. What follows can be no more than a tentative and provisional way of suggesting how such changes may have effected the production and transmission of knowledge.

With the massive expansion of knowledge in the nineteenth century, networks of knowledge production began to expand and cohere as disciplines, relatively insulated from each other (Hoskyns 1993; Collins 1998; and Chapters 10 and 11 of this book). Furthermore, this process was paralleled by the emergence of the subject-based school curriculum as a key institution for the socialization of young people (Young 1998). What is less widely acknowledged is that the expanding public legitimacy and objectivity of the natural sciences, and later the social sciences, was underpinned by what Ward (1996) refers to as 'codes of association'. These 'codes' were enshrined in institutions such as the university subject departments and specialist professional and academic organizations concerned with knowledge production, and also in the school subject associations concerned with what counted as school knowledge and how it could be assessed and examined (Layton 1984). Despite significant expansion and diversification over the past century, these specialist forms of social organization remain the major social bases for guaranteeing the objectivity of knowledge and the standards achieved as the proportion of each cohort of school students entering examinations increases.

It is not surprising that the contents of and relations between the subjects and disciplines of the curriculum as the dominant form of the social organization of knowledge should have been contested. As argued earlier in the chapter, they have been taken as a given, and underpinned the neo-conservative defence of the traditional curriculum. On the other hand, their emergence and expansion was undoubtedly associated historically with profound inequalities in the access to education on the part of different social classes that were in part a legacy of a previous era. It is this association between the form of academic specialization and social inequality that has provided the bases for the radical attack on the subject-based curriculum underpinned often by left-wing versions of postmodernist attacks on epistemology. From the point of view argued in this paper, such an attack is mistaken. It is difficult to demonstrate, as claimed or implied by the postmodernists, that the historical association of curriculum specialization and social inequality is causal in its origins. Equally untenable is the a-historical view associated with neo-conservatism that existing academic specialization must be treated as a given – the result of some form of natural evolution. The disciplinary model of specialization is now challenged, however, not for primarily epistemological reasons, but by a technical-instrumentalism that takes issue with its resistance to change and its uncritical deference to traditional authorities. The neo-conservative model is increasingly seen as (i) too slow in the production of knowledge, (ii) too inefficient and too elitist to ensure that the majority of the population gain the skills and qualifications they need, and (iii) too out of touch with the increasingly competitive global society in which we find ourselves (Gibbons *et al.* 1994, 2000). As a result, the universities are under pressure to move away from a reliance on disciplines towards more trans-disciplinary models of knowledge production, and schools are encouraged to shift from a curriculum based on subjects to one based on modularity, the mixing of academic and vocational studies, and generic skills (Qualifications and Curriculum Authority 1999).

This conflict between the neo-conservatives and instrumentalists can be seen as one between different modes of knowledge production and curriculum organization along the following dimensions:

- from insulation to connectivity between disciplines and subjects, and between knowledge and its application;
- from the separation of general and vocational knowledge and learning to their integration;
- from linear sequencing to modular choice as curriculum principles;
- from hierarchical to facilitative or collaborative approaches to pedagogy.

Neo-conservatives tend to endorse the first of each of these options and take for granted that knowledge is best produced and transmitted through insulated, specialist, linear and hierarchical modes. At the same time, they neglect the political and economic changes that are calling into question these principles, as well as the inequalities of access and outcome that are associated with them. The technical-instrumentalists, on the contrary, support moves towards more connective, integrated, modular curricula, and more facilitative approaches to pedagogy. Unlike the neo-conservatives, they are well aware of the changing global economy and its implications, and they interpret knowledge and learning needs from what they hear from employers who call for a more skills-based curriculum (Royal Society of Arts 1998). However, their curriculum proposals give scant attention to the cognitive and pedagogic interests that it was earlier argued underpin the production and acquisition of knowledge. As a result, their curriculum proposals provoke doubts about standards and end up unintentionally providing support for the neo-conservatives (Woodhead 2004). From the social realist perspective argued for in this chapter, both approaches are flawed. The 'curriculum of the past' (Young 1998, 1999) that is defended by neo-conservative traditionalism takes no account of the changing social context within which the curriculum is located. On the other hand, the so-called 'curriculum of the future' neglects the extent to which the capacity of any curriculum to be the basis for acquiring new knowledge in any field depends on *cognitive* interests, which will be expressed in the social networks, trust and codes of practice among specialists that give it an objectivity and sense of standards. Whereas the old curriculum was undoubtedly elitist, its critics, both instrumentalists and postmodernists, focus only on its elitism and resistance to change. They fail to recognize that the social organization of subjects and disciplines transcended its elitist origins as a basis for the acquisition and production of knowledge. Without the equivalent networks and codes of practice, a new curriculum will lose the benefits, albeit for the few, of the neo-conservative model without any gains for the many. There are few signs that the traditional groupings of subject specialists that have maintained standards have been extended by new types of specialist teacher networks needed to underpin multi-disciplinary curricula. Furthermore when such networks have been developed they rarely address the issue of cognitive interests.[7]

Postmodernist critiques tend to point to the voices that are silenced in the new curriculum model, as in the old. However, this is an example of the limitations of the over-dichotomized critiques discussed earlier, and does little more than to demonstrate that some kind of silencing (or expressed less emotively, selection) will be a feature of any curriculum. The issues of what kind of selection and what kind of learning are most important are not addressed from such a perspective. In re-emphasizing that both the emergent properties of knowledge and its wider social basis have to be taken into account, a social realist approach to knowledge offers a possible way forward both for the sociology of education and for curriculum studies.[8]

Conclusions

The social realist approach argued for in this chapter recognizes the 'social' character of knowledge as intrinsic to its epistemological status because the logical reconstruction of truth is always a dialogue with others set within particular collective codes and values (Collins 1998). This has important implications, then, for avoiding the 'educational dilemma' posed by the alternatives of traditionalism and instrumentalism, and their (so-called 'progressive') postmodern critics. For example, it provides the grounds for:

- avoiding both the a-historical givenness of neo-conservative traditionalism and a reliance on such notions as relevance, learner-centredness and experience in decisions about the curriculum;
- maintaining an autonomy for the curriculum from the instrumentalism of economic or political demands;
- assessing curriculum proposals in terms of balancing goals such as overcoming social exclusion and widening participation with the no less important 'cognitive interests' that are involved in knowledge production, acquisition and transmission;
- reorienting debates about curriculum standards from attempts to specify learning outcomes and extend testing to identifying cognitive interests and building the necessary specialist communities, networks and codes of practice to support them.

From a sociological point of view, these four implications of a social realist approach to knowledge take it beyond the alternatives posed by the two orthodoxies and their postmodern critics, and bring knowledge back into curriculum debate and into the sociology of education, as the historically located collective achievement of human creativity.

3 Durkheim, Vygotsky and the curriculum of the future

> Only the church has an art. It alone gives us a little comfort and detaches us from the world ... we are all children beside the liturgists and theologians ... The greatest ... imitate them.
>
> (Paul Valery 1991)

> the rules of classic art teach us by their arbitrary nature that the thoughts arising from our daily needs, sentiments and experiences are only a small part of the thoughts of which we are capable.
>
> (Paul Valery 1941)

Introduction

What principles should underpin the curriculum of the future? First, will the curriculum continue to be based on a clear separation between the theoretical knowledge to be acquired at school and the practical knowledge that people acquire in their everyday lives? And second, will the curriculum continue to take the disciplinary form that became established during the nineteenth century, or should it give far greater emphasis to the practical and social skills and knowledge that, many argue, adults are likely to need in a competitive global economy (RSA 1998)? Answers to these questions will depend, at least in part, on the assumptions that are made about the nature of knowledge, how and in what ways it changes and how the knowledge on which the curriculum is based differs (and should differ) from the everyday knowledge of communities and workplaces. As well as being concerned with these questions, this chapter continues the broader aim of this book, which in collaboration with others (see Muller 2000; Moore 2004 and Muller 2007 as well as Chapters 2 and 15 of this book) is to develop a more adequate basis for the sociology of education. It also breaks new ground for me as a sociologist in discussing the work of the Russian psychologist, Lev Vygotsky. Two of Vygotsky's ideas are of particular importance to me. One is the distinction he makes between what one can learn on one's own and what one can learn with a teacher, which is expressed in his concept of the 'zone of proximal development'. The second idea is what he refers to as the relationship between theoretical and everyday concepts, which lies at the heart of pedagogy and the curriculum.

The belief that the knowledge acquired through the curriculum is (or at least should be) cognitively superior to people's everyday knowledge has been the major rationale for the massive expansion of formal education in the past two centuries and for the reform of vocational programmes that had previously relied only on workplace learning. However, radical educationists, including nineteenth-century socialists, twentieth-century romantics and twenty-first-century adult educators who invoke the pedagogic potential of individual experience, have a long history of questioning these assumptions about the knowledge base and educational potential of the formal curriculum. Criticisms of the traditional curriculum have gained a new and wider credibility in the past decade. A growing tension has become apparent between the fluidity and openness to innovation of successful advanced economies – what some have termed 'fast capitalism' – and the persistence of relatively rigid divisions between the different school subjects and disciplines and between curriculum knowledge in general and the everyday knowledge that people use in employment and more generally in their adult lives. On the one hand it seems inconceivable that the curriculum should be immune from changes in society and from what some argue are changes in the mode and sites of the production of knowledge (Gibbons *et al.* 1994). On the other hand, the traditional curriculum, which institutionalized the separation of subjects from each other and of the curriculum from everyday knowledge, is an almost universal feature of education systems, and has been associated with the massive expansion of knowledge and economic growth of the past two centuries. We have here, in other words, a version of the distinction between 'conservative-traditionalists' and 'instrumental-rationalists' introduced in the previous chapter.

Muller (2000) sharpens the dilemma facing curriculum designers and gives it a greater analytical specificity by characterizing this tension between 'past' and possible 'future' curricula in terms of the contrasting principles of *insularity* and *hybridity.* The principle of insularity emphasizes the *differences* rather than the *continuity* between types of knowledge. It rejects the assumption that the divisions and classifications between types of knowledge are just a reflection of traditions inherited from medieval times and that they are maintained largely as a justification of existing professional interests and current power relations. These classifications have, it is claimed, both epistemological and pedagogic significance; in other words, they relate in fundamental ways to how people learn and how they produce new knowledge. The principle of insularity asserts that the demands of knowledge production and acquisition put limits on the possibilities for curriculum innovation – in particular the crossing of disciplinary and subject boundaries and the convergence of theoretical knowledge and practical 'know-how' and skills. There is, it is argued, a pedagogic (and, in relation to research, an epistemological) price to pay for dispensing with such boundaries. Not surprisingly, the principle of insularity is sometimes invoked to support profoundly conservative doctrines in defence both of the curriculum status quo and of claims that, despite the steady increase in numbers gaining higher level qualifications, both school and university standards are falling (Woodhead 2002). However, there are epistemological as well as political arguments in support of insularity.

The former are based on a view of knowledge – that what distinguishes knowledge from fact, opinion and practical know-how is that it is not tied to the history and social organization of its production or acquisition. As Descartes put it nearly four centuries ago, real knowledge is beyond all 'custom and example'.

The principle of hybridity, on the other hand, is a relatively recent idea. It rejects any claim that the boundaries and classifications of the curriculum reflect features of knowledge itself and are anything more than a product of history. It stresses not the differences but the 'essential unity and continuity of [all] forms and kinds of knowledge ... [and] the *permeability* of classificatory boundaries' (Muller 2000; my additions and italics). The principle of hybridity is defended not primarily on pedagogic or epistemological grounds,[1] but in terms of its consistency with the increasingly 'boundary-less' character of modern economies (Reich 1991). A curriculum based on the principle of hybridity is seen as providing a way of overcoming the traditional boundedness or 'encapsulation' (Engestrom 1991) of school or academic knowledge.

The 'social constructivist' view of knowledge and the curriculum that is implicit in the concept of hybridity has always appealed to radicals as a basis for exposing the vested interests associated with existing boundaries and their claims to universality. It is these arguments that are endorsed by postmodernists who follow Nietszche and argue that the debate is an old one, and hybridity is only superficially a new idea; for them neither epistemological nor pedagogic criteria have ever been more than a way of masking issues of power and interest.

There are, however, practical reasons why a curriculum based on the principle of hybridity appeals to education policy makers; it appears to converge with the new policy goals of social inclusion and accountability. Pressures for social inclusion require the curriculum to go beyond its traditional subject boundaries and recognize the knowledge and experience of those traditionally excluded from formal education. Likewise, pressures for greater accountability seek to limit the autonomy of the specialist knowledge producers. In both cases the insularity of academic knowledge is set against social and economic arguments for a 'responsive' curriculum that can be the basis for new kinds of skills and knowledge that transcend current disciplinary boundaries and academic/vocational divisions. In rejecting any link between specific knowledge classifications and either pedagogic demands or epistemological principles, the hybridity principle supports the belief that decisions about the curriculum should depend, ultimately, on market pressures and political priorities. A good example is the growing number of programmes launched in higher education that are designed with the primary purpose of attracting more students.[2]

The outcome of the tension between these two principles seems currently to point in two directions. One is towards the progressive disappearance and replacement of the disciplinary curriculum and, it could be argued, the weakening of an autonomous critical role for educational institutions. The other is the emergence of new divisions between *elite institutions* (both schools and universities), which continue to maintain discipline-based curricula, and *mass institutions* with curricula geared to more immediate economic and political demands. The issue with which this chapter is concerned continues the quest begun in the previous chapter. It is to find a basis for the curriculum that avoids these outcomes without reverting to the conservativism of the traditional model of disciplinarity, or accepting the uncertain consequences of hybridity and its ultimate renunciation of any distinctive pedagogic or epistemological criteria. In order to do this, the chapter discusses and compares some of the social and educational ideas of the French sociologist Emile Durkheim and the Russian psychologist Lev Vygotsky, as well as some of those who have built on their ideas and taken them further. Both theorists, albeit in different ways, gave priority to the *differentiation* of knowledge, especially the differences between theoretical and everyday knowledge, rather than to its seamlessness. Similarly, both theorists tried to locate the differentiation of knowledge within their social theories of the origins of higher forms of thinking.

The next section of this chapter describes the theoretical basis of the idea of insularity in the work of Durkheim (1995) and as it has been developed more recently by Bernstein (1971, 2000). It outlines Durkheim's and Bernstein's respective distinctions between 'sacred' and 'profane' orders of meaning, and 'vertical' and 'horizontal' discourses and knowledge structures. It argues that the strength of a Durkheimian approach as the basis for a model of the curriculum is that it recognizes that although knowledge is a social and human product, it is its *sociality* that gives knowledge an objectivity beyond the social processes associated with its acquisition and production. However, in treating the differentiation of knowledge in dichotomous terms (or in the case of Bernstein, in terms of a number of fractally related dichotomies (Abbott 2000; Moore and Muller 2002), Durkheimian analyses remain largely synchronic and static. In other words, they describe the features of different types of knowledge and their social bases, but give little attention to how the relationships between them may change over time.[3] Thus, while a Durkheimian approach provides criteria for distinguishing between the curriculum and everyday knowledge in general, it does not locate the historical roots of the forms in which these criteria are expressed. Hence it is somewhat limited as a basis for conceptualizing how new knowledge categories and curricula are generated, or for evaluating the different ways in which the curriculum and everyday knowledge are separated. Furthermore, in his concern with locating the foundations or the possibilities of knowledge in society (a kind of sociological Kantianism), Durkheim's approach is, I would argue, more a sociological philosophy than a historical sociology. In turning to Bernstein's development of Durkheim's approach, I suggest that, while still limited in the a-historical nature of his categories, he goes beyond Durkheim in two ways. First, he shows how different forms of knowledge progression can be conceptualized, and second, he provides a framework for analysing the different ways in which curriculum and everyday knowledge are separated.

The chapter then turns to a comparison of the social origins of thought and knowledge in the work of Durkheim and Vygotsky. It is particularly concerned with the implications, in their accounts of the evolution of modern scientific thinking, of the rather different ways in which they drew on ethnographies of primitive societies. It goes on to note the central role of pedagogy in both their social theories. I then examine Vygotsky's approach to the differentiation of knowledge as a basis for describing two very different approaches to considering his distinction between scientific and everyday concepts. The first of these treats Vygotsky's distinction as a dichotomy that has some parallels with Durkheim's distinction between 'sacred' and profane'. This is an approach followed by a number of neo-Vygotskians (e.g. John-Steiner *et al.* 1978). It argues that Vygotsky concentrates on the relationship between the two types of concept and how they can be used to analyse the learning process. In contrast, Durkheim pays less attention to the relationship between the types of concept, but is more explicit about the distinctive *social* origins of scientific concepts themselves (Durkheim 1983). The second approach is the one followed by Engestrom (1991), which is to interpret Vygotsky's distinction dialectically, in terms of his overall theory of human development. This means that the distinction between scientific and everyday concepts is no longer just a dichotomy, or even an account of the process of learning and development. It becomes part of an approach to the historical development of knowledge as human society changes, and how this process is linked to how individuals engage in learning and development. Potentially, such an approach offers a way of going beyond the analyses of Durkheim and Bernstein, and locating knowledge and the curriculum within a broader theory of social change. I shall, however, suggest that although Vygotsky breaks with the problems of Durkheim's synchronic analysis, a dialectical approach introduces new problems that, on its own, it is unable to resolve. By locating knowledge in the history of human beings' actions on the external world, a dialectical approach treats knowledge as a product of human labour. Furthermore, labour in the Marxist sense referred to purposive activity; hence the obvious parallels between Marx's theories of the labour process and the activity theories developed by Leont'ev and others who built on Vygotsky's ideas. Within such an analysis, knowledge and truth, as distinct categories referring to causes and explanations that are not tied to specific political purposes, disappear.[4]

Understandably, most Soviet theorists of Vygotsky's time claimed to have 'solved' the problem of a dialectical theory of knowledge in terms of Marx's theory that the emancipation of the working class was the necessary and logical outcome of history and therefore the arbiter of truth and objectivity. Vygotsky's interpretors in the west, such as Engestrom, have tried to avoid this Marxist dogmatism, as well as the relativism implicit in a dialectical approach. They attempt to retain the idea that resolving contradictions has emancipatory potential, but generalize the Marxist idea that the basic contradictions in any society are between social classes by claiming that they are a feature of social life in general. This approach has parallels with Dewey, who also held a non-dogmatic version of dialectical method. Dewey did not adopt a social class analysis but relied on his belief in a form of Darwinian social evolution and his hopes for the progressive democratization of American society as criteria for knowledge and truth (Rytina and Loomis 1970). Another alternative is reflected in Ollman's philosophy of 'internal relations' (Ollman 1976), and in the arguments developed by Bakhurst (1995), who draws on the Russian philosopher Ilyenkov. Bakhurst and others argue that a dialectical approach that overcomes the 'two worlds' of knowledge and practice is consistent with the idea that not only are we part of the world of which we seek knowledge, but that this world is already pre-socialized by us. It follows that any concept of knowledge cannot avoid being dialectical, at least in the most general sense. This is intellectually coherent in its own terms. However, if it is used as a basis for addressing specific issues of social or curriculum change, it does not seem to be able to avoid the problem of knowledge that the pragmatists and Marxist dogmatists try to avoid. Some kind of assumptions about knowledge have to be invoked. I conclude that a dialectical interpretation of Vygotsky is inadequate on its own. It needs to be combined with what I have referred to in Chapter 2 as a 'social realist' approach to the objectivity of knowledge. Towards the end of this chapter, I attempt to develop this 'solution' to the problem of knowledge that was left unresolved in dialectical approaches such as Marxism and pragmatism, and their tendency to collapse the category of knowledge into practice, and the category of truth into its consequences. In attempting to address the unresolved problems of a dialectical approach, I will draw on Durkheim's analysis of pragmatism (Durkheim 1983). I am not invoking a universalistic approach to truth or objectivity, nor the idea that truth criteria can be developed that are more than partially independent of specific contexts. I shall argue, instead, that a concept of knowledge that has some independence from the contexts of its production, acquisition and development in history is necessary both as a basis for a more adequate curriculum theory, and in accounting for the unprecedented role in social transformation that has been played by science since the seventeenth century. Second, I shall take further the argument developed in Chapter 2 that knowledge has emerged as the product of the codes, rules and practices of those involved in specialist fields of inquiry and the debates that have developed within them (Collins 1998). The chapter concludes with some observations on the implications of my comparison of Durkheim and Vygotsky's ideas for the questions about the curriculum with which the chapter began.

Durkheim, knowledge and the curriculum

Durkheim did not develop his approach to knowledge and concept development as an explicit part of his educational theory. It is only relatively recently, thanks largely to the work of Basil Bernstein, that its importance for debates about the curriculum has been recognized. Developing a *sociology* of knowledge had two purposes for Durkheim. First, it was part of his broader concern to establish the distinctive role of sociology as a social science of universal applicability. Second, he wanted to establish a sound (and therefore, for him, necessarily a sociological) basis for science and truth which would overcome what he saw as the fundamental weaknesses of the philosophy of his time and its domination by rationalism and empiricism (Ward 1996).[5] There are at least two possible reasons for the neglect of Durkheim's sociology of knowledge by curriculum theorists. One may have been that his focus was not on specific fields of knowledge such as the natural or social sciences, but on providing a sociological theory of knowledge and truth in general. Second, Durkheim's general social theory of knowledge was not, like his famous study of suicide, based on contemporary data, but on extrapolating from an analysis of ethnographic studies of religion in societies that had no institutions of formal education.

Durkheim's starting point in his analysis of primitive societies was the *social* reality of their religions; he saw religion as the prime example of 'collective representations'. Collective representations do not, for Durkheim, originate in individual minds; they grow out of the 'collective effervescence' of communities, and are the source of the most basic categories of human thought such as cause, time and place as well as the specific categories and ritual practices of different religions. Furthermore, he argued that these collective representations, though initially religious in content in primitive societies, were the paradigm of all advanced forms of theoretical knowledge. Crucial to his account of religion and the emergence of collective representations in general was his distinction between 'profane' and 'sacred' orders of meaning, which he argued was a feature of all the primitive societies that he studied.[6] The distinction for Durkheim was absolute: 'In all the history of human thought there exists no other example of two categories of things so profoundly differentiated or so radically opposed to one another' (Durkheim 1995: 53).

For Durkheim, the 'profane' referred to how people respond to their everyday world – in practical, immediate and particular ways. He distinguished the 'profane' everyday world from the 'sacred' world of religion, which he saw as invented, arbitrary (in the sense of not being tied to specific objects and events) and, equally crucially, *collective*. The sacred consisted of systems of related but unobservable concepts. In not being tied to specific observations or experiences, these systems of concepts had, for Durkheim, *an objectivivity* arising from their shared, social character, and from the fact that they were external to the perceptions of individuals. Furthermore, because they do not originate in individuals, sacred concepts are relatively fixed and unchanging as well as exhibiting a distinctive feature of knowledge and truth – individuals feel under external pressure to accept them. For Durkheim, when truth and knowledge are at stake, the issue of choice does not arise.

Religion was important for Durkheim, not as evidence for the existence of God but for two other reasons. First, being a shared set of collective representations it had an integrative function[7] in maintaining social solidarity, and second, he saw religion as the model for all the other types of abstract thought, such as modern science, that consist of unobservable concepts. In other words, the totems of the aborigines and the gas laws of the physicist were, in form at least, identical for Durkheim. He identified two key features of the 'sacred', which are summarized in what he referred to as 'the faculty of realization' and which gave the sacred its paradigmatic status as the basis of future knowledge. First, in so far as the sacred was constituted by a set of concepts shared by a community but not tied to specific objects or events, it enabled people to *make connections* between objects and events that, on the basis of everyday experience, did not appear related. This 'connecting' capability is crucial for scientists, but no less so for those in primitive communities who experience most natural events as external forces over which they have little control. Second, not being tied to the everyday world, the sacred enables people to *project beyond the present* to possible futures. In the case of primitive societies this capacity for projection referred to people's capacity to envisage some kind of 'after life' beyond their everyday world over which they felt powerless. By contrast, in modern societies, the same capacity becomes the potential to predict on the basis of scientific hypotheses and the evidence for them, and more generally to conceive of alternative forms of society (such as socialism). For Durkheim both these features distinguished 'theoretical' knowledge (in the sense of knowledge constituted by a system of concepts), whether religious or scientific, from everyday knowledge. At the same time the distinction was, for Durkheim, not a judgement about one type of knowledge being superior to the other; his stress was on their differences. As he pointed out, everyday living would not be possible if we could only rely on theoretical knowledge whether it was religious or scientific. Similarly, if our thinking was restricted to the 'profane' or the everyday it would only be possible to make sense of the world in very limited ways. Furthermore, everyday thinking, located as it is as responses to specific contexts, is no basis for developing objective knowledge of the world that transcends such contexts. Durkheim's argument was that *all* societies are characterized by a degree of specialization between these two types of knowledge. What distinguishes societies is not specialization per se, or the availability of abstract unobservable concepts, but the extent of specialization, the nature of the concepts,[8] and the extent to which they are criticized and subjected to empirical test.

Gellner (1992) argues that the significance of Durkheim's sociology of knowledge is that he makes a powerful case for the social (as opposed to individual) origins of reason or abstract thought; hence he broke with the individualism of Descartes and, though more ambiguously, Kant,[9] and what he saw as the abstract idealism of Hegel. Abstract or theoretical thought is not, for Durkheim, a characteristic or capacity of particular individuals, but a feature of societies – all societies.[10] In showing how the features of abstract thought, especially its scope and its systematic character, are related to its origins in social activities, Durkheim's sociology of knowledge is *synchronic*; it sees knowledge or concepts as collective representations which arise when people come together in societies. Where his theory is less adequate is in providing a *diachronic* account of the differentiation and expansion of abstract thought in modern societies, and its association with empirical methods and specialist forms of critical analysis. Gellner (1992) makes the interesting suggestion that if we are to have a full understanding of the growth of knowledge, Durkheim's theory needs to be complemented by Weber's account of how Protestantism in the seventeenth century (and the doctrine of predestination, in particular), as a particular expression of the sacred, formed the social basis for the emergence of the distinctive discipline of science and the risk-taking involved in entrepreneurship. However, to explore Gellner's suggestion further is beyond the scope of this chapter. In so far as Durkheim identifies a motor for the differentiation of knowledge, it appears to be the population pressures which he saw as determining the broader changes in the division of labour; however, he does not relate this argument directly to changes in his knowledge categories. Another problem with Durkheim's account is that he gives little attention to the internal stratification of knowledge within societies.[11] It seems likely that this neglect was partly a result of the dependence of Durkheim's sociology of knowledge on studies of small-scale societies with little stratification. The problem to which extrapolating from studies of primitive societies leads is that Durkheim's sociology of knowledge avoids the extent that relations of power, such as those expressed in divisions between mental and manual labour, shape relations between types of knowledge and convert them into hierarchies (Young 1998: Chapter 1). Furthermore, his emphasis on *differences* between types of knowledge in the societies that he studied neglects the tendency in modern societies for some profane knowledge to claim sacred status. It is this neglect of the link between power and knowledge which some radical and postmodernist critics of Durkheim have highlighted. However, in their critiques, as was suggested in Chapter 2, they themselves tend to reduce discussions of knowledge to questions of power, and neglect the very questions about knowledge with which Durkheim was concerned.

Durkheim's argument about the social origins of knowledge can be summarized as follows:

- All societies distinguish between the sacred and the profane and between common sense (our everyday response to events) and *theory* (our systems of unobservable concepts).
- It is the *social* reality of unobservable concepts (whether scientific or religious) that gives them their power (and claims to objectivity and truth) relative to our common-sense concepts, and enables them to transcend the specific instances and circumstances of everyday life.
- The development of knowledge is given little attention in Durkheim's work. His view is best described as combining the *continuity* of the separation of abstract and everyday thought and the *evolution* of abstract thought from its original religious form to its contemporary scientific forms (Horton 1974).

For Durkheim, continuity refers to the separation of theory and common sense in all societies, and evolution refers to the process by which religion (as the first form of theory based on unobservable concepts) becomes the social basis for science. He rejected what Horton (1974) refers to as the contrast/inversion schema associated with Levy-Bruhl, which emphasized the contrast between the mystical thought of primitive societies and the rational thought of modern societies. There is an important difference here between Durkheim and Vygotsky, who was much influenced by, but not uncritical of Levy-Bruhl in developing his account of the social origins of higher forms of thought, (Vygotsky 1987; Luria and Vygotsky 1992). This is a point that I will return to later in this chapter, and in Chapter 4.

A major problem with Durkheim's social theory of knowledge is that, while an evolutionary development of knowledge is implied, he says little about the process. His theory is strong in its distinction between theory and common sense, and the origins of the distinction in the separation of sacred and profane orders of meaning;

however, it says little about how one type of unobservable concept (e.g. force as a mystical idea or totem) evolves into another (force as a scientific idea – like gravity). Like most intellectuals of his time, Durkheim took science for granted as his model of knowledge, and therefore in effect equated the two. What distinguished his view of science was his emphasis on its conceptual rather than its empirical basis, and his demonstration that this conceptual basis has social origins. However, I next turn to some brief comments on how the leading English Durkheimian, Basil Bernstein, took Durkheim's ideas forward and applied them to the curriculum.

Bernstein's distinction between 'vertical' and 'horizontal' knowledge structures' (2000) is a development of his own earlier ideas about the classification of knowledge (Bernstein 1971) and Durkheim's sacred/profane distinction applied to the curriculum. He separates Durkheim's distinction between theoretical and common-sense ideas from the distinction between the sacred and the profane on which it was based. He also breaks up Durkheim's dichotomy and explores the different forms that theoretical concepts can take in terms of vertical and horizontal discourses, pyramidical and segmental knowledge structures, weak and strong grammars and explicit and tacit modes of transmission. As a result, we have a far more analytically powerful approach to the knowledge base of contemporary curricula. However, while undoubtedly an advance on Durkheim, the weaknesses as well as the strengths of the Durkheimian framework persist. Like Durkheim, Bernstein treats his categories largely in synchronic terms, and their relationship with each other and their development remain unclear. The idea of knowledge change appears only as a suggestive footnote to his overall theory.[12] However, his distinction between types of knowledge structure provides a valuable framework for analysing current curriculum developments, such as those which try to base the vocational curriculum on the tacit skills gained through work experience (see Chapter 9). On the other hand, as his theory does not, at least explicitly, account for how categories of knowledge change historically, it is difficult to see how on its own it can be a basis for conceptualizing a 'curriculum of the future'.

Verticality as a cardinal property of knowledge is defined more precisely by Bernstein than the sacred or science by Durkheim, in terms of sets of principles of generalizeability which are hierarchically related to each other. However, his analysis of verticality seems over-determined by (i) an idealization of physics which may be less pyramidical than he assumes (Knorr-Cetina 1999), and (ii) a view of the segmented structure of sociology which seems to deny the possibility that it, and therefore, as Moore and Muller (2002) point out, his own work, can provide explanations that go beyond redescription. This is a point that is explored in more detail in Chapter 15.

In searching for a more historical and dynamic approach to knowledge that can take account of the impact of societal change on the knowledge base of the curriculum, I turn next to the work of the Marxist psychologist and social theorist, Lev Vygotsky. The distinction between scientific (or theoretical) and common-sense thinking was, as in the case of Durkheim, at the centre of Vygotsky's social and educational theory. However, the differences as well as the similarities between the two theorists are important and, in particular, how these differences are linked to how each theorist interpreted their origins in the thought of primitive societies.

The social origins of knowledge and thought in Vygotsky and Durkheim

As a sociologist coming to Vygotsky's work for the first time, I was initially struck by the striking similarities between Vygotsky's distinction between scientific and everyday concepts and Durkheim's distinction between the sacred and the profane.[13] However, although Vygotsky was undoubtedly familiar with Durkheim's work, I have found very few explicit references to Durkheim in his writings, at least those that have been translated into English.[14] The key section on scientific and everyday concepts in his *Collected Works* (1987) makes many references to Piaget's distinction between spontaneous and scientific concepts, but does not explicitly refer to Durkheim at all.[15]

There are also parallels between Vygotsky and Durkheim in their approaches to the social origins (or genesis) of higher forms of thought, though again, Vygotsky does not refer explicitly to Durkheim. In his account of the social origins (or genesis) of thought, Vygotsky drew explicitly on the writings of Durkheim's French colleague, the social anthropologist, Levy-Bruhl. Vygotsky was interested in developing a theory of human development that showed that 'relations between mankind and nature are not all that have changed. Man himself has changed and developed. Human nature has changed [*in the course of history*]' (Luria and Vygotsky 1992: 41; my addition in italics). It was this concern to avoid an essentialist and a-historical view of human nature that led to Vygotsky being interested in the historical development of the human psyche (or human psychology, as he put it), and with this goal in mind he turned to studies of 'so-called' primitive peoples, and in particular the work of Levy-Bruhl. Vygotsky drew two important lessons from Levy-Bruhl. The first was his argument for a non-individualist theory of thought. Vygotsky agreed with Levy-Bruhl that 'the laws of individual psychology ... cannot provide explanations for the beliefs ... that emerge in any society'. Second, he was searching for the basis of a *developmental* theory that emphasized how forms of thinking *change* over time. Hence the importance, for Vygotsky, of Levy-Bruhl's premise that 'different types of society are associated with different types of human psychology' (Luria and Vygotsky 1992: 44).

Vygotsky points out that for Levy-Bruhl, 'the higher psychological functions of primitive man are profoundly different from those same functions in civilised man ... the very type of thinking ... (is) ... a historical variable' (Luria and Vygotsky 1992: 44). Vygotsky was not uncritical of Levy-Bruhl's characterization of primitive thinking as pre-logical or mystical, and pointed out that he neglected the practical (or in Marxist terms, the productive) side of life in primitive societies. Vygotsky's view was that even primitive man was capable of 'objective logical thinking whenever the purpose of his actions is direct adaptation to nature' (Luria and Vygotsky 1992: 45).

In own his last works, undertaken long after Vygotsky died, Levy-Bruhl somewhat modified the extreme dichotomy of his earlier views, and allowed a role for practical, non-mystical thought in primitive societies as well as recognizing that mysticism can still be found in modern times (Horton 1974). However, he retained the distinction between common sense and science on the one hand and mysticism on the other which was, as we shall see, diametrically opposed to Durkheim's position.

Unlike Durkheim, Vygotsky accepted Levy-Bruhl's distinction between primitive and modern thought, which he saw as the paradigm case for the idea that human thought varies between societies and develops over time. Vygotsky refers to Levy-Bruhl approvingly as 'the first [person] to have shown that the type of thinking, per se, is not a constant, but a variable, which develops throughout history' (Luria and Vygotsky 1992: 46). On the other hand, Vygotsky appears to have identified the developmental potential of primitive thought with just those 'actions in direct adaptation to nature' (Luria and Vygotsky 1992: 45) to which Levy-Bruhl himself paid little attention.

Vygotsky does not seem, at least explicitly, to have been aware of Durkheim's quite different analysis of primitive mentality. Horton (1974), in discussing Durkheim's review of Levy-Bruhl's *Les Fonctions Mentales dans les Sociétés Inférieures*, noted that:

> both he [Durkheim] and Levy-Bruhl are concerned to explore the distinction that is commonly made between 'primitive' and 'modern' thought [and that] both are in agreement about the social determinants of all thought and about the essentially religious nature of 'primitive' thought.
>
> (Horton 1974: 267)

However, as Horton goes on to point out, 'Levy-Bruhl sees "primitive" and "modern" thought as antithetical ... whereas Durkheim ... sees the change from primitive to modern as stages in a single evolutionary process'.

Durkheim, Horton argues, singles out Levy-Bruhl's 'law of participation',

> whereby for primitive man [it is possible to] participate in several entirely different forms of being. Whereas for Levy-Bruhl this 'law' was an exemplar of everything that is most opposed to the spirit of modern science, for Durkheim what Levy-Bruhl calls participation is at the core of all logical life.
>
> (Horton 1974: 268)

We have, therefore, three different approaches to the genesis of higher forms of thought. Levy-Bruhl saw the thinking of primitive man as characterized by a combination of mysticism and common sense. For him, in the process of civilization, societies have gradually dispensed with the mysticism of primitive thought, and replaced it with the empirical methods of science. Vygotsky agreed with Levy-Bruhl about primitive thought being a combination of the practical and the mystical; however, he gave much more emphasis to the practical, especially 'the invention of tools, hunting, animal husbandry, agriculture and fighting all [of which] demand from him *real* and not just apparent logical thought' (Luria and Vygotsky 1992: 45).

Thus, Vygotsky located the historically changing nature of man's psyche in these forms of human labour. The development of higher forms of thought, for Vygotsky, grew out of these practical activities as part of human development in general. Vygotsky did not appear to address exactly how higher (and later, scientific) forms of thought developed from this early practical activity.

Durkheim, on the other hand, interpreted the findings of the ethnographies of primitive societies very differently from Levy-Bruhl. First, as Horton (1974) points out, Durkheim stresses (i) the *continuity* between primitive religious classifications and the classifications of modern science, and (ii) the *difference* in modern societies between technical/practical classifications and scientific classifications (for a further exploration of this point see Chapter 4). Although he does not say so explicitly, Vygotsky would, one assumes, have rejected each of these propositions. He would have agreed with Levy-Bruhl that science is not in continuity with religion but is its antithesis. Furthermore, he would have rejected Durkheim's distinction between the technical and the scientific. Second, Durkheim differed from Levy-Bruhl in his characterization of primitive thought; for him the point was not that it consisted of common-sense practical thinking and mystical thinking, but that common sense (the profane) and religious or conceptual thinking (the sacred) were separate and different. It was the shared and therefore social character of the sacred and its separateness from everyday life, not its content, that gave it objectivity and enabled it to be the basis for science for Durkheim.

In contrast to Durkheim, it was in primitive man's *practical activity* that Vygotsky saw the 'germ' of knowledge that develops later into 'scientific' concepts. For Durkheim, on the other hand, the germ of modern science is to be found not in man's practical activities but in the socially based objectivity of the religion of primitive societies. These differences between Durkheim and Vygotsky lie at the heart of their different approaches to knowledge. For the former, the objectivity of knowledge is conceptual and located socially, originally in religion. For the latter, it is located in man's productive activities in history. I will return to this distinction in a later section, and in Chapter 4.

For both Durkheim and Vygotsky, and notwithstanding the latter's Marxism, there is a sense in which educational (or pedagogic) relations were the *primary* social relations, especially in the modern societies of their time. This similarity cuts across the more obvious differences between a liberal sociologist in capitalist France and a Marxist psychologist in Soviet Russia. How education was conceptualized as 'the social' by the two writers was different, and indicates why it may be useful to take them together. As someone sympathetic to the goals of post-revolutionary Russia, Vygotsky's primary interest was in developing Soviet citizens as an inseparable part of the goal of societal progress towards communism. Education had a central role in this process. Vygotsky argued that it was the capacity of human beings to learn, not from mere adaptation to the environment as is the case in animal learning, but from teaching (or pedagogy), that distinguished them from animals. Hence the key role of learning and development in his social theory, and the importance of his concept of the zone of proximal development which links learning to teaching in the broader context of the historical movement towards communism. In his social theory there are powerful similarities between Vygotsky's concept of learning as a social process and Marx's concept of the labour process – especially if labour is interpreted in the broader humanistic sense associated with Marx's early writings. It was not just that Vygotsky recognized that learning is a social process and inescapably linked to teaching, but that for him the purpose of education, and learning more generally, was social change.[16]

Durkheim's priorities were quite different from Vygotsky's. He was interested in how social order is maintained when societies are undergoing dramatic change.[17] Political instability and the progressive collapse of the credibility of the Catholic Church as the main bastion of social order in France were the realities that most shaped Durkheim's thinking. It was not surprising therefore that, as a democrat, Durkheim's primary political and theoretical interests were in finding a non-coercive basis for maintaining social order; hence the pivotal role he gives to education and morality. Thus, although education had a similarly central social role for Durkheim as for Vygotsky, the emphasis for each was different. For the former, the function of education was integrative rather than being oriented to social change and was moral rather than developmental. For the latter it was explicitly developmental, for the individual and for society. Bearing in mind these differences and similarities, the next section turns to a more specific consideration of Vygotsky's distinction between scientific and everyday concepts and their implications for the curriculum (or instruction, as he would have expressed it).

Locating Vygotsky's distinction between scientific and everyday concepts

As others have pointed out, Vygotsky's ideas about the development of scientific concepts did not form a fully developed framework for the curriculum. Furthermore, it is only recently that neo-Vygotskian researchers have begun to focus on the curriculum implications of his ideas (Hedegaard 1999). Two main approaches to Vygotsky's distinction can be identified in the literature. These are: (i) attempts to clarify and update it in light of recent research, and (ii) locating Vygotsky's distinction between scientific and everyday concepts within the broader (dialectical) method that he proposed for psychology. I shall give some initial attention to the first approach and then focus specifically on the second.[18] It not only brings out clearly the differences between Vygotsky and Durkheim, but provides a possible framework for going beyond Durkheim's a-historical distinction between the sacred and the profane. Furthermore, approaching Vygotsky's distinction through his overall method seems more consistent with his own position.[19] Although he does not engage in a specific discussion of dialectical materialism, an indication that he was thinking along these lines is suggested in his reference to:

> The dialectial leap ... [as] ... not only a transition from matter that is incapable of sensation to matter that is capable of sensation, but a transition of sensation to thought. *This implies that reality is reflected in consciousness in a qualitatively different way in thinking than it is in immediate sensation.*
>
> (Vygotsky 1987: 47; my italics)

His distinction between 'thinking' and 'sensation' is itself an indication of the differences he emphasized later between science and common sense. Whether, however, this remark supports his Soviet editor's assertion about his indebtedness to Engels and his 'creative use of the concepts of dialectical materialism and his unambiguously socialistic orientation' (Vygotsky 1987: 387) is far less certain.

I am not concerned to argue for a 'real' Vygotsky even if that were possible, or to predict how he might have developed his approach to concepts and knowledge if he had lived longer. My concern is to explore how Vygotsky's idea of scientific concepts and their relationship with everyday concepts can help us to conceptualize knowledge in a theory of the curriculum. In particular, I want to consider the extent to which Vygotsky's concepts and his use of them offers the potential for overcoming the problems of Durkheim's synchronic approach. My argument, as I stated earlier, will be that a dialectical approach to knowledge of the kind suggested by Vygotsky does offer some possibilities, but cannot, on its own, overcome the problems that a Durkheimian approach leaves us with.

Gellner (1992) reminds us that it was Hegel, in his critique of Kant, who first used the term 'dialectic' as an alternative to Aristotelian logic, to explore the implications of human beings being part of the world that they seek to understand. It was Hegel who recognized that this undermined the claims of rationalist and empiricist approaches to be able to free knowledge and reason entirely from history and from the knowing subject. However, it does not follow that this historical embeddedness prevents us from developing knowledge that is not bounded by that history. As Alexander puts it:

> Theoretical knowledge can never be anything other than the socially rooted efforts of historical agents. But this social character of knowledge does not negate the possibility of developing either generalised categories or increasingly disciplined, impersonal and critical modes of evaluation.
>
> (Alexander 1995)

The capacity to develop systematic and powerful theoretical knowledge of the kind that Descartes endeavoured to define is something distinctive to the post-Enlightenment era and, as such, our social theory and our curricula need to take account of it. It follows that we need a concept of knowledge that, while not context- or culture-free, is independent of specific contexts and activities, and has applicability across contexts. Hegel's dialectic of reason in history was, perhaps, the first attempt to suggest what the nature of such knowledge might be. As he put it:

> world history is governed by an ultimate design, that it is a rational process – whose rationality is ... an absolute reason ... a proposition whose truth we must assume; proof of its truth lies in the study of world history itself, which is the image and enactment of reason.
>
> (Hegel 1837, quoted in Gellner 1992)

Social theories since Hegel, including Marxism, activity theory and pragmatism, have all tried to tackle the problem of knowledge being both objective and historical by linking knowledge to human purposes rather than treating it as being 'for its own sake' and independent of history. However, in seeking to avoid giving knowledge a spurious autonomy from action and its consequences, these theories, as far as I can see, lead either to relativism or dogmatism. In the absence of a concept of knowledge or truth that is in some sense independent of 'the socially rooted efforts of historical agents', as Alexander put it in the earlier quote, judgements are unavoidably made on the basis of criteria that are treated as a given, and beyond argument (the example of Hegel above is a case in point). The only alternative (which is only an alternative 'in theory') is to make no judgements at all. In Hegel's idealist dialectic, criteria for knowledge and truth were linked to the movement of reason in history; in Marx's materialism, they were linked to the class struggle, and in pragmatism we are offered a demystified idealism that idolized a practical and instrumental view of science. This is not the place to rehearse the problems with a dialectical approach to truth, except to state that they easily reduce to instrumentalism, or the justification of 'what is' in specific cases. Hegel stands apart from the others, not least because he was less specific than Marx or the pragmatists about what reason in history actually meant. Whether he saw reason as an emergent outcome of history, or as itself defining truth, is outside the scope of this chapter. At times, he seemed to look to the emerging Bavarian nation state of his time as the culmination of history. However, this provided criteria that were no less problematic than those that were proposed later by Marx or the pragmatists. On the other hand, if we do not have any independent concepts of knowledge or truth, dialectical logic leaves us with an untenable relativism. I shall argue, therefore, that problems remain with a dialectical interpretation of Vygotsky's distinction between scientific and common-sense concepts, in that it does not treat knowledge as a distinct category. First, however, I shall review how he distinguishes between the two types of concepts. Then I will draw on Engestrom's dialectical interpretation of Vygotsky's distinction. I shall suggest that the problems we are left with are not specific to Vygotsky's approach, but are fundamental to the idea of dialectic logic itself. A point can, I think, be made about dialectic logic that parallels Hacking's (2000) observation about social constructivist approaches to knowledge. His argument is that at a very general level, the claim that knowledge is socially constructed is difficult to refute; on the other hand, enormous difficulties arise with attempts to extend the general idea to specific examples of social construction, such as the curriculum. What is needed and invariably absent is some idea about degrees or forms of 'social constructedness'. It may be that Vygotsky had some awareness of these difficulties in the case of the dialectic, and that this explains why, although he was intrigued by it, it remains undeveloped in his own writing.

Vygotsky's scientific and everyday concepts: differences, relationships and interpretations

Vygotsky identifies a number of features that distinguish scientific and everyday concepts. In relation to the purposes of this chapter it is useful to list them and to see where there are explicit parallels with Durkheim's ideas and where such parallels are absent. The main differences between the two types of concept for Vygotsky were:

1   They involve different relationships to objects. For Vygotsky, whereas a child's relationship to the world through his/her everyday concepts is through what he/she sees or experiences directly, with scientific concepts, the relationship is mediated by these concepts, and is not dependent on direct experience.
2   The absence of a system (of relationships between concepts) was, for Vygotsky, the cardinal psychological difference distinguishing everyday from scientific concepts.

Both of these features are expressed in almost identical ways by Durkheim in his discussion of the differences between sacred and profane orders of meaning.

A child (it could of course be an adult) uses everyday concepts while not being aware of doing so, whereas reflexive awareness is always a feature of the use of scientific concepts. Vygotsky draws a parallel with grammar, when he points out that anyone can use grammar to make sentences without knowing any grammatical rules.[20] There is a problem here, as the definition seems to refer to use as well as content. Is any concept scientific when it is used reflexively, or are some concepts scientific even when not used reflexively? There is not the same explicit concern with reflexivity and awareness in Durkheim, although when he writes of the 'faculty for idealizing ... substituting for the real world another different one, to which [people can] transport themselves by thought ... [through which] something is added to and above the real' (1995: 469), Durkheim is, I would suggest, making a similar point to Vygotsky.

Vygotsky also emphasizes the interrelatedness of the two types of concept in the following terms: 'The rudiments of systematization first enter the child's mind by way of his contact with scientific concepts and are then transferred to everyday concepts, changing their psychological structure from the top down' (Vygotsky 1962: 93). This interrelatedness of the two types of concept underlies for Vygotsky the inseparableness of learning from instruction, and is a proposition that is crucial both for the curriculum and for educational research. He argues that the two kinds of concepts develop in opposite directions: 'the development of a child's spontaneous concepts proceeds upwards and the development of his scientific concepts downward' (Vygotsky 1962: 108) and:

> Whereas scientific concepts begin with their verbal definition and develop 'as they are filled with further schoolwork and reading', spontaneous concepts are already 'rich in experience' but, because they are not part of a system, they provide no explanations and can lead to confusions.
>
> (ibid.)

As Vygotsky points out, these differences relate to the different ways the two types of concepts emerge – in one case usually in face-to-face meetings in concrete situations, and in the other in a 'mediated attitude towards the object'. In considering the relationships between the two types of concepts, we confront the biggest differences between Vygotsky and Durkheim. For Vygotsky, interrelationships between the two types were crucial – in a sense they encompass the process of learning. For Durkheim, who was more concerned with social order than learning, it was the differences between the two types that were crucial. I referred earlier to his comment that: 'there exists no other example of two categories of things so profoundly differentiated or so radically opposed' (Durkheim 1995: 53). He goes on to say: 'This is not equivalent to saying that a being can never pass from one of these worlds into another; but the manner in which this passage is effected ... demonstrates the essential duality of the kingdoms' (Durkheim 1995: 54). He then takes initiation rites as an example to dramatize this 'boundary crossing'. For example, 'It is said that at this moment the young man dies ... that the person he was ceases to exist and that another is instantly substituted for it. He is reborn under a new form' (Durkheim 1995: 54).

Durkheim is of course writing about religious rituals in primitive societies, and Vygotsky is concerned with learning and instruction in Soviet schools. However, there is an underlying point to which I will return. Unlike Vygotsky, Durkheim is not primarily concerned with a process; he is emphasizing the (social) power and objectivity of classifications which, he argues, apply just as much to the relationship between science and common sense today as they did to the separation of the sacred and profane worlds of primitive societies.

In his recent book, Daniels (2001) points out that Vygotsky's analysis stresses both the distinctions between everyday and scientific concepts, and their interdependence. However, while recognizing their distinctive strengths, Vygotsky's primary emphasis is, in my view, on the limitations of everyday concepts. For him, like common sense for Durkheim, everyday concepts lack any capacity for abstraction and generalization and fail to provide the learner with the resources to act in what he referred to as a voluntary (or free) manner. This is another of his crucial lessons for educationists today, particularly in the field of lifelong learning, where the idea of increasing the role of everyday concepts in the curriculum, in the form of a learner's prior experience and tacit knowledge, has powerful support among some educational professionals (see Chapter 13).

Present-day researchers building on Vygotsky's ideas point to some of the problems his distinction has left us. As Davydov notes, Vygotsky's distinction tends to imply an equivalence between science and the school curriculum. On the other hand, by emphasizing Vygotsky's point that thinking with scientific concepts involves self-conscious awareness, Wardeker (1998) seems almost to equate Vygotsky's idea of 'scientific' with being reflective. At the other extreme, Rowlands (2000) tries to claim that Vygotsky shared Lenin's objectivist view of knowledge. Vygotsky himself appears to have given very little explicit concern to the epistemological basis of the curriculum, or what he meant by 'science'. However, he did indicate that the historical development of knowledge was an important topic for future research when he stated that: 'while we learned a good deal about the development of scientific as opposed to spontaneous concepts (in our research), we learned little about the regularities specific to the development of sociological concepts as such' (Vygotsky 1987).

It may be useful to separate three ideas that are at least implicit in Vygotsky's analysis. They are: (i) the different sites of learning (whether or not learning takes place in school); (ii) how concepts are used (whether they are used reflexively or in a routinized or passive way); and (iii) the content of learning (the body of knowledge that a concept is part of). These possibilities can be represented in a diagram (see Table 3.1).

Not surprisingly, perhaps, given the conditions in the Soviet Union in his time, Vygotsky concentrates his analysis on how schools can help learners to move from (1) to (8) in the diagram with less attention to the intermediate steps and the possibility that the move in schools might be from (1) to (6). He gives little attention to the possibility of the moves from (1) to (3) – the reflexive use of everyday concepts (as, for example, in trade union and political activity) – or from (1) to (4), or how to prevent the move from (1) to (6) – the routinized acquisition of scientific concepts. It was V.V. Davydov [quoted in Engestrom 1991] who was later to point out that much of schooling consisted of the routinized acquisition of scientific concepts (6). It is these possibilities that have been explored within the sociology of the curriculum (Gamoran 2002). The move from (1) to (4) in the diagram points to the possibility, not explored by Vygotsky but not excluded by his analysis, that 'scientific' concepts can be acquired in a variety of contexts, not just school.

Site of learning	*Out of school*		*In school*	
⟍ Types of concepts Use of concepts ⟍	Everyday	Scientific	Everyday	Scientific
Routine	1	2	5	6
Reflexive	3	4	7	8

Table 3.1 Types of learning (elaborated from Vygotsky)

Vygotsky's distinction between scientific and everyday concepts is important for curriculum theory partly because it associates scientific concepts and their properties with the knowledge to be acquired at school. In other words, at one level Vygotsky, like Durkheim and Bernstein (with his distinction between vertical/horizontal knowledge), undoubtedly accepts the principle of insulation between theoretical knowledge and common sense and the specialization of curriculum knowledge that follows from it. There are, however, a number of specific problems with his distinction that I want to consider. First, whereas he stresses the importance of both the distinctiveness of the two types of concept *and* their interrelationships in the process of learning, those who have used his ideas have had difficulty in keeping these two ideas together. Neo-Vygotskians tend to stress *either* their distinctiveness (Rowlands 2000) *or* their interrelationships (Moll 1990). Those who focus on their distinctiveness tend to justify the givenness of school knowledge and an objectivist model of science (Rowlands 2000). Rowlands claims that this does not lead to a crude transmission model of pedagogy, which would certainly be at odds with Vygotsky's own stated views. For Vygotsky, it is precisely the reflexive features of scientific concepts that enable the learner to develop a self-awareness that distinguishes them from the common-sense concepts that he/she uses and takes for granted in everyday life. However, Rowlands's rejection of a one-way transmission pedagogy is belied by his frequent references to Lenin to support his view that Vygotsky had an objectivist view of knowledge. Lenin not only had an objectivist view of knowledge, but his view of the role of the Party undoubtedly involved a one-directional transmission model of pedagogy. On the other hand, others such as Goodman and Goodman (in Moll 1990) stress the interrelatedness of the two types of concepts, but tend to minimize their distinctiveness.

Let me summarize the argument so far. Vygotsky provides an original and suggestive account of how the two types of concepts are related in the processes of moving from the abstract to the concrete and vice versa. However, he is not specific about what he means by 'science', beyond not wishing to restrict its meaning to the natural sciences. Some commentators have suggested that as his examples refer either to Darwin's theory of evolution or to Marx, he must have favoured an explicitly Marxist interpretation of the term 'science'. One way of approaching the issue of Vygotsky's meaning of the term is proposed by Engestrom (1991). This involves starting from Vygotsky's explicit claim to draw his theoretical principles from Marx. It follows that in interpreting Vygotsky's conceptual distinctions we need to (i) interpret science in its Marxist sense, as knowledge leading to the emancipation of the working class, and (ii) treat his science/common-sense distinction not as a dichotomy, but as internally related concepts located both in history and in the process of individual learning and development. This approach has the advantage of offering an alternative to the a-historicism that characterizes Durkheim's and Bernstein's analyses. However, as I have already suggested, knowledge as a separate category tends to get lost within the framework of dialectical materialism. The idea of interpreting scientific concepts dialectically seems to fall into one of two traps. One is a crude kind of Cold War

Marxist-Leninism, as exemplified by Rowlands, which would appear to depend on a highly selective use of quotations, and an equally selective use of inferences from them. The other trap is a form of pragmatism which, though often linked to progressive, liberal or even radical goals, has its own problems in dealing with the question of knowledge. I shall now explore Engestrom's 'dialectical' interpretation of Vygotsky's distinction in more detail – and the possibilities and problems that it leads to.

Vygotksy's scientific and everyday concepts within the framework of dialectic logic

In his excellent and extremely comprehensive text, Engestrom (1991) locates Vygotsky's ideas within a dialectic approach, which was undoubtedly the framework that Vygotsky himself was exploring but never had time to develop in detail. There is no doubt that Engestrom offers a very distinctive perspective on Vygotsky's approach to concept formation. At the same time, by making clear what is involved in thinking about concepts within the notoriously (and perhaps inevitably) slippery terms of dialectic logic, his account also suggests why, for all its evocative power as critique, the dialectical method is unable to fulfil its promise as a theory for generating new knowledge.[21] This section of the chapter draws substantially on Engestrom's account.

Dialectical logic, whether applied to knowledge or human development generally, depends for its objectivity on its claims to know the unknowable – the future course of history. Engestrom begins by pointing out that in contrast and in opposition to other forms of logic, dialectical logic claims to be based not on abstractions but on the actual movement of history. It is this idea of historical change that offers the promise of solving the problem of the meaning of Vygotsky's 'scientific' concepts. Dialectics, Engestrom states, reverses the direction of conventional logic:

> instead of seeing 'concrete' phenomena as something sensually palpable and 'abstraction' as a conceptual or mentally constructed process, 'concrete' (things how they are) refers to the systemic interconnectedness of things. In other words, concrete phenomena are *the outcome* not *the starting point* of thinking.
>
> (Engestrom 1991; my italics)

From the perspective of the dialectical method, formal abstractions, such as those developed by Durkheim and Bernstein, can only separate arbitrary features of objects from their interconnections. In contrast, Vygotsky's scientific and everyday concepts, seen dialectically, are concrete abstractions that reflect and reconstruct (or claim to) the systemic and interconnected nature of the objects to which they refer.

In order to illustrate this argument, Engestrom gives the example of Marx and Engels's comparison between their concept of the proletariat as 'the most revolutionary class of bourgeois society – the gravedigger of capitalism' (Engstrom 1991) and the typical sociological definition of working class as 'the most oppressed and passively suffering poverty-ridden class, capable, at best, only of a desperate hungry rebellion'. In other words, Engestrom states, the Marxist concept of the proletariat was the real expression of the objective conditions of the working class. The truth of this proposition is borne out, according to the Russian philosopher Ilyenkov: 'as is well known, by the real transformation of the proletariat from a "class in itself" into a "class for itself"' (quoted in Engestrom 1991).

We have, therefore, an example of Marx's materialist transformation of Hegel's movement of 'reason' in history. Unfortunately history, if it can be claimed to 'bear out' anything, 'bears out' the opposite to what Ilyenkov claimed. In an ironic twist of history, it can be argued that in forcing capitalism to reform, the proletariat has succeeded in being its own gravedigger, not that of capitalism.[22]

Engestrom again quotes Ilyenkov, who states that a dialectical concept 'expresses a reality which, while being quite a particular phenomenon ... is at the same time a genuinely universal element ... in all the other particular phenomena' (Engestrom 1991). It follows that the task of concept formation is to identify these 'genuine universal elements' or 'germ cells' – as they were referred to by the Russian psychologist, Davydov (Engestrom 1991). Engestrom then poses the key question as to how such genuine concepts (or germ cells) emerge in the first place.

To answer this question, he turns to the argument of three other Russian philosophers, Arsen'ev, Bibler and Kedrov, that genuine concepts arise out of the interplay of forces involved in *any* productive activity. It follows that scientific concepts need not be limited to those developed and used within the historically formed activity called science. 'From our standpoint, *any* ... concept is in its potentiality ... scientific-theoretical' (Arsen'ev, Bibler and Kedrov quoted in Engestrom 1991; my italics). Thus, everyday thinking has in principle the same theoretical potential as the consciously elaborated concepts of science. Engestrom quotes Ilyenkov as making a similar point when he asserts that 'the universal laws of thought are the same both in the scientific and so-called everyday thinking' (Ilyenkov quoted in Engestrom 1991).

The distinction between scientific and everyday concepts does not itself, therefore, provide the criteria for knowledge or the curriculum. If we follow Engestrom's analysis, it is only by setting Vygotsky's distinction within the framework of the dialectical movement of history, and from this developing a set of methodological criteria for generating concepts, that the significance of his distinction emerges. The dialectic, as the quotation from Ilyenkov implies, refers to the 'universal laws of thought' (and of course, of history), which not only apply to scientific and so-called everyday thinking but to every field of knowledge.

Engestrom summarizes the dialectical approach as developed from Vygotsky by Davydov as follows:

> genuine concept formation ascends first from perceptually concrete phenomena to the substantial abstraction (or 'germ cell') which expresses the

genetically original inner contradiction of the system under scrutiny. It then proceeds to concrete generalization by deducing the various particular manifestations from this developmental basis.

(Davydov quoted in Engestrom 1991)

The problems with such an approach to the curriculum are first that it is methodological not substantive, and second that it assumes the universal applicability of dialectic logic, not only as an account of the movement of history, but as a methodology for the generation of new knowledge in every field and as a theory of learning and teaching and hence a basis for the curriculum.

Hedegaard's (1999) work provides an indication of the problems involved in applying such an approach to the curriculum. Let us take two examples of her argument. First she refers to Vygotsky's approach as 'a method of theoretical knowledge [that involves] relating concrete instances to general ideas ... and understanding generalities as concrete instances' (Hedegaard 1999: 29). However, it is far from clear what is distinctive about this 'method', or where the 'general ideas' come from. Later in the same paper, Hedegaard states that: 'The meaning of the concepts in a germ-cell model is dialectically formed through the concepts' relations to each other. For example in the subject domain of evolution the concepts species and population define each other' (Hedegard 1999: 29).

Again the 'dialectical' method seems to lose its distinctiveness altogether; it merely describes the way evolutionary biologists define concepts in their field, just as chemists relate atomic structure and the periodicity of the elements. We are left with a method that is either too general to have any applicability, or involves assumptions which do not necessarily apply in specific fields. What advantages does a dialectical interpretation of Vygotsky's ideas have over Durkheim's and Bernstein's descriptive categories?

1   It stresses the importance of a historical and dynamic approach to the development of knowledge and concepts, even though it provides no clear guide as to how such an approach could be developed.

2   It attempts to hold together three processes that are inextricably linked in human history but are invariably treated as separate by researchers in the current academic division of labour. These processes are (i) the movement of history as the transformation of our relationships with each other and with nature, (ii) the growth and development of knowledge, and (iii) the processes of learning and development. However, although Vygotsky refers to the interdependence of these processes in his own writing, he concentrated largely on the third. Resisting this tendency for specialization is even harder today.

3   Being a *historical* approach, a curriculum model derived from it overcomes, at least in principle, the weaknesses of distinctions such as those between the 'curriculum of the past' and the 'curriculum of the future'.

4   It defines knowledge, and therefore the curriculum, in terms of purposes, and not in terms of fixed notions of objectivity or 'knowledge for its own

sake'. However, as I shall argue in the next section of the chapter and take further in Chapter 4, the contrasting ideas of 'knowledge for a purpose' and 'knowledge for its own sake' are not necessarily as mutually exclusive as they may appear.

Despite the importance of these points as principles, the example of Hedegaard's research indicates that a dialectical theory operates at too high a level of generality when it comes to identifying specific curriculum options. While it claims to be a critique of other abstractions from the point of view of the real movement of history, in reality it is another abstraction claiming to be an account of the true development of history. Furthermore, insofar as it overemphasizes 'method', even in the theoretical sense, it plays down the importance of concrete analyses. I am not aware of any examples of the dialectical method being applied other than retrospectively or of it leading to the generation of new knowledge in any field. The problem of identifying the 'germ cells' remains unresolved. For example, it is difficult to envisage what kind of general rules could exist for identifying 'germ cells' in, say, chemistry and literature and history that go beyond the core concepts that would be identified by specialists in their fields. The rules for generating new 'germ cells' are formal, not substantive. There is no distinct 'knowledge category' within the dialectic, so knowledge has to be 'imported'. Invoking purposes such as 'the emancipation of the working class' or even 'overcoming contradictions' as criteria has the danger of reducing theory to a technology – it works (or it does not work) for particular cases, once the purposes are agreed.

My conclusions at this point are:

1   Vygotsky's science/common-sense distinction is a suggestive framework for a curriculum model. In emphasizing both the distinctiveness and the interrelatedness of the two types of concept, it offers some advantages over a Durkheimian analysis.
2   Locating Vygotsky's distinction within a dialectical framework offers a way of approaching his concept of science. It is useful in reminding us both of the non-givenness of knowledge categories such as science and the non-school-boundedness of curricula. However, it is difficult to make a case for the dialectical method offering a general theory of how knowledge in different fields develops.

I now want to suggest how a Vygotskian approach might be strengthened by introducing the idea of knowledge as a distinctive category, while retaining its historical dimension. This involves a consideration of Durkheim's discussion of pragmatism as a kind of dialectical approach (Durkheim 1983; Rytina and Loomis 1970), and his emphasis on the *social* objectivity of knowledge and truth.

Knowledge as a distinctive category:
Durkheim's social realist approach

In the previous section, I drew on Engestrom's work to locate Vygotsky's distinction between scientific and everyday concepts within the framework of dialectical logic as a dynamic and historical approach to how science and knowledge in general develop. However, the dialectical method assumes that (i) knowledge and truth can only be understood in terms of purposes and consequences, rather in their own terms as explanations located within frameworks of understanding shared by specialist communities, and (ii) logic can be subsumed into a particular view of historical development. These assumptions mean that in effect a role for knowledge as a distinct category (other than dialectical materialism as knowledge) is denied. Without a role for knowledge as a distinct category, such an approach cannot fulfil its claims to provide a generative theory of the curriculum. There are no good grounds for supposing that either the development of history or the generation of knowledge in different fields or the process of acquisition of knowledge can be subsumed within the principles of the dialectical method, except in the most general and therefore not very useful sense. As a result, approaches that adopt a dialectical approach cannot avoid the implicit acceptance of some knowledge as given and some concepts as having the capacity for generalization. Sometimes the consequences of this are trivial; sometimes, as in the case of the Soviet Bloc countries in the Stalinist era, they are not.[23] Examples of the more substantive content of the dialectical method that are sometimes referred to are the interrelatedness of concepts and the principle of contradiction. However, abstracted from the historicism of Marxism, neither is distinctive; the former is familiar to systems theorists, and the latter is familiar to those who have read the American sociologist Robert K. Merton and his idea that sociological research should focus on unintended consequences (Merton 1957). The question then is whether we are left with either the a-historical abstractions of Durkheim and Bernstein, or a historicism that claims to know the course of history, as the only alternatives for a curriculum theory to the conservatism of insularity or the relativism of hybridity which was where this chapter started. In the remainder of this section, I will take a number of steps in developing a possible, positive alternative. First I will draw on Durkheim's critique (Durkheim 1983) of the pragmatism of William James (and to a lesser extent of the early works of Dewey), to suggest that he does offer a *general social* theory of the objectivity of knowledge. Furthermore, I will suggest that it can be the basis for treating knowledge as a distinct category (in other words, that knowledge involves truth claims that have varying degrees of autonomy from its social origins or context of acquisition). Second, I will argue that Durkheim's approach to the objectivity of knowledge is complementary rather than antithetical, as is sometimes assumed, to a dialectical approach such as Vygotsky's.

As Rytina and Loomis (1970) demonstrate, although the content of Marxism and pragmatism are very different, the dialectical structure of the two theories, both of which have Hegelian roots, is remarkably similar: both, in Gellner's (1992) terms, are 'providentialist'; both reject the scholasticism of 'academic' philosophy in favour of fusing theory and practice; and both argue that the validity of knowledge and the objectivity of truth are practical questions, to be judged in terms of human purposes and outcomes. Knowledge is valid for both Marxism and pragmatism if it serves the betterment of mankind (even though they differed profoundly about what that betterment might involve).

Durkheim did not give much attention to Marxism, at least in his published writings. However, he makes a sharp distinction between his view that religion is a social phenomenon and the Marxist idea that religion is no more than 'a translation into another language of the material foundation of society' (Durkheim 1995: 471). For Durkheim, although social life 'bears the mark of its material foundation', collective consciousness is more than an epi-phenomenon – it has a life and an objectivity of its own. He was, however, much more concerned with pragmatism than Marxism, for quite specific reasons.[24]

Durkheim focused on the pragmatism of William James and to a lesser extent of Dewey and praised them for their 'heightened sense of human reality' in contrast to the pervasive rationalist and idealist philosophies of the time. For Durkheim, like the pragmatists, 'all that constitutes reason, its principles and categories, has been made in the course of history' (Durkheim 1983).

However, he was concerned that for pragmatism, truth and knowledge had no externally compelling character; they had only practical utilitarian value. Truth and knowledge in any objective sense were, if pragmatism was right, at best useful instruments for organizing everyday life. Durkheim's view was that the objectivity of truth and knowledge (and morality) are real regardless of whether they are or are not perceived as useful. First, the objectivity of knowledge is necessary for orienting people to their collective existence in society. This is the well known Durkheimian argument that in conditions of modernity, where social differentiation means that interdependence rather than similarity is the characteristic way in which people relate to each other, shared values (and particularly, knowledge as an expression of these values) have a key integrative role in society. In addition, however, Durkheim saw that the unique feature of both knowledge and truth is that they are compelling and that this obligatory character of knowledge was the major condition for the production of new knowledge – an insight that has informed much sociology of science.

Durkheim argued that pragmatism collapses truth into the sensations, instincts and the consciousness of individuals; in a similar way, Marxist dialectics linked truth to the emancipation of the working class in history, and in the Soviet era to the exigencies of Communist Party politics. Both theories, for Durkheim, neglect the fundamental obligatory character of truth – the former replacing it with individual benefit, the latter with political power. Durkheim's conclusions are first that the arguments for the objectivity of knowledge are social, not philosophical, and second that knowledge relates to the causes of things, not their consequences. Causality for Durkheim, whether religious or scientific, has a conceptual and also collective basis.

Why is Durkheim's argument about knowledge so important for the curriculum? It goes back to an earlier point that I made about the differences between

Durkheim's and Vygotsky's views of the social genesis of knowledge and higher forms of thought. I showed that Durkheim locates the origins of theoretical knowledge in the shared religious beliefs and rituals that brought people together in primitive societies. The rationale for religious belief for Durkheim was not that it solved practical problems, but that it gave people a sense that they could not generate from experience of who they were and where they were going. It also, although retrospectively, had another rationale; it was the paradigmatic basis for all conceptual thought, including science. Vygotsky locates higher forms of thought in early man's productive actions in finding food and building shelter. For Vygotsky, religion, because it did not contribute to human development and therefore the realization of man's destiny, was unimportant and would wither away. The important knowledge developed by early man for Vygotsky was what he acquired in appropriating nature and surviving. This difference underlies the fundamental separation of theoretical knowledge (originally religion) and common sense for Durkheim, and therefore the social basis of the separate reality of knowledge as a distinct category, and their equally fundamental integration for Vygotsky. Science, as the development and testing of unobservable, socially shared concepts, was not, for Vygotsky, a distinct theoretical activity as it was for Durkheim; it was an integral part of the way in which man appropriates nature in history. Hence, to the extent to which Vygotsky was a Marxist, epistemological questions about knowledge as a separate category distinct from practice did not exist; they were always resolved in practice, in the course of history. It follows that Vygotsky's distinction between scientific and common-sense concepts was a contingent one, to be overcome in practice and through learning. For Durkheim, the separation between theoretical knowledge and common sense was not contingent – it was real; the development of knowledge for Durkheim involved the progressive replacement of one kind of theoretical knowledge (religion) by another (science). Hence the necessary social basis of knowledge.

The complementarity of the two theorists can now be expressed as follows. Durkheim's sociology of knowledge neglected the technical appropriation of nature that was emphasized by Vygotsky, and cannot adequately account for how the unobservable concepts developed in early religions become the concepts of modern science with their power to transform the world. Vygotsky, on the other hand, by locating the genesis of thought in men's early practical activities, cannot adequately explain how these practical activities became transformed by theory. It is for this reason that the two theories can be seen as complementary, rather than mere critiques of each other. It follows that the curriculum must focus on both the social reality of knowledge and concepts that Durkheim stressed, and the process of transforming the world through concepts that was Vygotsky's priority. There is a sense in which Durkheim gives us the basis for a curriculum but no pedagogy, whereas Vygotsky gives us a pedagogy but no curriculum. Both recognized the importance of a historical perspective, but neither had a satisfactory theory of history. This argument is developed further in Chapter 4.

Conclusions

This chapter began by suggesting that there was a tension underlying the future development of the curriculum between the traditional principle of insularity and the increasingly popular arguments in favour of hybridity and their opposing assumptions about the nature of curriculum knowledge and its relationship with everyday knowledge. It went on to examine Durkheim's social theory of knowledge as the original expression of insularity and argued that a Durkheimian approach provides powerful arguments emphasizing the distinctiveness of theoretical knowledge and the role of the school curriculum in providing opportunities for people to acquire it. His arguments suggest that we should be cautious about blurring disciplinary and subject boundaries and weakening the specialist research and pedagogic communities associated with them. I suggested, however, that a Durkheimian analysis, in failing to emphasize the historical character of knowledge, can lead to a narrowly conservative view of knowledge as a given, and is unable to take account of the wider social changes that are shaping both knowledge and the curriculum.

To address these issues, I turned to the work of Vygotsky, who worked in the two decades after Durkheim's death – and, in particular, his distinction between scientific and everyday concepts. I discussed some of the significant similarities and differences between Durkheim's and Vygotsky's ideas and how they relate in part to their different interpretations of the social origins of thought in primitive societies. After concentrating on Vygotsky's distinction between science and common sense in some detail, I suggested that it needs to be understood within the framework of the dialectical method that he drew, albeit implicitly, from Marx and Hegel. From a Marxist perspective, scientific and everyday concepts and their interrelations are part of men's and women's attempts throughout history to transform the world. The chapter discussed Engestrom's dialectical interpretation of Vygotsky's ideas, and looked critically at the strengths and weaknesses of such an approach. In subsuming logic and knowledge into history, I argued that the dialectic method rejects knowledge as a distinctive category, and therefore cannot account for the distinctive feature of our era – the exponential growth of knowledge and its capacity for transforming the world. Although knowledge is always a product of people's actions in history, at least since the seventeenth century (and in some instances before), knowledge has transcended the contexts in which it was developed, in ways that would have been inconceivable in earlier eras.

Knowledge, like truth and morality, is inevitably external to learners and to those trying to create new knowledge, hence the significance of the boundaries and classifications between knowledge and common sense which Durkheim (and later Bernstein) wrote about. It follows that there is, I would argue, no alternative to what I will call a *social realist*[25] approach to knowledge and the curriculum. Such an approach is *social* because it recognizes, with Marx, Durkheim and Vygotsky, the role of human agency in the production of knowledge. Knowledge can never be taken as given in any more than a temporary sense; it is always a part of history and always fallible. Equally, the approach to knowledge and the curriculum that I am arguing for is *realist* because it recognizes the context-independent characteristics of knowledge, and that the powerful discontinuities between knowledge and common sense are not some transient separation to be overcome in the future, but the real conditions that enable us to gain new knowledge about the world. Knowledge is socially and historically constructed, but it cannot be subsumed into the processes of historical and social construction; in other words, we make knowledge out of knowledge. At the same time, this 'reality' of knowledge is itself, as Durkheim argued, social in origin. Whereas recognizing the sociality of knowledge without its reality can lapse into relativism or dogmatism, a focus on its objective reality without recognizing its sociality can become little more than a justification for the status quo. A curriculum of the future needs to treat knowledge as a distinct and non-reducible element in the historical process in which people continue to strive to overcome the circumstances in which they find themselves. In relation to the starting point of this chapter, these circumstances refer to the making, remaking and crossing of boundaries between disciplines and between school and workplace knowledge. These boundaries can be both 'prisons [and] ... tension points condensing the past and opening up possible futures' (Bernstein 2000: Preface). However, seeing these tensions between the legacy of the past and the pressures of the future as a historical process is not enough. The recognition that knowledge and truth are not just historical processes but are external and objective is important in two senses. The first is Durkheim's sense that knowledge and truth are always obligatory, and a necessary condition for new knowledge. The second sense of the objectivity of knowledge is that described by Gellner and associated with the growth of science in the centuries since the Enlightenment. This does not require us to accept what Durkheim (and Marx, though with very different implications) believed – that a single common scientific method was emerging which would gradually be extended in scope from the natural world to the social, human world. It does recognize, however, that there are rules, codes and values associated with different specialist traditions which make well grounded claims about knowledge and how it is generated and acquired. A curriculum with any claim to be 'for the future' cannot avoid treating the knowledge that has emerged from such traditions and specialist communities as a category in its own right, and endeavouring to ensure that learners have access to the rules for its production in its different forms, whether fields, subjects or disciplines.

The idea of truth as something external to individuals but social (and therefore essentially human) was a condition, Durkheim argued, both for the production of knowledge and for orienting us to our membership of society. For him, just as moral ideals are the norms for conduct, so truth is the norm for thought and, I would add, knowledge must be the norm for the curriculum.

The limitation of an approach that is over-reliant on Durkheim is that it can easily become too static a view of knowledge. Knowledge in science, as in all other fields, changes. The Marxist tradition of dialectics with which Vygotsky was associated with avoided this static view of knowledge by putting its confidence not in truth or knowledge, but in history 'being on their side'; that is, what

Gellner (1992) calls 'providentialism'. At least since the Enlightenment, it is knowledge not history that, for all its weaknesses and fallibility, and more successfully in some fields than others, has been the better guarantee of truth. Theories and methods and debates have been established in disciplines, and most (although not all) cross- or multi-disciplinary discoveries have originated within the disciplines, not external to them (although sometimes as a result of people trying to break out of them). Hybridity is best seen as an attempt to either challenge disciplinary authority or accelerate the 'break outs'. The dialectical method, if broadly conceived, is an attempt to give a historical, transformative and purposive dimension to hybridity. In the 1960s and 1970s, dialectics was widely defended, at least on the Left. However, although strong on aspirations and claims, it was weak on substantive method or results. Hybridity has emerged in recent decades in response to economic pressures, as an attempt to speed up new knowledge production and to overcome the separation of theory and practice. However, only in specific cases has it provided the conditions for generating new knowledge or concepts. When applied to the curriculum it collapses boundaries and limits the possibilities for the acquisition of theoretical knowledge.

New knowledge and new curricula are generated when researchers or learners acquire and build on existing knowledge and concepts from specific fields and disciplines to make sense of or transform the world. Insularity, Durkheim's sacred and profane, and Bernstein's vertical and horizontal knowledge structures are suggestive ways of describing the structure of knowledge and its social basis. Hybridity points to the historically contingent aspect of these structures without giving us much idea of where they are going or whether some structures are more contingent than others. Vygotsky's distinction between scientific and everyday concepts retains the distinction between theory and common sense that is found in Durkheim and suggests that the relationship between the two needs to be located not just in the classroom but historically, and understood in relation to a broader notion of human purposes. Vygotsky's importance for curriculum theory is not, in my view, in his specific concepts which are suggestive but either too general to be clear how they might be developed or, if used uncritically as in the Soviet era, open to abuse. His importance is rather his heroic attempt to hold together the processes of learning and the generation of new knowledge which over-specialization within research communities has forced apart. Who are the globalization theorists who are also theorists of pedagogy and the curriculum, as I am sure Vygotsky would have been if he were living today?

4 'Structure' and 'activity' in Durkheim's and Vygotsky's theories of knowledge

Introduction

This chapter builds on the argument developed in the previous chapter, which examined the curriculum implications of comparing the ideas of the French sociologist Emile Durkheim and the Russian psychologist Lev Vygotsky. This chapter returns to the contrasts between the two writers but focuses explicitly on their theories of knowledge. It starts from the position that any critical educational theory needs an adequate social theory of knowledge. However, as discussed in Chapter 2, with the notable exception of Basil Bernstein and a number of those who have worked within the framework that he established (Muller 2000; Moore 2004), the sociology of education has a poor track record in addressing this issue. Chapter 2 argued that sociologists of education have tended to reduce the 'social' to the activities, interests or beliefs of groups of 'knowers'. For somewhat similar reasons the broader field of educational studies is characterized by another divide, between those who emphasize the curriculum and those who focus on classroom practice (or pedagogy). As Alex Moore notes in the introduction to his recent book, curriculum studies seems to have been drawn away from 'fundamental and global questions of curriculum purposes and effects [and] ... the wider relationships between curriculum, society and culture' (Moore 2006:1).

The distinction between curriculum and pedagogy in educational studies has parallels with the well known distinction between 'structure' and 'agency' in social theory (Giddens 1979), and might be seen as a dividing line between the approaches adopted by Durkheim and Vygotsky, at least in how their ideas have been developed and used. This chapter takes a rather different and hopefully more productive approach. It argues that Durkheim and Vygotsky were both, in the broader sense of the term, epistemologists interested in the curriculum, *and* pedagogic theorists interested in classroom practice, even if in different ways one or the other focus is underdeveloped in the work of each writer. Although, as argued in Chapter 3, both were distinctive in their time by having explicitly *social* theories of knowledge, their respective approaches were very different. In this chapter, I concentrate on their social theories of knowledge, and the implications of the differences between them for how the sociology of education should tackle the question of knowledge.

In relation to Vygotsky, a lack of attention to his theory of knowledge in the literature is noticeable. This no doubt reflects the fact that his work has largely been taken up by psychologists and linguists, despite its much broader philosophical roots and its potential contribution to a range of disciplines. It may also have been, as Derry (2003) argues, that the fashion for postmodernist critiques of what is referred to as 'abstract rationality' has led to the distorted or at least highly selective contemporary interpretations of Vygotsky.[1] Durkheim, in contrast, has long been recognized as a sociologist of knowledge. However, the abstractness of his concept of the 'social' and the fact that he did not explicitly refer to his social theory of knowledge in his writings on education has meant that only recently has his sociology of knowledge been recognized as central to his educational theories (Moore 2004).

This chapter begins with the two major points about knowledge that the two writers under discussion have in common. First is the idea that knowledge is not located 'in the mind' or in the material world. For both Durkheim and Vygotsky, albeit in different ways, knowledge is the outcome of men and women acting together on the world; in other words, both had an unambiguously social theory of knowledge. Second both recognized that the acquisition and transmission of knowledge is central to education.[2] This does not of course mean, as some have supposed, that either relied on a mechanical or (electrical) metaphor of transmission.

In taking further a comparison of the ideas of the two thinkers, this chapter argues that while neither offers a fully satisfactory social theory of knowledge, both raise issues that the sociology of education and educational studies more generally cannot ignore.[3] It begins by referring to the similarities between ideas of the two writers that were referred to in the previous chapter and suggests that while both can be understood as adopting a social realist approach to knowledge,[4] the ways that they conceptualized social reality were very different. I argue that whereas the fundamental idea of Durkheim's theory of knowledge is the idea of 'social structure', Vygotsky's theory relies on the idea of 'social activity'.[5] Later in the chapter I will discuss in more detail the difference between the concepts 'social structure' and 'social activity'.

The first section of this chapter outlines Durkheim's theory of knowledge and the problems that arise from its particular concept of social structure and its neglect of the dimension of social activity. It draws on both his early anthropological work (Durkheim 1995; Durkheim and Mauss 1970), and some criticisms of it, and his later work on pragmatism (Durkheim 1983). I then go on to describe Vygotsky's social activity-based theory of knowledge and how it emphasizes just those issues that Durkheim neglects. I discuss how Vygotsky's emphasis on social activity appears to preclude him from treating knowledge as something that can be conceptualized as separate from its uses. The importance of being able to separate knowledge from its uses is of course Durkheim's key point in his critique of pragmatism (Durkheim 1983), and has profound implications for the curriculum,which were touched on in Chapter 3 and discussed in more detail later in this book. I then explore the contrasts between Durkheim's and Vygotsky's theories in more detail and develop more fully the analytical distinction between 'structure' and 'activity', after which the chapter turns to some issues raised by the leading contemporary Durkheimian, Basil Bernstein. I focus in this chapter largely on Bernstein's last book (Bernstein 2000); however, the ideas on educational knowledge developed in that book can be traced back to his earliest papers on the curriculum (Bernstein 1971). I show how both the strengths and some of the problems with Durkheim's approach that were discussed in Chapter 3 re-emerge in Bernstein's more developed theory of educational knowledge. I continue by tracing some of the ways in which Vygotsky's ideas have been developed, especially by the Finnish socio-cultural theorist, Yrjo Engestrom, and exploring how Engestrom's approach highlights the problems that an activity-based theory of knowledge can lead to. The chapter concludes by suggesting some of the educational implications of the distinction between structure-based and activity-based approaches to knowledge.

Despite being located within the different disciplinary traditions of sociology and psychology, and living and working in contexts as different as pre-First-World-War France and post-revolutionary Russia, Durkheim and Vygotsky had much in common as social theorists and educational thinkers. Both had social theories of knowledge that were closely related to their ideas about education.[6] Both shared a fundamentally evolutionary approach to knowledge and human development that was common to most progressive intellectuals in the early decades of the twentieth century. Both held *differentiated* theories of knowledge; they recognized that knowledge is not a seamless web – that theoretical or context-independent and everyday or context-bound knowledges have different structures and different purposes. Both saw formal education as the main condition for people to acquire the capacity for generalization, and both recognized that the acquisition of context-independent or theoretical knowledge was the main albeit not the only goal of formal education.

On the other hand, Durkheim and Vygotsky differed both on the aspects of human development that they saw as fundamental, and on how they conceptualized the social in their theories of mind and knowledge. It is also relevant that Durkheim had a far greater concern with education's integrative role in a society, especially when, as in the France of his time, the old religious bonds were weakening. In contrast, Vygotsky was living in a society in which a new concept of man – socialist man – was being created. It is hardly surprising, therefore, that they had different ideas about the social character of knowledge.

Both recognized that human beings are social in ways that have no equivalent among animals, and both interpreted social relations as fundamentally pedagogic. In other words, both saw that it is through the ability of human beings not just to adapt to their environment as animals do but to respond to pedagogy that they become members of society and create knowledge. They differed, however, in how they interpreted the origins of this fundamental human sociality. Although both were creatures of the Enlightenment and believed in science and social progress, Durkheim tended to looked backwards for the sources of knowledge and social stability, whereas Vygotsky looked forward to men's and women's potential for creating a socialist society. Before exploring the implications of these differences, I will now focus separately and in more detail on Durkheim's and Vygotsky's ideas abut knowledge.

Durkheim's theory of knowledge

For Durkheim, the fundamental sociality of human beings is the basis of his social theory of knowledge; everything that is human is social for Durkheim. Human society, he argued, originated in the collective relations found in the most primitive societies – the clan system in those he studied. For Durkheim, the sociality of early human beings was expressed in and was the basis for their membership of clans in the societies that he studied. It was in this ability to classify clans (and how the clan of which one was a member was distinct from others) that Durkheim and Mauss (1970) located the origins of logic (the grouping of things into discrete categories). Durkheim argued that totems associated with primitive religions (usually an animal, a bird or a fish) were collective representations which defined what clan someone was in (and therefore who they were). He built his social theory of the foundations of knowledge on his account of totemic religion and it was from this starting point that he developed his distinction between 'the sacred' and 'the profane', and his view of primitive religion as a kind of proto-science.

Durkheim set out to show that, despite being experienced by members of primitive societies as religious beliefs and practices, the collective representations which emerged from and constituted the clan structures are, in form at least, remarkably like the ideas of modern logic. He is, it can be argued, inverting the dominant rationalism of his time, which assumed that logical ideas are innate (at least in the Kantian sense). As he and Mauss put it:

> (it is not) that the social relations of men are based on the logical relations between things, in reality, it is the former which have provided the prototype for the latter ... men classified things because they were divided into clans.
>
> (Durkheim and Mauss 1970: 82)

We keep returning to Durkheim's ideas a century later, not because subsequent ethnographical evidence supports them (often it does not) but because, almost uniquely, he offers a convincing *sociological* account of the most basic categories of human thought (and therefore of the foundations of knowledge). The power, objectivity and generality of knowledge are for Durkheim located in the generality of society for its members. Furthermore, in making a distinction between the totemic classifications which hold primitive societies together, and what he and Mauss refer to as the 'technological classifications that [merely] reflect usage', he is suggesting how we might develop a social theory of the origins of distinctions that we largely take for granted, such as those between the analytical and the descriptive, between the theoretical and the everyday, and between what is necessary and what is contingent.[7] In other words, he is offering us the basis for a social theory of the differentiation of knowledge. His social theory of knowledge is therefore also the basis for a theory of the curriculum; it implies a set of principles for the selection of curriculum knowledge. This is a point to which I will return.

In a footnote to the book *Primitive Classification*, Durkheim and Mauss make a clear distinction between their idea of social classifications and the ways that members of primitive societies classify what Durkheim and Mauss refer to as 'the things on which they lived according to the means they used to get them' (Durkheim and Mauss 1970: 81). They saw the latter type of classification as 'mere divisions ... *and not schemes of classification*' (ibid; my italics).

Why did Durkheim make such a sharp distinction between religious or totemic classifications and what he referred to as technological (or practical/useful) classifications? My view is that this distinction is fundamental to his theory of knowledge and his theory of society, which are in a sense the same; this point needs some elaboration. Furthermore, in his tendency to elide the sociological meanings that he gives to religion, knowledge and society, it points also to some problems with Durkheim's approach. First, it is arguable that his whole theory of knowledge collapses if the reason for making the distinction between 'social' and 'technological' classifications is not accepted. The case that he makes for the social basis of knowledge assumes that the clans of which primitive men and women were members and the collective rituals that sustained them had an epistemological priority over any other forms of social grouping or relations in which they may have been involved. Second, despite his criticisms of Kant, Durkheim was at heart a rationalist, who accepted the idea that reason (and its specification as logic) was the unique quality that made people human (and different from other animals). Reason was also, for Durkheim, the basis of our objectively true knowledge of the world, and hence it was the foundation of science. On the other hand, Durkheim was deeply dissatisfied with the accounts of the origins of human reason that were prevalent in his time. These, and the problems with them that he identified, can be summarized briefly in the following very schematic terms:

- *Rationalism* – this refers to the argument by Kant and his followers that reason is innate in the human mind. For Durkheim this was an unproveable assertion and therefore, like faith, an unreliable basis for knowledge or truth. Furthermore, it was also unable to account for the great diversity of beliefs in different societies.
- *Empiricism* – this is the claim, by those such as John Locke, that reason is grounded in experience (or the sensations that our mind receives) that is disciplined by scientific method. For Durkheim, sensations are an unreliable and inadequate basis for explaining the universality and compelling force of logic in human affairs.
- *Hegelian dialectics* – Hegel grounded reason in history and ontology; in our being as humans. This was a view of reason and logic with which Durkheim did not explicitly engage. As an admirer of Comte's positivist sociology, he would presumably have seen Hegel's approach as unscientific.
- *Dialectical materialism* – this views the grounds for knowledge and truth in human labour, and the contradictions that arise as people struggle through

their labour to appropriate the material world. Durkheim dismisses this (Marxist) view with the argument that 'the world of representations is superimposed upon its material substratum, far from arising from it' (Durkheim 1995: 461). Although recognizing that the material world always 'left its mark' on human affairs, Durkheim asserts the 'sui generis' reality of social or collective representations.

Durkheim's social (or more specifically, societal) theory of knowledge and reason was his attempt to overcome the weaknesses he saw in these four approaches.

Third, Durkheim separated the two kinds of classification because he thought that logical classification must be prior to any classification related to usage. In other words, men lived in clans and developed a sense of themselves as clan members before they developed classifications.[8] As he and Mauss put it in explaining why they were not paying attention to technological classifications, 'we have tried above all to throw some light on the [social] origins of the logical procedure which is the basis of scientific classifications' (Durkheim and Mauss 1970: 82). An understanding of 'the word' precedes an understanding of 'the world' was the way he was to express this idea later in his account of the medieval French universities (Durkheim 1977).

Fourth, Durkheim was seeking an answer to why we find logic so compelling; in other words, where, he asked, did its undoubted power over our thinking come from? For Durkheim this power could never arise out of its usefulness in terms of satisfying specific needs (see Chapter 15). Consequences, he argued, are inevitably unreliable criteria for truth. The power of logic has to refer to factors that are a priori and external to any specific human activity. In other words, to restate a key Durkheimian point, the compelling power of logic, and hence knowledge, has to come from society as a reality *sui generis.*

His explicit dismissal of the importance of what he and Mauss refer to as 'technological' classifications arises from (i) his focus on the *foundations* of knowledge or logic, and (ii) his concept of society *as a whole* as the grounds for truth and objectivity and the basis for the humanity of all men and women and their sense of identity. As Worsley (1956) argues, it is the morphology of the societies that he studied – in particular their clan structure – that Durkheim took as his model for the social origins of the basic categories of logic, and hence of the foundations of knowledge. In linking the classes of clan, sub-clan and tribe to the rules of logic, he claims to have the basis for extrapolating a social theory based on primitive societies to the collective representations of any society, however complex.

Undoubtedly Durkheim does focus on societies as wholes, which is not surprising given the lack of differentiation in these primitive societies; they were *the* exemplar of 'mechanical solidarity'. Furthermore, he gives little attention to the activities that take place within them or their internal structures. The question is 'does this matter for his theory of knowledge?' The problem can be illustrated in relation to hunting and gathering that were the means of subsistence in the aboriginal societies that he studied. These activities themselves play no part in his account. He refers to society and social relationships in largely abstract terms, with no reference to their content or to the specific activities and interests or members. Another example of his separation of structure and content is to be found in his descriptions of how the totems that represent deities are associated with different plants and animals and become symbolic repositories of spiritual forces. Durkheim implies that any plant or animal could be arbitrarily assigned as a totem; it is their function that was important to him.

Worsley (1956) argues that this neglect of the survival or subsistence activities of members of the aboriginal societies which he studied is a weakness in Durkheim's theory of knowledge.[9] The members of these societies did not cultivate the land, they had no flocks and had few techniques of food preservation. As a result, procuring food through hunting and gathering was a very high priority. This meant that the ways in which particular areas of land were classified and the different seasons were distinguished were vital for a clan's survival. For Worsley, these subsistence classifications warrant the same epistemological importance as the clan relations that Durkheim focused on. However, it is only clan relationships that Durkheim was concerned with; it was as if man's relationship to the material world was of secondary importance. Durkheim did not appear to take account of the fact that religious beliefs such as totemism and clan relations develop in specific environments and that clan-based societies also develop forms of systematic and relatively objective classifications that arise from needing to identify and use animals and plants for food and clothing. In other words, it could be that there is not just a clan (and therefore a societal) basis for classifications, but a material basis as well.[10]

The general point is that for Durkheim, the universality of the categories of thought that he is concerned with arises from the generality of the collective representations that he identified, and not from the specific social experiences of survival in particular environments. He separates the collective clan activity of primitive societies from the activities of clan members as they wrestle their livelihood from nature, without seeing that this may introduce problems for his theory of classifications. In his critique of Durkheim, Worsley (1956) wants to relativize the fundamental categories of thought to the specific circumstances of particular societies. From Durkheim's point of view, this would remove both their fundamental objectivity and their societal character.

Durkheim makes a powerful case for the social basis of the foundations of knowledge or logic. As Cuvillier (1955) puts it, truth for Durkheim is a social reality, but it cannot be explained in terms of the practical needs that lead societies to develop particular kinds of 'technological' classifications. Durkheim contrasts thought which is speculative (with roots in the 'sacred') with action, which he expresses as a form of 'sudden release', or immediate response to need – in other words, as 'profane'. As a result, his theory offers a sociology of the foundations of knowledge and truth, and a theory of the basic differentiation of knowledge; on the other hand, it does not take us very far as a theory of the development of specialized knowledge. We have a starting point for a social theory of knowledge, but a number of problems are left unresolved. One is how science, with foundations modelled on what is general to any society, is used to transform the very specific worlds of everyday life. A second problem is how Durkheim's categories of 'sacred' and 'profane' might relate to a social theory of the curriculum – a point that is taken up in the work of Basil Bernstein.

I now turn to Vygotsky's theory of knowledge, which is distinguished from Durkheim's in three ways. First, as indicated earlier, it is a far less developed aspect of his thinking. Second, it does not separate the foundations of knowledge from 'technological classifications', or specific knowledges such as science and technology. Third, it locates the origins of knowledge not, like Durkheim, in social structures that are general to societies, but in the human activities that have historically been involved in transforming the natural world.

Vygotsky's theory of knowledge

Whereas Durkheim quite explicitly developed a theory of knowledge in his books *Primitive Classification* (with Marcel Mauss 1967) and *The Elementary Forms of Religious Life* (Durkheim 1995), Vygotsky's primary focus was on human development, or the development of mind, not knowledge. As I argued in Chapter 3, he wanted to show that: 'Human nature [*and specifically, human minds*] has changed in the course of history' (Luria and Vygotsky 1992: 41; my addition in italics).

Again in contrast to Durkheim, who set out to counter arguments of those like Comte and Saint Simon who associated specialization and the division of labour with societal fragmentation, Vygotsky's focus was on the individualism that dominated the psychology of his time. His interest was in conceptualizing a social and cultural theory of mind that countered prevailing essentialist and a-historical tendencies in psychology. So it was with somewhat different purposes that Vygotsky turned to anthropological studies of primitive peoples. Like Durkheim, he did not himself undertake any ethnography; unlike Durkheim, he seems to have relied largely on the secondary analyses of Levy-Bruhl, rather than on original ethnographies.

Vygotsky drew an important and fundamental lesson from Levy-Bruhl that brought him close to Durkheim: that thought and mind are social. However, whereas for Durkheim it was the formal similarities between the minds of primitive and modern man that were important, Vygotsky took over Levy Bruhl's view that it was the differences between the two that mattered. As he put it: 'the higher psychological functions of primitive man are profoundly different from those same functions in civilised man ... the very type of thinking ... [is] ... a historical variable' (Luria and Vygotsky 1992: 44). Also in contrast to Durkheim (and Levy-Bruhl), Vygotsky stressed the crucial epistemological importance of the practical subsistence activities of members of primitive societies. Vygotsky's view was that even primitive man was capable of 'objective logical thinking whenever the purpose of his actions is direct adaptation to nature' (Luria and Vygotsky 1992: 45). Unlike Durkheim (and like Levy-Bruhl), Vygotsky saw no positive role for religion. Whereas for Durkheim, religion was the structural precursor of science, Vygotsky saw the germ of modern science and technology in the 'tools, hunting, animal husbandry, agriculture and fighting all [of which] demand from man real and not just apparent logical thought' (ibid.). These were just those activities that Durkheim dismissed as contingent and 'merely technological' forms of classification.

In contrast to Levy-Bruhl, who did not differentiate between science and modern thought (both for him constituted the largely undifferentiated and superior common sense of modern societies), Vygotsky made a clear distinction between science and everyday or common-sense concepts that, as I argued in Chapter 3, had significant similarities with Durkheim's distinction between the 'sacred' and the 'profane'.

We can conclude this brief account of Vygotsky's ideas about knowledge by suggesting that he located his social theory of knowledge in just what Durkheim disregarded – man's struggle to appropriate nature for his survival. Thus, in a broad sense, he was a materialist and, at first sight, Vygotsky's historical approach to knowledge appears more grounded in the realities of social existence than Durkheim's. However, it has a number of problems. First, he seems to take for granted the progressive transformation of mankind's pre-scientific struggles for survival into modern scientific forms of thought. There is no space in his theory for identifying the conditions for this transformation on the lines developed by Max Weber and powerfully argued for in contemporary terms by Ernest Gellner (Gellner 1992). Second, the relationship between Vygotsky's evolutionary theory of the development of knowledge and the emergence of higher forms of thought and his theory of the development of the human mind in children is unclear. The developmental link that he wants to make between 'the real logical thought demanded by primitive man in animal husbandry and agriculture' (Luria and Vygotsky 1992) and the higher forms of 'scientific' thinking associated with the pedagogy of formal education is more implicit than explicit. The development of Vygotsky's distinction between scientific (theoretical) and everyday concepts appears to have arisen more from his critique of Piaget than from any explicit relationship to his genetic and materialist account of human development. Finally, Vygotsky appears to take for granted the issues that were of primary concern to Durkheim – namely the objectivity and compelling power of logic and the necessarily social foundations of knowledge.

Further aspects of the differences between Durkheim and Vygotsky

As I argued in Chapter 3, there are significant formal similarities between Vygotsky's idea of theoretical concepts and Durkheim's idea of the 'sacred' in terms of the criteria that they specify for each. Both are expressed as involving systematic relationships between concepts and being independent of specific contexts. Both provide the potential for speculation, connection and generalization. Both are separate from everyday practices (although the emphasis placed by the two writers on this separation is different), although derived from them. Vygotsky distinguishes between reality reflected in consciousness (theoretical concepts) and in immediate sensation (everyday concepts) as qualitatively different ways of thinking. He refers to their relationship as a 'dialectical leap', but we are left in considerable doubt as to what he means by this. In Chapter 3 I suggested that it was useful to see Vygotsky's approach to the two types of concept as dialectical in the straightforward sense that he sees them as embedded in and related to each other in an ongoing process. This appears to be in stark contrast to Durkheim's view that 'in all the history of human thought there exists no example of two categories (the sacred and the profane) so profoundly differentiated or so radically opposed' (Durkheim 1995: 53).

For Durkheim, society (as a structure that is independent of the social activities that have generated it) shapes and constitutes the forms of social classification regardless (almost) of the activities of any specific society. Vygotsky, on the other hand, saw just these activities – the working on and transforming nature – as the fundamental basis of human development in history (and therefore of knowledge). The question that remains is what is the relation between this view of social activity and how it develops, and Vygotsky's distinction between theoretical and everyday concepts. It has been argued by Wertsch (1990) and others that Vygotsky had an over-teleological view of history, and endorsed an abstract view of rationality that was a legacy of an uncritical view of the Enlightenment.[11] However, regardless of whether this is a correct view of Vygotsky's ideas about rationality, human society would seem to be impossible without some notion of teleology or purpose. Likewise, postmodernist critiques of his ideas about scientific concepts may well say more about the critics than about Vygotsky. He was after all working in a very particular time in post-revolutionary Russia. The next section focuses on the differences between Vygotsky and Durkheim in terms of the activity/structure distinction introduced earlier in this chapter.

Durkheim and Mauss argue that what they referred to as primitive classifications:

> are not singular or exceptional ... on the contrary [they] seem connected ... to the first scientific classifications ... [having] all their essential characteristics. They are systems of hierarchized notions ... standing in fixed relationships to one each other and together form a single whole ... like science, they have a purely speculative purpose. Their object is not to facilitate action, but to advance understanding, to make intelligible the relations which exist between things ... [they] are intended, above all, to connect ideas, to unify knowledge.
> (Durkheim and Mauss 1970: 81)

Durkheim is able to develop his social theory of the foundations of knowledge by arguing that the structure of society (in the case of the examples he takes, this refers to the way that clans are distinguished in primitive societies) is homologous with the structures of logic, and therefore with the foundations of all knowledge. The strengths of such a theory are that:

- it treats society as the foundation of knowledge and as separate from and not reducible either to other social relations or institutions, to individual members, or to the ways knowledge is used (as in the case of technology and tools);

- it highlights classifications or rules of exclusion and inclusion within a hierarchical system as necessary features of society and of any knowledge that claims objectivity;
- it makes explicit the link between identity and knowledge, ie. between the clan (or society) that I am a member of and my knowledge of the world as a member of a society or clan (an important point picked up by Bernstein and developed in Chapter 10);
- it offers a justification for a social and a priorist theory of knowledge that unlike pragmatism does not rely on uses or consequences as criteria of truth and unlike Hegel and Marx does not rely on a providential view of the workings of reason or of the clash of social classes in history.

However, in avoiding 'technological' types of classifications that arise from the exigencies of survival and need, and by assuming that the principles that he identified about the social basis of knowledge in the most primitive societies hold for every society, Durkheim treats the foundations of knowledge as almost outside of both society and history. He is assuming in effect that though social, the foundations of knowledge have no history – they are almost universal. The problem with this conclusion is that it can rob the idea of 'the social' or 'society' of any content – in other words, it robs it of any culture that is specific to particular societies. It is also at odds with debates within philosophy that have led to changes in ideas about logic (Collins 1998). Whatever one thinks about the wider relevance of ideas such as 'fuzzy logic', why they have emerged at this time and in some senses as responses to developments in computer science is an interesting sociological question. Also, being only concerned with foundations, Durkheim's theory robs knowledge of its content. The challenge to Durkheim posed by Worsley and other social anthropologists is that even in those primitive societies, the clan structure was not the only basis for the development of social classifications. A social theory of even the foundations of knowledge may be more complex than Durkheim hoped. His rejection of the epistemological significance of technological classifications remains difficult to justify.

Despite the similarities between Durkheim and Vygotsky summarized earlier in this chapter, I suggested that the latter could be seen as beginning with just what the former avoided – the activities of man in his struggle to appropriate the natural world. Unlike Durkheim, Vygotsky takes man's productive relationships with the natural world as his starting point. At the same time, his concept of human development involves the emergence of higher forms of thinking, which do not automatically arise from man's relationship with the natural world but depend on the pedagogy of formal education, and the specific development of science as a social institution. Unlike Durkheim, Vygotsky sees science as replacing religion; it was not as a kind of proto-science. He sees no need for a model and an explanation of the emergence of theoretical knowledge with some autonomy from practical concerns. How then, for Vygotsky, are these systems of theoretical concepts developed from practical subsistence activities, and how do they gain their objectivity? Knowledge ('scientific concepts' is probably the nearest he gets to referring to knowledge) is not a separate social category for Vygotsky; it is a result of the evolution of man's relationship with his environment. For Vygotsky, knowledge, we can assume, develops in the process of mediation between consciousness and the world, as theoretical and practical concepts shape and develop each other. The seamlessness of the relationship between science and technology in Vygotsky's evolutionary account of the growth of knowledge and the blurring of scientific and everyday concepts with technology are at odds with his stress on the importance of the distinct roles and forms of theoretical and everyday concepts in the pedagogy of formal education.

We have, therefore, two social theories of knowledge. One is structure-based: it sets the foundations of knowledge apart from the lived world (at the same time, as a social theory it has its origins in that lived world and human beings need to make sense of it) and provides us with the categories for speculating about the world. However, once we move out of Durkheim's primitive societies with their clans, it is far from clear how one specifies his concept of society and its generality, or the nature of the knowledge that is being referred to.

The second theory of knowledge is social activity-based: it arises from our collective activity in trying to shape the world to our purposes; it remains embedded in the world, and the objectivity of the explanations it provides arise from the success or failure of our efforts at transforming it. This 'dialectical' or pragmatic model of the relations between theory and practice that is expressed in the interdependence of scientific and everyday concepts is not adequate on its own. It requires some notion of purpose, some teleology, however provisional, and a more explicit notion of the separateness as well as the embeddedness of theoretical concepts from the everyday. Without these additional elements, one is left with a 'logical utilitarianism' (to use Durkheim's term for criticizing pragmatism) that does not account for the 'hard' objective character of truth, or for the remarkable growth of science and technology, and their impact on society, in the past two centuries. There are thus two problems with Vygotsky's theory of knowledge. The first is that his idea of scientific or theoretical concepts is too general, and too lacking in specificity in the generalizations that it offers. His criteria for theoretical concepts do not provide us with any way of differentiating concepts in the various fields of specialist knowledge that are the basis of curricula. The second problem is that whereas Durkheim offers no way of conceptualizing how science transforms the everyday world, Vygotsky focuses only on the process of transformation between scientific and everyday concepts, and does not distinguish between science and technology. We are left with only formal criteria for distinguishing theoretical concepts from any other. I shall return to these problems in a brief discussion of post-Durkheimian and post-Vygotskian developments.

Post-Durkheimian approaches to knowledge

Almost the only post-Durkheimian developments in the sociology of knowledge are those associated with the work of Basil Bernstein and his followers.[12] This is not the place to describe the complex body of his ideas. I will, however, pick up a number of issues that I have raised in relation to Durkheim and which reappear in

Bernstein's work. They refer to his concept of classification, his idea of the social, and his model of science. Bernstein first drew on Durkheim's idea of the relationship between classifications and social order in his justly acclaimed paper, 'On the classification and framing of educational knowledge' (Bernstein 1971). In that paper, he distinguished between curricula based on strong classification between different fields of knowledge and strong framing between school and everyday knowledge, and those characterized by weak classification and weak framing. Like Durkheim, his focus was on relations between knowledge contents, not the contents themselves. This can lead to a rather static and a-historical view of knowledge and curriculum categories that allows strong disciplinary boundaries to be treated as themselves almost beyond history and as the only condition for knowledge production and acquisition. It does not provide a framework that deals adequately with new forms of knowledge classification that may not be disciplinary in the traditional sense or with the historicity of disciplinarity itself. Bernstein returned to the issue of knowledge in one of his last and most original papers (Bernstein 2000), in which he distinguished between vertical and horizontal knowledge structures. His model for vertical knowledge structures has some parallels with Durkheim's clan model of primitive society. Also like Durkheim, Bernstein relies on a somewhat idealized notion of science (in his case physics) in terms of which less vertical forms of knowledge are compared, inevitably unfavourably (for a further discussion of this issue see Chapter 15). On the other hand, following Durkheim, Bernstein's great strengths are that he offers us a sociology of *knowledge* as something *sui generis*, not just as a sociology of knowers and their interests and standpoints (Moore 2004). Educational knowledge – or its selection and pacing in the curriculum – becomes, from his perspective, something to be studied sociologically as a phenomenon in its own right, with its own distributional consequences, not just as another social institution or, as he once put it, 'as a relay of other institutions and structures'. Bernstein also takes up a point that was referred to but not developed by Durkheim when he argues that knowledge classifications are both identity relations and hierarchical relations as well as knowledge relations – they include and exclude. This point is pursued in relation to professional knowledge and the threats to it inherent in the processes of privatization and marketization in Chapter 10.

Post-Vygotskian developments

Given that Vygotsky's ideas about science and knowledge were implicit rather than explicit in his theory of human development, it is not surprising that they have been vulnerable both to being used in oversimplified ways and to being the subject of simplistic criticisms. Post-Vygotskians have tried to go beyond his formulation of the theoretical/everyday distinction, and what they take to be his rather narrow concentration on formal schooling. However, such developments rely on two highly problematic assumptions that are prevalent in much contemporary educational research. These concern (i) the very idea of science, or indeed any knowledge, being able to make claims to truth and (ii) the possibility that schooling may not provide special conditions for the acquisition of theoretical concepts. This is not the place to challenge these critiques. Their underlying assumptions have been discussed in Chapters 1 and 2, and a possible alternative approach is outlined in Chapter 15.

The Finnish researcher Yrjo Engestrom is an exception to most other post-Vygotskians. I discussed his broad philosophical approach in Chapter 3. Here I want to explore how he has gone beyond Vygotsky's theoretical/everyday distinction in quite distinctive ways (Tuomi-Grohn and Engestrom 2003). Engestom argues that in any classroom, workplace or community it is possible to develop what he refers to as 'theoretically grounded concepts' which go beyond the distinction between theoretical and everyday concepts, and provide the tools for actors to understand and change the world. It is not the purpose of this chapter to examine his ideas in any detail. I will restrict myself to making two observations. First, in disconnecting the acquisition of theoretical concepts from its institutional location in specialized educational institutions such as schools, colleges and universities, where it was located by Vygotsky, Engestrom seems to be denying that there may be institutional specificities to the acquisition of particular types of knowledge. This could have serious practical implications, especially in developing countries (see Chapters 13 and 14 that deal with this question in the South African context). Second, although Vygotsky stressed the interrelationship of theoretical and everyday concepts in the process of learning, he also stressed their distinctiveness, and did not argue that their differences could be blurred in the interests of solving particular problems; it follows that Engestrom's formulation of 'theoretically grounded concepts' represents a break with, rather than a development of, Vygotsky's ideas. As I suggested earlier in the chapter, it may be that by his focus on the embeddedness as well as the distinctiveness of theoretical and everyday concepts, Vygotsky did not, like Durkheim, see it as necessary to try and articulate more precisely the nature of their distinctiveness.

Vygotsky emphasized the embeddedness of theoretical and everyday concepts as the basis for a pedagogy that would enable learners in schools to develop higher forms of thought. This embeddedness also implicitly provided the grounds for his theory of knowledge. However, he does not, as far as I am aware, discuss the possibility of different types of theoretical concept (as in the case of concepts associated with different disciplines and school subjects), or the possible relationships between them. As a result, the Vygotskyian tradition has, with few exceptions, focused on the relationship between theoretical and everyday concepts as a developmental process and neglected the content and structure of theoretical concepts. In relativizing his idea of scientific or theoretical concepts, neo-Vygotskian revisionists such as Wertsch seem to be in danger of losing what was distinctive about his pedagogic theory and its links with his theory of knowledge.

The one post-Vygotskian who took what might be described as a more Durkheimian approach to knowledge was the Russian V.V. Davydov. Davydov started with Vygotsky's critique of crude 'transmission' models of pedagogy and his observation that 'direct instruction in concepts is impossible ... .[The teacher] who attempts to use this approach achieves nothing but a mindless learning of words...' (quoted in Engestrom 1991). He pointed out that much teaching in schools is like this, and is likely to continue in that way. This, he explains, is partly due to inadequacies that he sees in Vygotsky's definition of scientific concepts.[13] However, his criticisms are of a completely different kind to those referred to earlier. Whereas postmodernist critics seek to weaken Vygotsky's emphasis on science and schooling, Davydov sets out to strengthen it by making it more explicit. He argues that a failure to specify the content of scientific concepts means that it is hard to distinguish them from empirical or everyday concepts. It is worth elaborating on his ideas a little, as he remains, in my view, an important example of someone who tried to build on Vygotsky's largely implicit theory of knowledge.

On the assumption that everyday knowledge gives us only 'abstractions' – in the sense that it never provides 'the whole picture', Davydov followed Marx in arguing that teaching theoretical knowledge must involve 'ascending from the abstract to the concrete'. It followed for him that teachers need a theory of the development of knowledge to enable them to identify topics which embody the core or 'kernel' concepts of any particular field. The problem with Davydov's formulation relates to the issue that I raised in Chapter 3 about Vygotsky's implicitly dialectical theory of knowledge. There is no general theory of the development of knowledge as is claimed by dialectical method; we only have accounts of the development of different fields such as physics and history. His approach thus lays itself open to a theory of knowledge defined bureaucratically, and knowledge selection becoming a state function as in the Stalinist era – and, albeit in a very different way, in some recent developments in England (see Chapter 6). One fruitful line of inquiry might be to treat Davydov's approach as a form of genericism (Bernstein 2000 and Chapter 10), and to compare it with western approaches to genericism such as critical thinking, meta-cognition and thinking skills, which play down content and stress processes.

Conclusions

When I wrote the paper on which Chapter 3 was based and began thinking about the contrasts and similarities between Durkheim's and Vygotsky's ideas, I was struck by the extraordinary and largely neglected similarity of one of their core distinctions – Durkheim's 'sacred' and 'profane' sources of meaning and Vygotsky's 'scientific' and 'everyday' concepts. However, as I tried to locate the two sets of distinctions in the whole body of the thought of each writer and in their approach to knowledge, I became increasingly aware of the differences between them. As I have set out to show in this chapter, they offer, in effect, two very different approaches to developing a social theory of knowledge with very different implications for the curriculum and pedagogy.

Daniels (2001) describes the aims of pedagogy as: 'helping children make links between their everyday understanding and ... schooled knowledge (or scientific concepts)'. With the somewhat different emphasis referred to earlier, the purpose of the curriculum for Davydov is to 'teach theoretical understanding'. Both of these formulations derive from Vygotsky and, in my view, it is hard to see

Durkheim disagreeing with them. However, as researchers or curriculum developers we are still left with the big questions. What concepts? What theories? What selection of knowledge? And on what basis do we decide?

Vygotsky addresses the pedagogic questions in his discussion of the interrelationships between theoretical and everyday concepts. He does not, at least for me, deal adequately with the foundational or the content questions. What are the non-arbitrary grounds for curriculum choices?

Durkheim does address at least the first of these types of question about foundations, in terms of the externality and objectivity of knowledge that needs to be the basis of the curriculum. Durkheim's model for the social basis of knowledge is, however, limited by depending on the idea of 'society as a whole'; he therefore addresses only the foundations of knowledge. His concept of the sacred (as the basis for speculative thought and the development of science) and his criticism of the seamlessness of pragmatism and other social constructivisms is more helpful to curriculum developers and critical educational theorists, and has been taken further by Bernstein with his typology of knowledge structures and how they can embody weak or strong classification and framing, or, as he later expressed it, the principle of verticality. However, as I argued earlier, his concept of vertical knowledge is over-reliant on an idealized notion of science, and on the debatable assumption that it provides a model for knowledge in general.

Contrasting the theories of Durkheim and Vygotsky has emphasized their differing weaknesses and strengths rather than leading to a new theory. They remind us of two things that are important for the sociology of education. First, it must have a theory of 'what is worthwhile knowledge'. Vygotsky's theoretical/everyday distinction and Durkheim's concept of the sacred as it was developed by Bernstein offer powerful resources for such a theory, as well as the basis for a critique of the trends to vocationalism, curriculum relevance and modularization which increasingly dominate government policies across the world. The sociology of education must also develop a theory of pedagogy that directs our attention to the activities of teachers and students that provide the necessary conditions for students to acquire powerful theoretical concepts – and in the broadest sense, to be educated. In furthering this goal, Vygotsky and Durkheim are undoubtedly complementary.

5 Curriculum studies and the problem of knowledge
Updating the Enlightenment?

Introduction

This chapter reflects on the field of curriculum studies. It concludes by asking two questions that set curriculum issues in a more historical and philosophical context. They are: why should a focus on the curriculum be concerned with the Enlightenment? And in what sense might the Enlightenment inheritance of the modern curriculum need updating?

The chapter has two aims. First it argues for a central role for curriculum issues in educational policy, in opposition to recent trends to give more emphasis to setting and achieving targets, outcomes and widening participation at almost any cost. I will elaborate on this point as it applies to policies for secondary schools and further education in England.

Second, I want to pick up on some of the issues raised in previous chapters, and to reinstate the issue of knowledge as integral to curriculum theory, in contrast to such issues as assessment, evaluation and guidance, on which postgraduate studies and research in curriculum studies increasingly seem to focus. It is not my argument that these issues are unimportant, but that they cannot be dealt with adequately in the absence of a theory of the role of knowledge in education. My assumption is that *the acquisition of knowledge*[1] is the key purpose that distinguishes education, whether general, further, vocational or higher, from all other activities. It is for this reason that debates about knowledge are crucial; by this I do not mean specific knowledge contents, although they are important, but the concepts of knowledge that underpin curricula.

A number of trends in educational theory, not only in the sociology of education, have contributed to the marginalization of knowledge in curriculum studies. I will mention three. The first is the unintended consequences of the work in the sociology of educational knowledge that began in the 1970s (Young 1971). I have discussed this in some detail in Chapters 1 and 2. Here I want to stress the irony that the intention of this work was to give centrality to the role of knowledge in education. However, the issue was conceptualized as identifying the interests of those with power to select knowledge for the curriculum. The problem, as Chapters 1 and 2 argued, is not that it is wrong, as some critics claimed at the time – social interests and the preservation of privileges are always to some extent involved in curriculum design as in all social arrangements – but that it is only a partial perspective that can easily become *the* way of conceptualizing the curriculum. It leaves us with no independent criteria for curriculum decisions, only competing interests.

The second trend has been in the philosophy of education, and is symbolized in the later writings of the philosopher of education, Paul Hirst (Hirst 1993), in which he rejected his earlier *forms of knowledge* thesis and argued that the curriculum must be based on *social practices*. As with the 1970s sociology of knowledge, the idea of 'social practices' provides no grounds for distinguishing curriculum knowledge from the knowledge we acquire in the course of our everyday lives.

The third trend has been the influence on curriculum studies, and on the humanities and social sciences generally, of postmodernist ideas. The writings of the French philosophers Michel Foucault and Jean-François Lyotard are used to critique the subject-based curriculum on the basis that it excludes all voices except those of the professional or academic elite (see Moore and Muller 1999 and Chapter 1 for more detailed discussions of this argument). Like the social constructivist theories of knowledge referred to earlier, postmodernism offers a superficially radical challenge to existing curricular models, However, like the earlier trends, postmodernism offers no alternatives, and leaves the curriculum theory on the sidelines of any serious debate.

It is these developments, together with the not unrelated social and political changes associated with neo-liberal economic policies, and an increasingly interventionist role on the part of the state, that have contributed to the crisis in curriculum theory. In policy terms, we have a national curriculum for primary and secondary schools, a post-compulsory curriculum, a vocational curriculum and, increasingly, a higher education curriculum, all of which take for granted the assumptions about knowledge on which they are based. On the other hand, we have a marginalized curriculum theory which offers critiques of the interests involved in existing curricula, but no alternatives.

There are three starting assumptions for the rest of my argument in this chapter. First, each of the three developments in educational studies that I have referred to collude, albeit unintentionally, with the marketization that now drives educational policy and which is in a deep sense anti-educational. Second, in denying a distinctive role for knowledge that transcends specific social practices, interests and contexts, these approaches remove the grounds for a critical relationship between theory and curriculum policy and practice. Third – and positively – I will argue, as an alternative, for a knowledge-based theory of the curriculum that recognizes the distinction between the type of knowledge that can be acquired at school, college or university and the common sense or the practical knowledge that we acquire in our everyday lives. To put it more generally, because the world is not as we experience it, curriculum knowledge must be discontinuous, not continuous with everyday experience. Important though it is, the difficult pedagogic issue of developing strategies for overcoming this discontinuity is not something that I will be concerned with in this chapter. At this point I will merely suggest that Bernstein's concept of recontextualization is a fruitful starting point

(Bernstein 2000), which I explore in relation to the vocational curriculum in Chapter 11 and is also developed by Barnett (2006). Judith Williamson, in an article in the *The Observer*, expressed my point about knowledge most lucidly in the following terms:

> Whether in astrophysics or literature, *there is a body of knowledge* to be learned and renewed. Most would like [it] to be useful and many would like it to be easy. However it is not often the former and rarely the latter. What really matters about knowledge is that it is true or rather that we can learn or find the truth or truths as best we can, in any field. This is what education and more specifically, universities are for.
>
> (Williamson 2002; my italics)

In other words, education presupposes the possibility of both knowledge and truth.

Concepts of knowledge and the 14–19 curriculum

Let me begin by taking an example, from current policy on 14–19 education, of the problem that arises from neglecting the question of knowledge. In 2003 the government proposed that:

- the National Curriculum at Key Stage 4 should be reduced to three compulsory subjects: English, maths and science (it began in 1988 with ten);
- modern languages and design technology, like history, geography and all other subjects, would become optional;
- 14-year-olds will be able to take GCSEs in areas such as engineering, health and social care, and leisure and tourism.

Four years later as I revise the paper on which this chapter is based, the principles underlying these proposals have since been taken further with (i) the options to offer Asian languages as alternatives to French, Spanish and German, (ii) reduced-content science syllabuses, and (iii) the opportunity for 14-year-olds to opt for work-related (but not vocational or applied) diplomas. The hope, as with the majority of recent reforms of the secondary curriculum, but not yet borne out in practice, is that (i) more students will achieve more qualifications at higher grades, (ii) they will benefit from the opportunity of a wider range of choices, and (iii) they will be better prepared for future employability.

There were a number of rather different responses to these proposals in 2003. For example:

- They were largely welcomed by the serious press and respected educationalists as at last giving a proper value to vocational subjects and the importance of student choice.
- The new proposals were seen as a half-hearted attempt to move towards the fully skills-based curriculum by those claiming to be radical and to have a

'grasp of the future' (see, for example, the recent Royal Society of Arts report on the Future of Schooling (RSA 2003).

- The proposals for the 14-plus curriculum, together with the target of achieving 50 per cent participation in higher education, were sharply criticized by those on the Right such as Chris Woodhead as 'dumbing down' and 'giving in to anti-elitist dogmas' (Woodhead 2002). However, the only alternative these critics offered was a return to a mythic 'golden age', when vocational education took the form of craft apprenticeship, academic studies followed in the footsteps of Thomas Arnold's Rugby, and the majority left school at 15 or earlier to do unskilled factory jobs, which of course no longer exist.

There was surprisingly little critical comment at the time from specialists in curriculum studies (or the sociology of education). This, I suggest, reflects the marginalization of the issue of knowledge in curriculum studies that I referred to earlier. Without a theory of what knowledge is important and its role in the curriculum, curriculum specialists are left with little more than a sense of unease about the likely consequences of premature vocationalism, and a reluctance to appear elitist by defending the subject-based curriculum – but no viable alternative. The space has been vacated by curriculum theory, and the only serious alternatives to government curriculum policies appear to come from the Right.

My problem with the government proposals is that they focus almost entirely on the *extrinsic* purposes of education. They assume that future employment is the main motivator of young people's willingness to go on learning. Quite apart from whether they are correct about what motivates young people and whether as a country we want growing numbers with GCSEs in leisure and tourism or even whether an expanding service economy can absorb them, such a policy seriously neglects the *intrinsic* purposes of education. By this I do not mean simply that the old idea of 'education for its own sake' has been forgotten; I mean the failure to consider a number of more fundamental educational questions. For example:

- Why do we want to persuade more young people to extend their schooling?
- What is it that is distinctive about the kinds of knowledge that can be acquired in school or college?
- Is it just that we want more young people to participate in full-time study, regardless of what they are learning?
- Is achieving a qualification, when qualifications no longer actually qualify someone to do something, a sound goal for educational policy?

The official reason for allowing 14-year-olds to choose leisure and tourism instead of, for example, geography or history, is presumably that employment-related knowledge will be more meaningful to them. However, this assumes that the differences between the kind of knowledge acquired in studying geography or history and the knowledge that might be acquired in a course in leisure and tourism (such as how to book a flight or a holiday) are not significant. What does such an assumption signify? Does it, like the 1944 Education Act, assume that only some students have the ability to acquire disciplinary knowledge in subjects like history or geography, or is there an assumption that such knowledge differences are no longer important?

Few would openly endorse the assumptions of the 1944 Act and its spurious reference to parity of esteem between three types of school for three types of pupil with three types of mind, so I will not consider them further. The argument that knowledge differences between subjects and sectoral fields such as leisure and tourism are not important has wider implications that I want to examine in the rest of this chapter. I shall in the process move beyond the specific case of geography/history and leisure and tourism to address more general questions concerning the knowledge basis of the curriculum.

I do not seek to defend any particular expression of a subject-based or disciplinary curriculum, and in particular not the one that was established, initially in the public schools, in the last decades of the nineteenth century. This would in effect be endorsing the position of conservatives like Chris Woodhead, who focus on the list of subjects associated with the traditional grammar school curriculum and neglect the principles and form of social organization that such a list presupposes. As I suggested in Chapter 2, the subject-based curriculum established at the end of the nineteenth century had credibility not just from its association with elite institutions, but from three more fundamental principles on which it was based that were not necessarily made explicit at the time, and that arguably transcend its particular institutional, historical and, in England, social class context. These were:

- A clear separation was accepted between the knowledge that can be acquired at school and the knowledge that people acquire in their everyday life.
- It was assumed that the knowledge acquired through the curriculum is cognitively superior to people's everyday knowledge – in other words, that the curriculum could take people beyond the everyday knowledge available to them through their experience.
- School subjects were located within communities of specialists whose members included not only school teachers, but university teachers and researchers. These groups often took the form of specialist subject teaching associations, many of which were first established in England at the beginning of the twentieth century.

Whereas right-wing conservatives focus only on the list of subjects, radical educationists concentrate on the extent to which the specialist subject communities were, at least originally, located among members of privileged institutions and privileged sections of society, and excluded the voices of the majority. Both groups neglect that there may be crucial social conditions for knowledge acquisition and production that are independent of the specific social contexts in which they are located.

The radical criticisms of a knowledge-based curriculum have a contemporary importance because they have gained a new and wider credibility in recent years. Policy makers, supported by some educationalists, have recognized a tension between the flexibility and openness to innovation of leading sectors of the economy and the rigidity of divisions in the curriculum. Existing curriculum divisions are seen by reformers as associated with elite institutions and as barriers to widening participation, especially for disadvantaged groups.

The question is whether we are left in the trap of two unacceptable alternatives. The first is the right-wing view that knowledge is essentially a given and that attempts to change the disciplinary structure of the curriculum are doomed to lead to dumbing down. The second 'modernist' view is that we have no alternative but to allow the curriculum to respond to market pressures for more choice, and more employment-related options. The highly questionable assumption of the latter view is that the consequences for learners can only be good. The more likely possibility or even probability is that large numbers of each cohort will leave school with more qualifications, but knowing very little.[2] If this is a trap, my view is that it is a trap partly of our own making – a product of inadequate theorizing.

Insularity and hybridity in the curriculum

I want to give some focus to how we might escape from this trap by drawing on my analysis in Chapter 3 that characterized the tension between 'past' and possible 'future' curricula in terms of the principles of *insularity* and *hybridity* (Muller 2000).

Let us first return to the principle of insularity – it goes back a long way – to the establishment of research laboratories in the eighteenth century (Shapin 1994) and to the disciplines that became the basis of the university curriculum in the early nineteenth century (Messer-Davidow 1993). Insularity emphasizes the *differences* rather than the *continuity* between types of knowledge – and specifically the differences between theoretical and everyday or common-sense knowledge. It rejects the view that the divisions and classifications between types of knowledge in the curriculum are a mere reflection of social divisions of earlier times. Curriculum classifications, it is argued, not only have social and political origins; they also have an *epistemological* and *pedagogic* basis. In other words, they relate in fundamental ways to *how people learn* and *how they produce and acquire new knowledge*.

The principle of insularity asserts that the conditions for new knowledge production and acquisition put limits on the possibilities for curriculum innovation – in particular: (i) the crossing of disciplinary boundaries, (ii) the incorporation of everyday knowledge into the curriculum, and (iii) the involvement of non-specialists in curriculum design. There will be, it is argued, a pedagogic price to pay for dispensing with such boundaries. Not surprisingly, this principle of insularity can be invoked uncritically in defence of the curriculum status quo. It is, however, worth making two points here.

First, insularity in the sense used here refers to *relations between contents* of knowledge, not to the specific contents themselves. In other words, insularity is not an argument for a particular list of subjects or contents, but only for the necessity of boundaries between different fields of knowledge and between theoretical and everyday knowledge.

Second, insularity is not primarily a political principle, although it may be used for political purposes. It is based on a view of knowledge that: (i) it cannot be equated solely with social needs or interests, or with its uses or purposes, and (ii) it draws on, but is not based on experience. As Descartes put it nearly four centuries ago, in a quote referred to in an earlier chapter, real knowledge is 'beyond all custom and example'. My argument is not that we have to agree with Descartes that true knowledge is achieved though introspection, but that, like him, we need to ask the question: what are the conditions for knowledge acquisition and production? What, as he would have expressed it, is our *discourse on method*? This implies not accepting uncritically the Enlightenment philosophers' claims for knowledge and truth, or, like the postmodernists, rejecting them. It means going beyond their limitations – in particular, their individualistic and a-historical view of knowledge and reason, and their tendency to equate knowledge only with the natural sciences.

The principle of hybridity, as I argued in Chapter 3, is a more recent idea. It rejects the claim that the boundaries and classifications between subjects and disciplines reflect features of knowledge itself, and sees them as always a product of particular historical circumstances and interests. It stresses, as Joe Muller, the South African social theorist, puts it, the 'essential unity and continuity of all forms and kinds of knowledge [and the potential] permeability of all classificatory boundaries' (Muller 2000). In other words, for hybridizers, anything goes with anything else – a kind of modular utopia!

The principle of hybridity is frequently defended in terms of its consistency with what is seen as the increasingly 'boundary-less' character of modern economies and societies. A curriculum based on hybridity is no more than a recognition of contemporary reality, it is claimed. It challenges the tendency for schooling to become 'learning for its own sake'[3] and appears to offer a way of making the curriculum relevant to more young people. At the same time, by being more inclusive and adaptable, a curriculum based on the principle of hybridity is seen as supporting the political goals of equality and social justice.

In the 1970s, the principle of hybridity was expressed in ideas such as interdisciplinary studies and an integrated curriculum. In the more market-dominated period since the 1990s, it has been expressed differently – with a far greater emphasis on individual access and choice. Practical examples of the principle of hybridity are:

- modular or unitized curricula;
- the University for Industry's adoption of the slogan that learning must be in 'bite sized chunks';
- the incorporation of experiential learning and workplace knowledge into the curriculum;
- the blurring of distinctions between academic and vocational knowledge.

The principle of hybridity assumes a fundamentally relativist view of knowledge that has always appealed to radicals as a basis for exposing the vested interests associated with existing knowledge boundaries and divisions.

Chapter 3 argued that there are specific political reasons why a curriculum based on the principle of hybridity has appeal to education policy makers today; it appears to converge with the new policy goals of choice, social inclusion and accountability. Choice and social inclusion require the curriculum to recognize the knowledge and experience of those traditionally excluded from formal education. Likewise, accountability requires limitations to be placed on the autonomy of subject specialists to define divisions and hence what counts as knowledge.

The insularity of academic knowledge can therefore be set against the social and economic arguments for a more 'responsive' curriculum that could be the basis for new kinds of skills and knowledge that transcend current boundaries. In rejecting the links between specific knowledge classifications and either pedagogic requirements or epistemological principles, the hybridity principle implies that decisions about the curriculum will (and should) depend, ultimately, on market pressures or political decisions; in other words, on political not educational priorities. What is the likely outcome of the tension between these two principles?

One outcome follows from treating insularity as an expression of educational conservatism and a defence of privileges that has to give way to the hybridizing pressures of a democratically elected government in the new global economy. According to this scenario, we can expect the progressive disappearance and replacement of the disciplinary or subject-based curriculum. To put it more starkly, the principle of hybridity treats those features of the curriculum that set it apart from everyday reality as fundamentally anachronistic and out of date. The future is assumed to be one of increasing homogeneity, in which the acquisition and production of knowledge are no longer distinct phenomena – but just two among many increasingly diverse social practices.

A more likely outcome, however, is that new divisions will emerge between elite institutions such as public schools and the remaining grammar schools, which are able to maintain subject-based curricula, and the remaining schools and colleges, which are unable to resist the pressure to develop curricula aiming to be relevant to immediate economic and political needs.

An alternative approach to the curriculum

The alternative approach for which I want to argue rests on very different assumptions that I have earlier referred to as a social realist theory of knowledge:

- It rejects the conservative view that knowledge is given and somehow independent of the social and historical contexts in which it is developed.
- It assumes a view of knowledge as socially produced and acquired in particular historical contexts, and in a world characterized by competing interests and power struggles. At the same time, it recognizes knowledge as having emergent properties that take it beyond the preservation of the interests of particular groups. In other words, we have to be prepared to speak about and argue for cognitive or intellectual interests.

- It rejects a view of knowledge as *just another set of social practices*. It sees the differentiation both between fields and between theoretical and everyday knowledge as fundamental to what education is about, even though the form and content of the differentiation is not fixed and will change.

The challenge for curriculum theory is to identify the nature of this differentiation, and to explore how to develop curricula that are based on it but not inconsistent with the wider goals of greater equality and participation. The approach to differentiation that I have found most useful draws on Bernstein's distinction between vertical and horizontal knowledge structures (Bernstein 2000). I do not intend to go far into his analysis in this chapter. Suffice to say, his argument is that knowledge boundaries and classifications are not only 'prisons ... [they can also be] tension points condensing the past and opening up possible futures'.

As I suggested earlier, the curriculum established in the late nineteenth/early twentieth century was both a list of subjects and a set of codes, rules, practices and forms of association, developed by those involved in specialist fields of inquiry. What Bernstein's analysis offers is a way of distinguishing those conditions that are necessary for the acquisition and production of knowledge and those associated with the social interests within which these processes were located – for example the public school/Oxbridge link at the turn of the twentieth century. Such an approach depends on a number of assumptions. It assumes that (i) the codes and practices associated with subjects and disciplines such as geography, history and the sciences are designed to set the curriculum apart from the everyday knowledge that students bring to school, (ii) these rules and codes are explicitly associated with formal educational institutions which are, at least in part, separated from the demands of family and everyday life, and (iii) it is this separation of the curriculum from everyday life that gives the knowledge acquired through it an explanatory power and capacity for generalization that is not a feature of everyday knowledge tied to practical concerns.

Certain principles for guiding curriculum policy necessarily follow. For example:

- The curriculum cannot be based on everyday practical experience. Such a curriculum would only recycle that experience.
- The content and forms that the curriculum takes are not and should not be static; new curriculum forms and content will always emerge.
- It is important to be extremely cautious about replacing a curriculum based on specialist research and pedagogic communities with one based on the immediate practical concerns of employers or general criteria for employability such as key skills.
- Providing access to concepts with explanatory power is not something limited to school subjects as we know them. However, it does depend, as in the case of professional fields such as engineering, architecture, medicine and accountancy – as much as in the case of academic disciplines – on knowledge shared by specialist teachers, university researchers and professional

associations. Not to rely on such forms of organization, as in the case of some of the new so-called 'vocational' fields such as leisure and tourism, is to seek a short cut to increasing participation which can only perpetuate educational and ultimately social inequalities.

- A 'curriculum of the future' needs to treat knowledge as a distinct and non-reducible element in the changing resources that people need access to in order to make sense of the world. The task of curriculum theory from the point of view argued here is to reassert this priority in the new circumstances that we face.

The 'curriculum of the past' and the 'curriculum of the future': a critique

I want to draw my argument in this chapter together with reference to a distinction between a 'curriculum of the past' and a 'curriculum of the future', which I have already referred to in Chapter 2, and which I first proposed in my book *The Curriculum of the Future* (Young 1998). I see the two concepts rather differently than I saw them in 1998, when I had not fully realized the importance of any curriculum model being based on an explicit theory of knowledge. The distinction that I made then between the two curriculum models can be summarized in terms of a number of key dimensions on which the organization of knowledge in the curriculum can vary:

- between the insulation of disciplines and subjects and the forms of connectivity between them;
- between the insulation of theoretical and everyday or common-sense knowledge and their integration as, for example, in Engestrom's concept of theoretically grounded practice (see Engestrom 2004 and Chapter 4);
- between the assumption that knowledge forms a coherent whole, in which the parts are systematically related, and the assumption that knowledge can be broken up (modularized) into separate elements and put together by learners or teachers in any number of different combinations.

The 'curriculum of the past' took for granted that knowledge is best transmitted and acquired through insulated, specialist forms that are consistent with its disciplinary coherence. It disregarded the possible impact of political and economic changes that call these principles into question, as well as the inequalities of access that were associated with them. However, 'the curriculum of the past' was located in a history of real social networks, and real trust among specialists, which gave it an objectivity and a concept of standards that transcended its social origins in elite institutions. The idea of a 'curriculum of the future' still remains a tendency and an idea, and can hardly be said to exist in any institutional form. It certainly has yet to establish an equivalent basis of trust as a way of promoting high quality learning. New forms of association and trust, and new types of specialists, will have to be created if it is to fulfil the claims made for it. The present unresolved tension between the two curriculum models leaves us with, at best, pragmatic modifications of the 'curriculum of the past'. They avoid fundamental questions regarding how to establish the new networks of specialists that take account of global economic changes but do not lose the crucial autonomy that was provided by the old subjects and disciplines.

Conclusions

Originally I had thought that I would begin the paper on which this chapter is based with the theme of its subtitle, 'Updating the Enlightenment?'. However, the relationship between the Enlightenment and the modern curriculum turned out to be a much longer-term project. Instead, I offer as an end note no more than a brief historical background to remind readers that the questions about knowledge and the curriculum with which I have been concerned are far from new. My interest in going back to the Enlightenment arose from trying to understand what it was about the Enlightenment ideas, and especially its ideas about knowledge and truth, that led to such severe attacks from the postmodernists. Debates around postmodernism tend to be polarized between a defence of reason and knowledge as in some way beyond history and society, and a totally relativist position that rejects any objective view of knowledge or any so-called meta-narrative of progress in history. Both positions are, I would argue, absurd. I want therefore to make a number of preliminary points in linking this broader debate to the issues in curriculum studies raised in this chapter.

First, in contrast to prevailing tendencies to polarize positions, I think we have to work with the tension between the objective claims of reason and knowledge and their inescapably contextual and historical character. Second, we are not limited, like many Enlightenment thinkers thought they were, to equating real knowledge only with the mathematical sciences. Third, it is difficult, I would say impossible, to formulate any sort of debate in the field of curriculum, as in any other area of policy, without some idea about progress, however cautious we need to be about its specific expression. Finally, there is Hegel. I am a late beginner in trying to understand the possible contemporary relevance of Hegel. However, I am convinced that we cannot afford to neglect him if we want to get beyond the kind of polarities that he attempted to reconcile, but which are still very much with us; obvious examples are those between the particular and the universal and between the objectivity of knowledge and its rootedness in history that I touched on briefly in Chapter 3.

Let me explain briefly why I think Hegel may be important for curriculum theory. It was Hegel who most fully recognized the dramatic implications of the Enlightenment; for the first time in history, it was no longer necessary to rely on tradition or divine revelation in dealing with issues of epistemology, ethics and aesthetics. As Habermas put it, 'Hegel inaugurated the discourse of modernity' (Habermas 1990) of which we are still part. Modernity for Hegel was unique because it was *self-grounding* and it is the implications of this momentous development that we are still grappling with in curriculum theory – one example is in

English literature and the debate about the canon; another is what on earth should be taught in school history? A third is the debate about content in school science. Hegel's idea that dialectical reason is the driving force of history is somewhat alien to us today. However, his legacy was not a position in the sense this is usually understood; it provides a framework for a debate.

Callinicos, in his excellent introduction to social theory (1998), states that Habermas distinguishes three positions staked out by those following Hegel. First, there were the Left Hegelians, the most famous being Marx. They retained Hegel's concept of history as a dialectical process, but moved it from the realm of ideas to the revolutionary tendencies of the working class. Second, there were the Right Hegelians, who associated absolute reason with the state of their time (and therefore with the end of history). They were the forerunners of modern liberalism (John Stuart Mill and perhaps, in our time, New Labour and Francis Fukuyama). Finally, and much later, there was Nietszche's response to the questions that Hegel posed; he set out to unmask both Right and Left as mere expressions of the will to power. In his total rejection of the Enlightenment, he was the forerunner of today's postmodernists.

The point of this digression from curriculum issues is that Hegel's identification of the self-grounding of reason and knowledge, and the difficulties that are posed by no longer being able to rely on tradition or divine revelation, are still with us today in relation to the curriculum as much as in other contemporary policy debates. Some, the successors to the Right Hegelians now seen as technocrats, want to halt history; some, like the Left Hegelians, invoke popular voices as expressions of social contradictions; and others claim that there is no rational resolution to problems, only power. I think that I am trying to find a way between the first two.

My conclusions to this digression are first that the Enlightenment changed everything – we cannot go back to tradition or God in deciding what to teach: we have only reason, knowledge and history. Second, we know more about how knowledge is acquired and produced than was known at the time of Hegel and his successors, and circumstances have changed. However, the fundamental issues which they were the first to face have not changed. Hence, in rethinking curriculum theory we have to keep going back to the questions that Hegel and his successors raised.

6   Education, knowledge and the role of the state

The 'nationalization' of educational knowledge?

Introduction

This chapter is concerned with the role of government in education, and the interventionist trend in educational policy, which, I argue, is in danger of undermining the fundamental purposes of schools and formal education in general, and therefore the conditions needed if progressive policies such as widening participation are to achieve their goals.

I am primarily concerned with two issues. The first is the question of knowledge that has recurred as a theme in the earlier chapters of this book. In particular, I want to emphasize the importance of distinguishing between different types of knowledge, and what role they have or should have in education. The second issue concerns recent efforts to achieve improvements in the outcomes of schooling and raise standards, and how this is taking the form of an excessive instrumentalism, where education is increasingly directed to political and economic goals, and justified by them. I shall argue that this instrumentalism, which was briefly discussed in Chapter 2, necessarily reduces the space and autonomy for the work of specialist professionals, both teachers and researchers. The implicit and sometimes explicit assumption of instrumentalists is that specific *educational* purposes – what in the English tradition has been referred to as 'education for its own sake' – are little more than a mask for preserving privileges.

The main expressions of instrumentalism in current educational policy are marketization, where educational institutions find themselves increasingly in competition for students and resources, and regulation (or quality assurance, as it is sometimes referred to), where external bodies of various kinds lay down criteria with which individual institutions have to comply. Both of these directly or indirectly reduce the autonomy of educational institutions and their professional responsibility for maintaining or raising their own standards. In the public debate, the serious alternatives appear limited to what amount to two forms of nostalgia – one from the political right, and one from the left. The one from the right argues against regulation per se. It invokes a return to the idea of the 'scholar professional'; at the same time, it invariably avoids (or accepts) the elitist implications of the system of which the scholar/professional was a part. The alternative leftist nostalgia, which goes back to the Italian Marxist and educational theorist,

Antonio Gramsci, has few voices today. It sees, or used to see, specialist professionals such as teachers as potentially the organic intellectuals of a future democratic and socialist society (Sassoon 1988). However, sadly, at least as far as I am aware, the Left such as it is long since gave up trying to think through either the kind of society in which Gramsci's vision might be possible, or the role of government and professionals in such a society.

In seeking a way of opening up these issues, I draw on two critical traditions from the sociology of education – the sociology of educational knowledge and, less directly, the research on privatization and choice in education. I shall draw on the analysis developed in earlier chapters and argue for a focus on the *conditions for the acquisition of knowledge* as the central educational research issue. With regard to the debates about privatization and choice, I shall argue that we need to rethink our use of the categories 'public' and 'private' at a time when government is seeking not just to privatize the public sector, but to use the private sector as a model for the public sector. Finally, I shall turn to the political philosopher Michael Polanyi, and suggest that his idea of the 'republic of science' may give us a possible alternative for how education and professional work generally might be governed in a way that takes more account of the specific goals of education to promote the acquisition of knowledge.

Theoretical background

My discussion of the sociology of educational knowledge cannot avoid returning to *Knowledge and Control* (Young 1971). The primary purpose of that book was to unmask the ideological assumption of the official curriculum – that it always expresses some interests. 'Interests', in the sense in which it was used then, referred primarily to social class and power relations; however, the argument is equally applicable to gender or ethnic relations and was taken up in these terms in the 1980s. Despite its strengths in reminding us always to question official versions of the world, the approach had a fundamental flaw which I discussed in some detail in Chapters 1 and 2. It only needs a brief recapitulation here. In arguing that all knowledge is social (an inescapable truth, if you do not give authority to divine revelation), it led to the position that curricula were no more than a reflection of the interests of those in power. In other words, it is power, not knowledge, that counts in education, as elsewhere. This led to a relativism that was not, to say the least, very helpful in debates about the future of the curriculum.

More recently, a new approach to the sociology of educational knowledge has been developed, which informs the main argument of this book, and this chapter in particular. It was initially outlined in Chapter 2. It is concerned not just with a critique of knowledge, but with the conditions for knowledge as the key research question for the sociology of education. In contrast to the earlier sociology of knowledge, it takes a *social realist* rather than a *social constructivist* position on knowledge. It recognizes that knowledge cannot be reduced to the activities and interests of those who produce or transmit it.

My interpretation of social realism rests on a number of assumptions which are crucial to the rest of this chapter. They are:

- The question of knowledge (what is it that people need to have the opportunity to learn or know?) is central to any educational policy.
- Knowledge about the world, if it is to be the basis of the curriculum, refers to concepts that take us beyond both the contexts in which we find ourselves, and those in which such knowledge is acquired and produced.
- The crucial implications of this idea of knowledge for the curriculum are that we make a distinction between knowledge produced by specialists (usually in disciplines) and the knowledge that people acquire through their experience in families, communities and workplaces.

Two contemporary fallacies

I want to illustrate why these rather abstract issues about knowledge are important, especially in relation to how knowledge is organized in curricula[1] and disciplined in research, by referring to two fallacies in current thinking – I will call them 'internalist' and 'externalist'.

The internalist fallacy is typical of the 'conservative neo-traditionalist' approach described in Chapter 2, and is associated with right-wing think tanks such as Politeia. It involves an a-social view that knowledge is given, and something that has to be acquired by anyone who wants to see themselves as 'educated'. For those identifying with this position, knowledge changes only occur as internal features of the knowledge itself. This enables them to defend existing orderings of knowledge and the social structures that they serve. A good example is Chris Woodhead's response to the Tomlinson Report published by Politeia (Woodhead 2004). Superficially, it appears ironic that the academic curriculum that those on the political Right want to defend is most threatened by just those market forces that they want to encourage. However, this irony may mask the assumption that the elite schools will always be able to protect themselves from market forces.

Such views are, however, correct in one sense: they recognize that there is something special about knowledge. However, they are wrong in seeing this special character of knowledge as a given, and not itself social and historical. One consequence is that Woodhead's critique can only shore up existing knowledge structures and the social inequalities associated with them. His recommendations for the future, as I indicated in Chapter 5, offer little more than a return to an earlier era, when most of those not going to university either became apprentices or had no choice but unskilled manual work.

What I refer to as the externalist fallacy is far more common today, and has parallels with the technical-instrumentalist ideology discussed in Chapter 2. Rather than treating knowledge as given and only characterized by internal changes, it sees nothing special about any particular ordering of knowledge – all are contingent. It follows that there is no reason why the curriculum, and all kinds of research, should not be determined as far as possible by social and political goals. This externalism can take a variety of forms. The currently fashionable approach is to identify educational outcomes such as social inclusion, widening participation and economic competitiveness and use these outcomes to develop targets to drive the curriculum and research priorities.

Despite their fundamental differences, both positions have one thing in common: they fail to take account of the conditions for producing and transmitting knowledge.[2] Whereas the internalists treat the existing knowledge structures as a-historical givens, the externalists treat knowledge as just another instrumentality which can be manipulated to serve the goals of whatever government is in power.

It was the English sociologist Basil Bernstein who first began to look at the conditions for knowledge acquisition and production and provide a way of moving beyond the two fallacies. He saw school and university curricula developing on the basis of what he referred to as the strong classification of different fields of knowledge and strong framing between educational and everyday knowledge structures. The key condition for the acquisition and production of knowledge for Bernstein was insulation: insulation between disciplinary fields, and insulation between educational and everyday knowledge. This is obviously a highly contentious argument, but it gives us a starting point and leads to two important questions:

1   Can these conditions be maintained as further and higher education are continuously expanded and made ever more subject to external regulation?
2   How far do current innovations for promoting greater participation (e.g. work-based learning, e-learning, work-related foundation degrees and curriculum modularization) undermine (or preclude) the conditions that Bernstein claimed were necessary for acquiring and producing knowledge?

With these broad issues in mind, I will turn briefly and by way of illustration to three specific policy issues that are discussed in more detail in other chapters of this book.

The role of academic disciplines in educational research

Successive UK governments have introduced various strategies to, as they would put it, 'make educational research more useful'. They seek to direct educational research to political and wider social goals and away from the criteria and priorities of individual researchers working within disciplines. Examples of such strategies are the shifting of funding towards national programmes like the Learning Society and the Teaching and Learning Research Programme (TLRP), the requirement of those bidding for research funding to take account of a broad range of 'users' of research findings, and the encouragement of universities to bid for government tenders and the inevitable narrowing of research agendas that this involves. I will argue in Chapter 7 that in weakening the autonomy (and, by implication, the conditions for knowledge production) of educational research, these strategies are in danger of undermining the scope for real advances in educational knowledge that might, in the longer term, contribute to improvements in policy.

The crisis in the professions

In Chapter 10, I draw on a less well known strand of Bernstein's work to analyse the crisis faced by professions assailed by state regulation in the case of teachers and medical professionals, and by the encroachment of the market relations in the case of law and accountancy. In his last book, Bernstein (2000) argues that professional knowledge emerged in the nineteenth century as a product of the tension between the 'inwardness' of academic disciplines and the 'outwardness' of practical demands (e.g. for better health, legal advice and new roads and railways). This tension led both to new professional fields such as accountancy and to new disciplines such as molecular biology and mechatronics. By the mid to late twentieth century, the balance between inwardness and outwardness was shifting towards the latter, and led to a new form of control – what Bernstein calls genericism. Genericism refers to giving precedence to rules, procedures and practices that are not specific to individual occupations or fields of study. Policies which emphasize genericism invoke the needs of consumers and customers; however, in practice, most generic procedures and criteria are generated by governments and government agencies. Genericism involves a shift in power away from professional and disciplinary specialists towards regulatory agencies and their more generic criteria. The basis for the development and application of new specialist knowledge by professionals is weakened, and their autonomy is reduced.

Reforming the 14–19 curriculum

From the point of view of the two fallacies I referred to earlier, the 14–19 curriculum represents a contradictory case. In giving precedence to the generic criteria of a four-level diploma over the knowledge-specific criteria of subjects, whether academic or vocational, the Tomlinson proposals (Tomlinson 2004) represent an example of what I have referred to as the externalist fallacy. The Labour Government (DfES 2005), however, in rejecting the report's proposals for a single diploma structure and reasserting the autonomy of distinct subject-based A-levels, adopted a position that is indistinguishable from that taken by Chris Woodhead and the right-wing think tank, Politeia, already referred to. Where the Tomlinson Report and the Government have similarities is that neither considers the conditions for knowledge acquisition or progression, whether in academic or vocational pathways. This example is discussed in more detail in Chapter 11.

Implications: the nationalization of educational knowledge?

In each of the cases I have referred to, we can note a shift from a reliance on generalizing principles associated with specialist professionals to a reliance on procedural principles associated with regulatory agencies. To put it another way, it is a shift from an *epistemological* form of accountability (which is associated with notions of truth and objectivity shared within disciplinary communities) to an *administrative* form of accountability, which relies on generic and invariably but not always quantitative criteria that are applicable to all professional and research fields. I want to consider two implications of this shift.

First, I want to suggest that it represents an example of the 'nationalization' of education. In using the term nationalization, I do not mean it in the sense that the term has been traditionally used to refer to the public ownership of privately owned businesses. I am referring to how activities which traditionally have had significant (professional) autonomy, whether in the public or private sectors, increasingly have to comply with goals specified by government or national regulatory bodies. The examples that I have referred to were the discipline base of educational researchers, the autonomy of members of professions, and the specialist knowledge base of subject and vocational teachers in schools and colleges. Each is being constrained in the interests of making their activities more accountable to regulatory bodies or the procedural principles enshrined in a national framework. What follows from my earlier argument drawn from Bernstein's sociology of knowledge is that these new forms of accountability will inevitably weaken the classification and framing of knowledge. As a consequence, the insulation which he argued was a key condition for the knowledge production that might be the basis of rigorous educational research and high quality professional work would also be threatened. The balance is being shifted from strong classification associated with internal criteria defined by specialists to weaker classification but greater regulatory control by regulatory bodies (and indirectly, by government).

I do not want to imply that the relative autonomy of members of professions, subject specialists or educational researchers should be beyond criticism. There are well known examples of when their practices involve little more than preserving privileges or maintaining out-of-date practices. Furthermore, in each of the examples that I have referred to, there is a warrant for dissatisfaction; early student drop-out at 16-plus, weak educational research and medical malpractice are real enough issues, to which the relevant professional specialists have given far too little attention.

My concern is not to oppose government interventions per se – an appropriate role for government is a necessary condition for democracy. It is with the nature of the government's recent interventions and the over-instrumental view of knowledge and education that they involve.

Second, I want to suggest that the issue we need to debate is not only that education is being privatized (as in cases such as 'failing' LEAs being handed over to engineering companies like Jarvis and a diverse range of bodies applying to establish academies) but the form in which it is being *nationalized*. The term 'nationalization' is far from adequate.[3] I am searching for a way of describing the shift from a view of public education as a professional practice with significant autonomy from state intervention, to the present situation when public education is increasingly a state-directed practice, under national rules and accountability procedures. I am aware that many of the processes I am referring to as nationalization borrow the language and strategies of the private sector – examples such as niche marketing and branding are even referred to in university circles – and so might be seen as examples of privatization. However, the power of intervention is the power of the state, and, more specifically, that of the elected government. It is state power that is being used to bring education in line with government goals. My own view therefore is that it is not adequate to refer to this process as privatization if we want to question the boundaries between what should and should not be the province of central government intervention.

How then should we describe what this process of nationalization involves? I suggest that educational institutions (like other public sector institutions such as hospitals) are increasingly becoming (and being seen by government as) delivery agencies, whether of research results, overseas students, qualified teachers, exam passes, higher rates of participation, or whatever the government identifies as their preferred outcomes. I am not arguing we should oppose these outcomes – far from it. It is the consequences that may follow when such externally imposed 'outcomes' drive educational institutions and policy that I am concerned with.

The combination of regulation, quantitative targets and tight funding associated with the emergence of the 'delivery agency' model of public education means that the specificity of what it is to be an educational institution is progressively reduced; the dominating priority becomes delivering targets and outcomes – not what the targets are, or how they are achieved.

A new and distinctive feature of this nationalizing process under the present Labour Government has been the substitution of Labour's former goal of promoting greater equality of opportunity by the new goal of overcoming social exclusion. The rhetorical power of social inclusion as a slogan is indicated by how difficult it is to challenge it without appearing to be conservative or elitist; who could be opposed to social inclusion except a reactionary old elitist? This response is of course an example of the classic 'third way' or 'New Labour' strategy for pre-empting debate about real and often difficult alternatives. The problem with giving priority to overcoming social exclusion is that a focus on inclusion can easily preclude debates about what people are being included in and about the possibility that more social inclusion might be associated with greater inequality. One example that illustrates this possibility is the GCSE results. Over 90 per cent of each cohort are now 'included' in the sense that they achieve at least some graded results. It is, however, not at all clear that this indicates a reduction in inequality.

We are dealing, I suggest, with a new stage in the expansion and development of public education, and we may need new concepts for understanding it. The history of this expansion up to now has involved two struggles. One has been over extending access to education to a far wider section of the public, and the other has been over the nature of the education that is provided. In England most of the efforts of the Left and Labour movements and indeed Labour governments have been directed to the former struggle. However, unlike its predecessors, the present Labour Government is no longer driven by a popular movement demanding expansion, but by its own goal of transforming what it sees as 'conservative' educational institutions, and their tendency, as government sees it, to exclude those they think will not benefit from the programmes that they offer. What is obscured by seeing educational institutions as 'conservative' is an important distinction between two kinds of conservatism which I will loosely refer to as 'political' and 'educational'. It is important to see these as analytical and not descriptive distinctions; in practice they can often be found together. 'Political' conservatism takes a variety of forms. Some are a legacy of the historical conservatism of the wider society; examples are the preferential funding treatment of Oxford and Cambridge Universities, and the charitable status of the public schools and a variety of other educational institutions. Other examples may be found in the characteristic inertia and resistance to change of formal educational institutions and subject fields. In contrast, 'educational' conservatism has its origins in the culture-conserving and transmitting role of educational institutions and the need to defend those specific structures that are the inescapable conditions for knowledge acquisition and production that I referred to earlier in the chapter. Examples of 'educational' conservatism might be the support for disciplines and certain forms of pedagogic authority and the resistance to breaking the curriculum up into 'bite sized chunks' (a less than felicitous phrase usually associated with Lord Dearing; whether this is justified or not, I do not know). My argument is that there is a danger that in not distinguishing between these two forms of conservatism, we forget to ask what in a particular case is being 'conserved' and for whom. As a consequence the excessive instrumentalism underpinning the delivery model of education and research may, in the interests of overcoming resistance to change, be undermining the conditions for access to knowledge which is the historic purpose of education and its expansion.

Let me summarize my main argument so far. It is that in so far as educational institutions are forced into delivery models based on administrative principles, the specificity of education, the epistemological basis of good research and professional work, and the possibilities of student progression are undermined.

In the three cases referred to I have suggested that the conditions crucial to each – the disciplinary basis of educational research, the specialist knowledge of subject and vocational teachers in the 14–19 curriculum, and the autonomy of professional expertise – may be threatened, not primarily by privatization, but by new forms of government intervention.

In each case we have examples of a centralizing or 'intervening' state, not primarily a 'privatizing' state. Furthermore, it is a state that might be even more likely to undermine the conditions for knowledge production and acquisition than one based more directly on the market; the example here is the USA, where a tradition of high quality postgraduate education and research is sustained in the *private* universities.

If we consider current policy solely through the lens of opposition to privatization, we may get trapped into thinking that what is needed is a larger role for the state. On recent evidence, at least in the English case, this could even accentuate the dominance of what I have referred to as the 'delivery model'. It follows that as analytical concepts in the field of educational policy, both the state/private dichotomy and privatization may have outlived their usefulness. It is the state that is intervening into professional and academic domains, not the private sector. We are in new circumstances, and we may need new theoretical tools for critique and for thinking about alternatives. New Labour's election slogan in the last general election was 'Forward not Back'. My suggestion is that we may need to go back if we want to go forward. In the final section of this chapter, therefore, I turn to the ideas in Michael Polanyi's *The Republic of Science*, which was written in 1962. I want to propose that, despite the paper being written over 40 years ago, and in a very different political context, it offers us a way of thinking about knowledge production and the role of the state that takes us forward from existing critiques of over-regulation and the rather narrow current debates about privatization.

The state and knowledge:
Michael Polanyi's *The Republic of Science*

In 1962 Polanyi faced a similar problem in relation to science to the one that I have suggested we are facing today in schools, colleges and universities. He discusses the state interventionist approach to the funding and control of science that was popular at the time but which many would think crude today. It involved setting specific political goals for scientific research, and was expressed in its most extreme form in the Soviet Union with Lysenko's environmentalist biology; an example of the externalist fallacy I referred to earlier taken to its limits. Of course, the reality of the natural world undermined Lysenko and his ideology, as it was bound to in the end. In contrast, education as a set of social institutions has a less straightforward role in resisting and undermining ideologies, not least because in the universities we are involved in creating as well as undermining them. Deeply flawed educational ideas such as 'child-centredness' and outcomes-based and competence-based approaches to vocational education are as likely to originate in universities as in government departments. Likewise their superficially modern equivalents such as 'personalized learning' and 'individual learning styles' keep being 'discovered', despite the substantial body of research documenting their fundamental weaknesses.

Polanyi did not argue that state intervention in science was always and in principle wrong, and that scientists should be left to themselves – this would be an example of what earlier in the chapter I referred to as the internalist fallacy. He takes a more subtle approach, by comparing the relative unboundedness of so-called 'free' economic markets with the boundedness of 'markets for ideas' in the sciences and other fields of knowledge. Science was not, for Polanyi, just a collection of bodies of powerful knowledge; it consists of sets of institutions, with their rules, codes, traditions and core values. The distinctiveness of the sciences as institutions is the unique value they place on innovation and the creation and defence of new knowledge. It is this value that distributes rewards, shapes research priorities and, albeit indirectly, influences the school and university science curriculum. This does not mean that the sciences (whether natural or social) are or should be beyond public criticism; they are public institutions largely funded by public money. Polanyi argued that the role of the state is not to try to direct scientific priorities, but to support the sciences in realizing their core value – the creation of new knowledge. Despite demands for a more externally or user-driven approach, this model still largely applies in the case of the Science Research Councils in this country.

We can envisage education as a set of specialist institutions that has some parallel with science as Polanyi conceived of it. It has its own rules, codes and traditions, but directed to a rather different core value – the acquisition and transmission as well as the creation of knowledge. This model, I suggest, provides the basis for an alternative role for the state in supporting educational research and the educational profession in promoting the acquisition, application and creation of new knowledge. It would involve less direct state intervention and regulation and more self-regulation. As a corollary, it would require the professional education community to re-affirm its core value of promoting the acquisition of knowledge, ask what the conditions for this are in the current context, and how far, in following political and economic imperatives in recent years, this value has been lost sight of.

7 Rethinking the relationship between the sociology of education and educational policy

Introduction

The topic of this chapter is far from new, although it is not as old as sociology itself. It was, for example, not a problem that would have worried Comte or Saint Simon, the founders of sociology as a social science, or even their French successor, Durkheim, who was more explicitly concerned with education. However, it is certainly an issue that sociologists have wrestled with since Max Weber wrote his famous essays, 'Science as a vocation' and 'Politics as a vocation' (Weber 1948). More than 50 years later the argument between Howard Becker's 'Whose side are we on?' (Becker 1967) and Alvin Gouldner's 'Sociologist as partisan' (Gouldner 1968) set the terms of the debate when I started teaching sociology at the end of the 1960s. This chapter is not an attempt to review those earlier debates; it has two much more limited aims. The first is to ask what might be learned from my experiences of trying, as a sociologist, to influence education policy in two very different contexts: England in the last three decades of the twentieth century; and South Africa since Nelson Mandela was released from prison in 1990. Both contexts, I am assuming, have something in common with the problems that many sociologists of education have faced in the past three decades. As such, the chapter is personal and reflexive, and makes no claims to be a comprehensive statement of the range of different positions or of the circumstances of the two countries in the periods under discussion.

The second aim of the chapter is to make an argument for how sociology should relate to educational policy that derives from the social realist theory of knowledge developed in previous chapters. Most of us have been torn, at different times, between the opposing dynamics of 'sociology as critique' on the one hand and 'sociology as reconstruction or policy intervention' on the other. As the South African sociologist Joe Muller points out in his book *Reclaiming Knowledge* (Muller 2000), this enduring dilemma is well expressed by Fritz Ringer when, with reference to French academics at the turn of the twentieth century, he asks: 'Are they intellectuals, prophets and sages; or are they scientists, specialized researchers or technical innovators? Are they critics of power or expert advisers to politicians, direct or indirect moulders of public opinion?' (quoted in Muller 2000). Positions on these questions (Ringer writes) 'are rarely held in full consciousness; they are implicit orientations ... a permanent substratum of thought, a part of the cultural preconscious, and a vital source of the cognitive dispositions at work in the intellectual field' (quoted in Muller 2000). Likewise, most of us will have hoped that there was a 'third way' that embraced both options, which we might call 'critical reconstruction' or 'critical policy intervention'. Such an approach would aim to explain the origins of policies, analyse how they work (and do not work) *and* seek to provide some basis for making prescriptions about future policies and how to implement them.

Most of the current pressures from government and research funders in the UK are directed towards sociology as 'supporting policy intervention', or policy-relevant research, as it is more frequently called. Policy-oriented programmes, such as the Economic and Social Research Council's (ESRC) Teaching and Learning Research Programme, which give priority to the needs of those assumed to be 'users' of research, get a growing proportion of ESRC funding, and university departments are encouraged to bid for centres and programmes linked to the evaluation and implementation of government policies. At the same time resources, both financial and intellectual, for critiques of policies or for developing concepts and theories that are not directly related to policy goals, are less and less easy to obtain.

The public scepticism about more fundamental (frequently referred to with some irony as 'blue-skies') research and scholarship in the social sciences is compounded by those who identify with the role of sociologist as critic, and at the same time adopt a postmodernist stance on epistemological issues. For if, as some argue, all knowledge is an expression of an interest or from a standpoint, it is difficult to make any publicly defensible case for critique or scholarship in the social sciences. Research and theory from this point of view are little more than politics or interests in disguise: either you agree with the particular standpoint or you do not (see Chapters 1 and 2).

Two issues are important if we want, as I do, to defend the claims of the sociology of education as an activity and a field that gives priority to cognitive values and theoretically based explanations and not just to particular standpoints. The first is to identify the material and institutional circumstances in which we find ourselves as sociologists of education, and the second is to be clear about what we mean by scientific knowledge in our field and in the social sciences more generally. The circumstances in which social science research has been located in recent years in the UK have been paradoxical. On the one hand there have been significantly more funds available for research in education than ever before. On the other hand, there is far more pressure on researchers to 'deliver' the kind of findings that governments and funding agencies want. This situation makes clarity about what we mean by knowledge in the social sciences uniquely important.

My argument in this chapter makes three assumptions that follow from discussions in the earlier chapters. The first is that we can distinguish clearly between knowledge and opinion or common sense, rather than seeing the former as merely one form of the latter, as some current theories in the social sciences are inclined to do. The second is that we can give grounds for claiming that explanations in the social sciences are not just from a point of view or a particular standpoint, even though points of view and values are inevitably involved. The third assumption is that sociological explanations offer distinct cognitive or epistemic gains over, for example, the views and opinions of policy makers, administrators and practitioners. This does not mean that sociological explanations will be necessarily accepted by policy makers or that they should be uncontested, or the views of others disregarded; questions of power, ideology and perspective are always involved in the social sciences. However, good sociological research can make unambiguous claims that it provides cognitive gains or better explanations. The most famous and still relevant example is the early demonstration by Jean Floud and her colleagues (Floud *et al.* 1956) of the social class basis of eleven-plus selection for grammar schools.

We also need to have some idea what the conditions are for generating sociological knowledge – what Basil Bernstein, in one of his last papers, referred to as 'vertical discourses' (Bernstein 2000)[1] – and what features distinguish vertical discourses from those such as educational policy that in his terms would be described as 'horizontal'. At the same time we have to recognize the limits of the knowledge claims of social scientists.

My more general point is that *theoretical* debates about educational policy or practice within disciplines and *political* (in the broadest sense of the term) debates about preferences for particular policies and their likely efficacy need to be recognized as distinct and different forms of thinking. They represent, as it were, boundaries to be maintained and crossed but not blurred. Recognizing the importance of the distinction between 'theoretical' and 'political' debates is, I would argue, necessary if sociologists are to develop the kind of knowledge about policy that can offer cognitive gains to policy makers over and above the latter's knowledge and experience. This distinction relates to the epistemological importance of the university as a key site of knowledge production and of disciplines such as sociology that are associated with universities and are separate from government departments and agencies involved in policy design and implementation. It also highlights the limitations of arguments that equate good research with policy relevance and include users in decision-making about research except in defining very broad sets of priorities. It is also an argument against the uncritical replacement of what Gibbons and his colleagues (Gibbons *et al.* 1994) refer to as Mode 1 or discipline-based knowledge by Mode 2 or trans-disciplinary knowledge.

My argument is that we should invert the paradox that sociologists have to face of increases in both funding and control of research which I referred to earlier. To the extent that increases in funding for the sociology of education assume that it can make a greater contribution to policy development, it needs to be more independent of specific policy priorities and outcomes. I want to reach this conclusion by reflecting on my recent experience of working on curriculum policy and review in South Africa, and will contrast this with my longer experience as a sociologist working on similar issues in the UK, first as a policy critic or critical sociologist in the 1970s following the publication of my book *Knowledge and*

Control (Young 1971), and then in the 1990s, as one of a number of educational researchers who tried to shape policy in the field of post-compulsory education and training (Finegold *et al.* 1990; Young 1998).

I consider the South African case here for two reasons. First, I was personally involved in policy development in South Africa in the early 1990s and more recently (a decade later) in a retrospective review of education policy since 1990. Second, there are, I suggest, particular lessons to be learned from the South African experience that have much wider implications. Since 1990 there have been much closer links between researchers and senior policy makers in South Africa than in the UK. After the complete exclusion of most university-based sociologists from education policy debates during the decades of apartheid, the two communities were able to open up to each other after 1990. However, what was distinctive about the situation in South Africa after 1990 was that ideas which often stayed within the research community in the UK were frequently taken up by policy makers. As a result, the South African case highlights issues concerning the responsibilities of university-based researchers that are easily taken for granted in a country like the UK, where for most sociologists it is unlikely that their ideas will ever become policy, at least in the short term.

A brief account of the background to my working in South Africa is, I think, necessary. My first professional involvement there began in 1990, shortly after Nelson Mandela was released, and a range of democratic organizations were legalized, including the African National Congress (ANC) and the South African Communist Party. I was invited to help develop policies on curriculum and qualifications for the post-compulsory sector for a future post-apartheid government. It was not long after the publication by the Institute of Public Policy Research (IPPR) of *A British Baccalaureate* (Finegold *et al.* 1990) in the UK. A decade later, in 2000, I was asked by the Human Sciences Research Council in South Africa to contribute to an educational policy review 'round table'. All the researchers and policy makers who were invited were asked to reflect on the previous decade, and on why South Africa's democratic government, elected in 1994, had found it so difficult to implement policies that had been developed, often by the same people, between 1990 and 1994.[2]

The round table provided a unique opportunity to reflect on the theories and research with which I and others had been associated a decade earlier, in light of what had happened since. This kind of opportunity is rare in the UK, partly because theories and research have a much less direct influence on policies and policy debates, and partly because politicians and educational policy makers in this country all too rarely reflect on the failure of past reforms and the lessons that might be learned from them. The endless string of new policies of the past two decades, especially in the field of vocational education and training, are a good example of what might be called policy amnesia or 'change without memory' (Keep 2006).

By the year 2000, when the policy review round table took place, South Africa was in the first year of its second ANC-led government, and a number of the policies developed in the early 1990s were at various stages of being implemented.

Two of these policies are particularly relevant to the argument of this chapter. They are:

- the introduction of a national framework for all qualifications: school, university, vocational and professional;
- the development of an integrated system of post-compulsory education and training that incorporated the upper secondary school curriculum, the curriculum of the technical (now FET) colleges (see Chapter 12), and work-based training in a single system.

Bearing in mind the massive task of replacing the racially divided systems of the apartheid era (there had been 18 separate racially based systems of education under apartheid), it was not surprising that growing doubts were being voiced about the feasibility of such ambitious policy goals. Among the questions posed at the round table were the following: Did the problems of implementation that were experienced after 1994 mean that the policies developed by the democratic movement in the pre-1994 period and the theories underpinning them were fundamentally flawed? Or were these difficulties primarily a reflection of the inevitable problems of implementation faced by any new policies, especially in circumstances where there is a lack of capacity at all levels?

There was (and still is) a significant lack of capacity in South Africa – both in the resources available to schools and colleges, and in administrative experience and educational expertise – at every level of the education system. However, my concern was, given this lack of resources, why had theories and policies that had been current within academic communities in many western countries, but not necessarily reflected in actual policies, been taken up so readily by those involved in developing policies in South Africa in the early 1990s? Was this because these ideas appeared to fit in with the widely held democratic vision of the anti-apartheid movement, despite the fact that they took little account of the social and educational realities of post-apartheid South Africa (or even, often, the social and educational realities of their countries of origin)?

My argument at the round table and in the book based on it (Kraak and Young 2001) was that in the early 1990s the emphasis had been on the envisioning and advocacy role of theories in shaping policy rather than their analytical role. There is only space here to briefly elaborate this distinction. It relates to a particular view of the differences between concepts in the natural and social sciences. Whereas the powers of explanation and prediction provided by concepts in the natural sciences have been dramatically increased by their progressive mathematicization, this has been paralleled by a reduction (some would argue the disappearance) of their role in providing visions of the future, at least in any specific sense. On the other hand, the extent, if at all, to which concepts in the social sciences can be expressed mathematically is problematic and deeply contested. Some would argue that 'theories' in sociology are nothing more than competing visions or possibilities, even if this is sometimes masked by obscure jargon or over-elaborate statistics. I take the view that there are some social science disciplines where the mathematicization of concepts is appropriate – demography and some parts of economics are good examples. However, even in the most empirically grounded research in sociology, we rely on concepts and ideas that are neither entirely separate nor separable from everyday life. It follows that concepts in sociology rely on public as well as disciplinary meanings, and always to some extent represent visions and views of the world; in other words, they cannot escape being visionary even when their explicit aim is to be explanatory. However, sociological concepts are not and need not be just visions; they are also part of systems of interrelated concepts, and are linked, either explicitly or implicitly, with ways of making sense of the social world and our experience of it. Despite this, the capacity of the social sciences to offer explanations on the lines of those in the natural sciences is extremely limited. To the extent that such explanations are developed, they rely for their claims to objectivity on the rules, procedures and reflexive practices of particular disciplines. Sociological concepts, as Giddens (1993) and others have noted, not only have their origins in attempts to make sense of the social world; they also become part of the world, and themselves become visions which need critical analysis. Globalization and lifelong learning are good contemporary examples. Hence, because sociological analysis always involves a combination of vision and explanation, one task of the sociologist is to make clear the distinct and different assumptions and purposes of each. In the context of the dramatic democratization that took place in South Africa in the early 1990s, it was understandable that the distinction between vision and explanation was not seen as important. Furthermore, in the circumstances of the emerging democratic movement there was little emphasis on the difference between social theories developed within academic and political communities, which tend to be critiques of other theories, and theories about policy implementation, which necessarily involve many other factors not necessarily considered by particular disciplinary communities.

I argued in the previous section that an understanding of the relationship between theory and policy needs an understanding both of the intellectual field in which theories are developed and of the changing context in which theory/policy relations are worked out. The next section considers aspects of the intellectual field of sociology of education in South Africa by focusing on a number of specific issues that were debated after 1990.

Key issues in the sociology of education in South Africa after 1990

Although the issues briefly considered in this section arose in South Africa, and in some cases were highlighted by the specific circumstances of that country, they were not independent of debates in the international community of sociologists of education. As a result, they have, I would argue, a more general significance for the relationship between sociology and educational policy, to which I will return.

Educational reform and economic change

The government proposals for integrating education and training in South Africa after 1994 were based on an optimistic scenario about how capitalism was developing, which was current among social scientists in western countries in the late 1980s and early 1990s. The best-known examples of this type of analysis were Piore and Sabel's flexible specialization thesis (Piore and Sabel 1984) and the different versions of post-Fordism developed by Robin Murray and others in the journal *Marxism Today*. In contrast to the earlier deskilling thesis, which began with Braverman's (1976) critique of Henry Ford's view of mass production and Marxist theories about the inevitable collapse of capitalism, the new theories argued that democratic forms of production premised on overcoming the division between mental and manual labour were emerging that lay at the heart of capitalism's search for higher levels of productivity. At the same time, the argument for integrating education and training not only linked to this progressive economic thesis about capitalism, it fitted in well with the democratic and integrationist educational philosophy of the democratic movement in South Africa.

However, as has since become apparent, these socio-economic theories related even less to the realities of South African capitalism than they did to capitalism in most industrial countries of the west. As many commentators were to observe, it was only in very special circumstances, such as those found in Emilia Romagna in Northern Italy, that the transformation of Fordist production showed evidence of the more democratic possibilities associated with post-Fordism, multi-skilling and flexible specialization. In South Africa, as in the UK, Fordism either persisted or was replaced by what became known as Hi-Tec- or neo-Fordism. There were parallels and similar problems with the economic arguments for integration (or unification, as it was referred to in the UK) of education and training that were made by the IPPR authors (Finegold *et al.* 1990; also see Chapter 11). Both appear with hindsight to be examples of the separation of the 'visioning' role of social theories – providing alternative possible futures – from the explanations about why such a vision might be a real possibility. This is not to dismiss the importance of a visioning role for theories in the shaping of policy development, especially in times of political transition. However, what should distinguish social theories from policy proposals or political priorities is that their visions should be related to explanations about how the world is changing. This link between vision and explanation is crucial if a vision is to stand a chance of becoming reality. Without such a link, visions are likely at best to remain utopias.[3]

Conflating political and educational discourses

Education policy documents in South Africa in the early 1990s were full of slogans drawn from the struggle against apartheid and calling for democratization, participation, consultation and integration. All appeared to fit in with dominant progressive educational ideas, especially those held within the adult education community. What the slogans did not recognize was the extent to which education practices and institutions have a specificity of their own, and that the language of democratic politics, and specifically that of trade union struggles, cannot be straightforwardly applied to issues concerning teaching and learning. This is not to dismiss the value of interrogating education through the lens of democratic theory, nor to undervalue the active involvement of students in their own learning. What is important is that the nature of the specificity of education is recognized, and where possible demarcated. Obvious examples of where democratic theory is likely to be at odds with the specificity of educational practices are the necessary authority relations between teachers and pupils that are expressed in the concept of peda- gogy (Christie 2002) and the cognitive superiority of particular fields of specialist subject knowledge over everyday knowledge. There are parallels between the democratic educational slogans that were common in South Africa in the 1990s and the argument for focusing on 'the politics' of school knowledge in books such as the one that I edited with Geoff Whitty (Young and Whitty 1977). At the time I certainly did not recognize the dangers of dismissing the specificity of educational practices and institutions, and seeing everything as at least potentially 'political'.

Social constructivist views of knowledge and the curriculum

The idea that educational knowledge is 'socially constructed' that was the theme of Chapters 1 and 2 of this book is another example of a set of ideas which has been widely debated (and sometimes endorsed) among academics in western countries since the 1970s, but which has had relatively little direct impact on curriculum pol- icy. In South Africa the situation was very different. The idea that the curriculum is a social construct fitted well with critiques of the apartheid curriculum and was readily taken up by policy makers (Muller 2000). It provided the conceptual basis for curriculum policy makers to make a break with the past. It appeared to hand the power to create a new curriculum to teachers, students and more broadly to 'the democratic forces', by legitimating the abolition of syllabuses that were associated with the oppressive regime of the apartheid era. The social construction of knowl- edge became a slogan for opposing the idea that the role of the curriculum is to enable learners to develop their thinking through an engagement with specialist bodies of knowledge that are not available to them in their everyday lives. Expertise and specialist knowledge, from which Black South Africans had been excluded under apartheid, all too easily became associated only with privilege. As a result, a new 'outcomes-based' (OBE) curriculum was proposed, largely free of content and limited to expressing the broad educational goals of the democratic movement. Not surprisingly, overworked teachers, often lacking specialist qualifi- cations and confronted with vast classes, did not know what to do with such ideas.

The role of qualifications in educational reform

After 1990 and in the period leading up to the first ANC-led government in 1994, the recently legalized independent trade unions had a uniquely powerful role in shaping the educational reform agenda in South Africa. Under apartheid, many

Black workers undertook skilled jobs but were denied the opportunity to get qualifications and therefore were still paid as unskilled workers. It made sense for the trade unions to argue for a qualification system that could be used to recognize the skills of Black workers without requiring them to undertake further study, and therefore would be a basis for upgrading their wages. Hence the appeal of an outcomes-based or standards-based qualifications framework, provided it was linked to opportunities for the assessment of skills acquired at work. This issue is explored in more detail in the specific case of RPL (the recognition of prior learning) in Chapter 13.

The idea that an outcomes-based approach to qualifications could drive reforms of the whole education and training system reform originated in Australia and the UK, where it had more to do with keeping qualifications in the hands of employers than with improving the pay of workers. Furthermore, when linked to funding, qualifications, as drivers of reform, also give governments more control over educational institutions (see Chapter 8); hence their popularity with governments adopting neo-liberal economic policies (Allais 2003). What was not fully grasped by those on the Left supporting qualifications-driven reforms in South Africa (and similar groups in the UK) was that on their own, qualifications are only definers of outcomes; they take for granted the processes and institutions that generate the outcomes. Furthermore, it was the infrastructure for certifying existing skills as well as institutions for promoting skill development that were so lacking in South Africa.

Political culture and educational reform

The struggle against apartheid defined the experience of many South Africans in the 1980s and earlier. This emphasis on struggle created a political culture that played an important role in overthrowing apartheid. However, it was at odds with the kind of culture that was needed for implementing reforms and creating a new and fairer education system in the period when the political battle against the legal and constitutional basis of apartheid had been won. A political culture of struggle sees conflicts as positive and necessary. They are either resolved in crises or lead to violent clashes; they demand immediate short-term 'victories'. Such a culture endorses confrontation and mass action as primary strategies. In contrast, a political culture conducive to the implementation of progressive educational reforms accepts that change is incremental and slow and that it relies on expertise and on individual as well as collective effort. With the experience of opposing apartheid still vivid in many people's minds in South Africa, voicing ideas such as support for an incremental approach was not easy. It could appear as if the project of political transformation was being put into reverse. Though dramatized in the South African case, this clash between political cultures is not unique to South Africa. One issue that it highlights is the importance of the distinction between types of 'conservatism' that I discussed in the previous chapter. There is a 'political' conservatism that denies access (in South Africa on racial grounds) and sustains inequality in the interests of protecting privilege; it needs to be opposed unambiguously. However, there is a no less important 'educational' conservatism, inherent in all pedagogic relationships and in the acquisition and production of knowledge, which is likely to be a condition for reducing inequalities.

Past practice, policies and institutions

An assumption widely held among policy makers associated with the democratic movement in South Africa in the 1990s was that anything associated with the old apartheid regime was to be rejected. Examples were apprenticeship, school inspection and a syllabus-based curriculum. Each of these policy instruments had been used in South Africa prior to 1990 to perpetuate racial inequalities. However, it does not follow that any of them are to be rejected per se. There are parallels in the UK, such as the attempt to make a break with key aspects the old vocational qualifications when NVQs were introduced in 1987 (Raggatt and Williams 1999) (see Chapter 9). Both the South African and UK cases can be seen as examples of the over-politicization of educational issues. In many ways the old system in South Africa, with its 18 distinct education systems divided on racial grounds, had nothing to commend it; like Nazism, it was an evil system. However, there were educational institutions and examinations which, although part of a racist system, were not just part of that system. Examples are Fort Hare University, where Nelson Mandela was educated, and the 'matric route' to university, which had been a progression route to university for at least a few Africans, many of whom are now in leadership positions. The horrors of apartheid made it difficult to accept that the apartheid system had any positive features.

Even a racist society like South Africa under apartheid had to create technicians and engineers at the same time as excluding the majority of Africans. For a long time it did both relatively effectively and technical colleges linked to an apprenticeship system were in place by the 1990s which were beginning to open up to Africans. Bearing in mind the length of time that it takes to establish trust in new institutions, it seems likely that, where possible, reforms should focus on expanding access and therefore public trust in existing institutions rather than necessarily seeking to replace them.

A number of conclusions can be drawn from what is, in so many ways, the unique case of South Africa. First, theory and policy discourses have their origins in different communities and need to be treated in their own terms if theory is to inform policy. Second, it is important, as discussed earlier, to distinguish between the visionary and analytical aspects of social theories. Third, problems arise when educational policy issues are over-politicized. This is something that the Left often points out about the Right, as in the case of left-wing critiques of marketization. It is less often addressed by those on the Left in relation to their own theories and debates. Fourth, the South African case illustrates the importance of recognizing that educational goals and practices have a specificity of their own. Sociology of education is inclined, understandably, to stress what educational practices have in common with other social practices. However, no less important are the ways in which they are different. In other words, we need a theory of both the 'content' and the 'context' of educational policy and practice, as well as the relationship between the two.

Educational policies and social theories in South Africa: the changing context

Up to now, this chapter has concentrated on problems associated with sociological theories and concepts being used uncritically in policy contexts. The other issue I want to raise that draws on the South African case is the relationship between sociology and educational policy, and how it is shaped by the wider context as well as by the intellectual field itself. My analysis here is indebted to and draws substantially on Muller's excellent and detailed account (Muller 2000).[4] In the South African case, the relevant period since the 1980s can be expressed in terms of four phases, as follows.

The 1980s: sociology as critique

This was the period when the structure of apartheid was beginning to crack under internal and external pressures, and at the same time military oppression of the resistance movement was increased. There was no scope for sociologists to collaborate with government, and only ad hoc links were possible with opposition movements (mainly trade unions). Sociologists were mostly based in the universities, which offered relative security but no power or influence over policy. The major question they faced was which theory should be the basis of their critiques. The debates of the time were concerned largely with whether South Africa represented a form of capitalist exploitation that happened to be expressed in racial divisions, or whether it was a specific form of racist capitalist state designed to protect white rather than specifically social class interests. Such debates, like many similar ones in western countries in the 1980s, were to become almost irrelevant in the 1990s.

1990–1994: sociology as visioning

In this period following the release of Nelson Mandela, many sociologists became actively involved in constructing education policies for the post-apartheid era. The most influential example was the National Education Policy Investigation (NEPI). However, this was a time in which the emerging democratic movement was free to meet and debate but still had no power. Not surprisingly, the distinction between vision and explanation tended to disappear; policy became equated with visioning and politics tended to lead theory.

1994–1996: sociology and policy reconstruction

Many university-based sociologists in South Africa developed close links with the new democratic government during this period, and often were employed directly by it. Social science research became identified with the development of policy frameworks which it was hoped would become the basis of future policy and legislation. At the same time, the lack of fit between the theories taken over from western academic communities that were implicit in the new policies, and the problems being faced in curriculum reform and the design of a new qualification system, was becoming increasingly apparent.

1996 and after: sociology and policy implementation

A focus on new legislation and the beginning of a period of policy implementation followed the election of the second ANC-led government in 2000, and the inevitable problems developed. These were paralleled by an emerging tension within the academic community that had been masked in the earlier period of opposition, between sociologists as critics and those who saw themselves as policy constructors (or reconstructors). However, this split took on a different and, I would argue, more productive significance to that typically found in a western European country such as the UK. Both senior civil servants and academic social scientists had a common history in the struggle against apartheid. As a result they shared a legacy and goals from that time that informed both theory and policy, and partly minimized the more negative consequences of the inevitable differences between the circumstances of the two groups.

Sociology of education and education policy in the UK since the 1960s

This section returns to the UK context and an inevitably brief and schematic discussion of the changing relationship between sociology of education and education policy since the 1960s. Its aim is to serve as a contrast with the South African case, and thus to address more general issues about the relationship between sociology of education as an intellectual field and the changing context in which it is located. Although Karl Mannheim was appointed to a Chair in Sociology of Education at the Institute of Education in 1946, government policies and political debates only began to take seriously the findings of sociological research with the publication of Floud *et al.*'s *Social Class and Educational Opportunity* in 1956. Sociology of education at the time was dominated by the 'political arithmetic' tradition established by Booth and Rowntree which saw it as a kind of neutral 'science for government'.[5] The close relationship between sociology and educational policy depended not only on the rigour of sociologists' research, but on a degree of consensus between researchers and policy makers, which only began to be seriously challenged by the end of the 1960s. Publications such as *Knowledge and Control* (Young 1971) heralded sharp debates within the discipline, and a break with policy was associated with the emergence of 'sociology of education as critique', initially from a phenomenological but later from a Marxist perspective.

An assumption of what became known in the 1970s as the 'new sociology of education' was to see policy as the exercise of power and the role of sociology as unmasking the power relations implicit in policies. It identified with teachers (and with their students) as agents of progressive educational change, supported by sections of the working class (usually represented by elements within the trade union movement and the Left of the Labour Party). However, as has been discussed in some detail in Chapters 1 and 2, this 'new' sociology of education was open to the charges of curricular relativism, and a naive view of policy which assumed that teachers were the key agents of educational change. Both problems, together with a drastically changing political climate, contributed to a fragmentation of the field in the 1980s; postmodernism and 'standpoint' or voice discourses emerged as dominant perspectives and much empirical research in the sociology of education became indistinguishable from policy evaluation. It was not surprising that the field appeared to lose purpose and direction. The 1990s saw the emergence of a new anti-conservative consensus and support for New Labour by many sociologists of education. The more critical strands became the basis for challenging the trend towards marketization of education and a growing emphasis on individual choice in educational policy; they also exposed the persistence of racial and gender inequalities. However, these latter developments tended to marginalize any broader concerns with a theoretical basis for the field. As a result it became over-associated with an advocacy role, and lost much of its autonomy and distinctiveness as a discipline. Many sociologists became absorbed in policy research or what became known as policy sociology. Despite a number of theoretically focused special issues of the *British Journal of Sociology of Education*,[6] this trend has continued since the election of a second and third Labour government as research agendas have become ever more policy-driven.

This all too brief and over-schematic account of the recent history of the sociology of education in the UK demonstrates two points relevant to the overall argument of this chapter. The first is the extent to which sociology of education has been shaped both by intellectual developments within the field, such as the disenchantment with Marxism and its 'replacement' by postmodernism, and by the changing context in which the field has been located. The second point concerns the typical conditions under which sociology has an influence on policy. It appears that its most influential periods were when there was the greatest consensus between researchers, politicians and policy makers (as in the 1950s and 1960s). The case of the 1990s, when sociologists of education, although fragmented, formed a much larger if looser academic community, is more complex. However, I would argue that consensus was again a condition for influence, although this condition applied only to some sections of the field. At the same time, such a consensus necessarily involved a weakening of the disciplinary or 'vertical' features of the sociology of education.

Discussion

Not surprisingly, there is a parallel between the shift from social constructivism to social realism discussed elsewhere and changes in my own thinking about the role of sociology of education and its relationship to policy and practice. In *Knowledge and Control* (Young 1971), a conflict model of the sociology/policy relationship was at least implicit. It assumed that theory would always and inevitably be in conflict with policy. In contrast, many of the projects on which I worked in the field of post-16 education policy in the 1990s reflected what might be described as a collaborative model, which sees theory as separate from but aiming to inform policy.[7] A collaborative model explicitly recognizes a division of labour between theory and its role in the analysis of policy on the one hand, and policy making and implementation on the other, as well as the very different constraints that each context imposes on those involved. However, it is not only a greater awareness of context that characterizes the collaborative model; it involves a shift in how educational change is understood. This shift can be expressed in terms of moving from a 'transformative' to an 'evolutionary' model of educational change. With hindsight, we can see that the 'new sociology of education' of the 1970s identified with a 'transformative' approach to educational change; its goal was to empower radical classroom teachers and their political supporters in their efforts to change the system from the bottom up. The 'evolutionary' model that characterized much research with which I was involved in the 1990s, and well represented in the paper by Howieson *et al.* (1997), was more cautious but arguably more realistic; it saw the primary role of sociology as educating the policy makers (and, indirectly, the politicians) and hence having more of a top-down influence on the direction of change. This shift of models reflected not only a recognition of the weaknesses of the earlier theories, but the desire on the part of researchers, after 18 years of Tory government, not just to sit on the sidelines and write critiques but actually to try and influence the development of policies. It also assumed that a consensus between sociologists and policy makers could be established. However, there was a price to be paid. The policy maker invariably seeks support for his or her policies from researchers. As a result, a collaborative approach to the theory/policy relationship involves a loss in the autonomy, and hence weakens the critical element in sociology. As Muller (2000) points out, Foucault stated the dilemma clearly when he wrote:

> I absolutely will not play the part of one who prescribes solutions. I hold that the role of the intellectual today is ... not proposing solutions or prophesying, since by doing that one can only contribute to the determinate situation of power that must be criticised.

> (Foucault, quoted in Muller 2000)

Foucault's argument seems telling. However, it has two problems. First, it takes for granted the legitimacy of and support for social science as a critique of policy as if it were self-justifying, which it is not; any specialist intellectual activity needs support. Second, Foucault implies that in refusing to provide solutions or make predictions, the sociologist is somehow excused from 'contributing to the determinant situation of power'. This kind of 'on the fence' position seems to neglect both the institutional location and the material base of the social sciences, which necessarily involve them in power relations and decisions, whether they explicitly endorse them or not.

A conflict model of theory/policy relations polarizes the two, and sees policy as invariably inhibiting rather than supporting progressive change. Theory, this model assumes, is radical and capable of emancipating educational practice; hence the conflict. However, on the evidence of the different cases of the early 1990s in South Africa and the 1970s in England, the model makes unjustifiable assumptions about the power of theory. It assumes that if policy and practice are 'set free' by critiques based on theory, they almost inevitably become 'radical' and 'transformative'. In each case, not only is the critical role of ideology neglected, but there is a failure to give sufficient emphasis both to the material conditions in each case, and to the necessary elements of 'conservatism' of educational institutions. The collaborative model, on the other hand, has the opposite problem. In its efforts to take the context in which policy makers work into account, it can easily neglect the power relations that are involved in accepting the framework of assumptions of the policy makers. However well-intentioned policy makers are, conflicts of interest are likely to remain between them and others with less power in the system; it is not just a question of different contexts in which people face different problems. Making explicit the links between policy frameworks and power relations must continue to be one of the critical roles of sociology. In the UK the collaborative model appeared peculiarly attractive to many researchers on the Left in the period 1992–1997, when the Labour Party was in opposition, and in the early years of the 1997 Labour Government. It was easy for sociologists to forget the constraints on policy makers and to overestimate the influence of researchers and hence the strengths of the collaborative model. Again, there are parallels with the 1990–1994 period in South Africa, when opposition policy makers were not constrained by any association with government or by implementation issues. With hindsight, I think the collaborative model, which was adopted by many sociologists of education in their attitude towards Labour Party policy in the 1990s, neglects the importance of researchers retaining their autonomy to develop theories which may not be attractive to policy makers. In other words, the collaborative model tends to assume that the struggle is over, rather than endemic to the relationship between sociology and policy. A failure to assert their autonomy in the pre-1997 period put sociologists of education in a weak position when Labour took over government in the UK and began to modify some of the policy positions it had adopted in opposition. South African researchers faced a similar dilemma in moving from being 'critics' to 'reconstructors' in the period after the election of their first democratic government.

Conclusions

The lessons for sociologists of education that I draw from my comparison of the UK and South African cases are (i) that it is important to make explicit the ways in which sociological knowledge can claim a degree of objectivity, (ii) that there are important conditions which make the creation of such knowledge possible, and (iii) that attempts to undermine such conditions must be resisted. At the same time, it has to be recognized that the conditions for this objectivity are not easily won.

They cannot rely on the outmoded claims of positivist social science or a comfortable consensus that can hide real differences. It also has to be accepted that serious attempts to establish a social realist theory of knowledge have not progressed very far. Claims to objectivity have to be based on the intellectual grounds and the traditions and values of the discipline that go back more than a century. With regard to the sociology/policy relationship, and notwithstanding the importance of seeking evidence for and against policies, it is my experience that the relationship between theory and policy is more conceptual than empirical, at least in any narrow way. It is about providing new ways of seeing old problems that can lead to both new questions and new possibilities. There is always likely to be a tension between knowledge based on disciplinary expertise and knowledge based on political priorities. It seems likely that neither conflict nor collaboration adequately characterizes the relationship between research and policy. The tension between the two will in my view never be resolved in a definitive sense; it will inevitably vary according to both political circumstances and the state of the discipline.

Sociologists of education need to make explicit their broad political and educational purposes and their commitment to the codes, rules and practices of their discipline. In that sense, we can do no better than follow the examples laid down for us by Max Weber and Emile Durkheim in the early years of the twentieth century. Whereas Durkheim's goal was to establish the distinctiveness of sociology, Weber drew on a wide range of disciplines in developing his sociology. Their two approaches are not incompatible, and are mirrored in the different approaches of the two most significant sociologists of education of the last decades of the twentieth century, Pierre Bourdieu and Basil Bernstein. Though frequently acknowledging his debt to Durkheim, it was Bernstein, not Bourdieu, who drew on linguistics and psychology as well as his own discipline in developing his sociology. Bourdieu offers us an approach to theory/policy relations by reminding us that seeing intellectual fields as sites of power struggles is not incompatible with having a commitment to truth and objective knowledge (Bourdieu 1975). Bernstein addresses a slightly different aspect of the question I have been concerned with in this chapter. He reminds us that education is never just a relay for other social forces, as social reproduction theories and, increasingly, government policies tend to assume. Education has a social specificity of its own that centres on the conditions for the acquisition of knowledge that can never be reduced to politics, economics or problems of administration (Bernstein 2000).

Part 2

Applied studies

8 Contrasting approaches to qualifications and their role in educational reform

Introduction

This chapter focuses on some of the implications of a recent trend for governments (in the UK and elsewhere) to use qualifications as a main driver of educational reform,[1] especially but not only in the field of vocational education and training. The chapter is not directly concerned with the issue of knowledge that has been a recurring theme in this book. However, the emergence of a new approach to qualifications (I refer to it in the chapter as the outcomes-based approach) raises some of the epistemological issues with which this book is concerned in a peculiarly acute way. I am not suggesting that qualifications cannot provide some indication of what a person knows and can do; nor do I argue that they have no role in educational reform. Qualifications are an element of social reality of the education systems of all societies; they do, to an extent, motivate learners, they are used by employers to screen applicants for jobs and increasingly, as this chapter argues, they are used by governments as part of how they control educational institutions. However, what I question is that qualifications expressed as outcomes or standards can provide an adequate basis for teachers to develop the curriculum. This can only lead, as is argued in greater detail in Chapter 9, to a collapse of standards (I use the term here in the older sense of raising (or lowering) standards) as opposed to the relatively new idea of writing or setting standards as precise statements of outcomes).

Outcomes-based qualifications, if seen as a basis for the curriculum, lead almost inexorably to an extreme version of social constructivism which in effect does away with the idea of a curriculum at all. The consequences, in the case of South Africa, of attempting to adopt such an approach to reform and the possible alternatives are made very clear by Allais (2003, 2006) and by Young and Gamble (2006).

Emerging trends and issues in qualification reform

The issues discussed in this chapter arise from three recent developments, with implications that most countries are or will soon be facing. The first is the growing interest of governments in the idea of a national qualification *framework*, based on outcomes defined according to a common set of criteria, and including all types of qualification, whether they are school- or work-based, general, vocational or professional in purpose. Furthermore, the qualification frameworks such as those in various stages of implementation in New Zealand, Scotland and South Africa are designed to include all levels of qualification, from those certifying basic skills to postgraduate degrees.

The origin of the idea of a qualification framework based on outcomes can be traced back to the NVQ framework introduced by the National Council for Vocational Qualifications (NCVQ) in the UK in 1987.[2] As far as I am aware, this was the first attempt to establish a national qualifications framework that was based on outcomes that were defined independently of any specific learning programmes provided by educational institutions. Although the NVQ framework was restricted to including only vocational qualifications, Gilbert Jessup (Jessup 1991), a leading figure in its design, saw the idea of an outcomes-based framework as having a much wider potential. He envisaged that learning outcomes could be the basis for a comprehensive framework for all education.

What was not recognized at the time of the launch of NVQs in 1987, but has since become much clearer, is that the concept of qualifications based on learning outcomes is not just a technical or administrative matter. In other words, like the closely related notion of competence, the idea of defining learning in terms of an outcomes-based framework implies both a very specific set of ideas about learning as well as the possibility that any type of learning (formal or informal) can be included in the framework. If there is to be formal comparability between different qualifications within a framework, the criteria for learning must be precisely specifiable in advance of any assessment and, of course, of the learning itself. It follows that qualifications defined within an outcomes-based framework disregard learning that might be important and valid for the learner but is not specifiable in advance or indeed may not be specifiable at all except in very general terms.[3]

Some kind of broad pre-specification of outcomes is of course a feature of all qualifications, in so far as one of their functions is to communicate something about a person's capabilities to a user, whether an employer involved in recruitment or a tutor considering whether to accept someone on a course. However, with the launch of NVQs, not only did the pre-specification of outcomes become much more detailed, but other features of traditional qualifications, such as a recognized syllabus and an assumed and sometimes explicit requirement to attend a course of study, were excluded. The definition of outcomes that are a feature of all qualifications changed from being a guide for those devising assessments and curricula and an indication of a person's capabilities, to claiming to be a precise definition of a person's competence or what he or she could do. In other words, the precise specification of outcomes was designed to replace the kind of tacit assumptions or judgements which, in more traditional qualifications, were used to compare one individual with others. There was also an assumption in the NVQ approach that precisely defined outcomes would not only free qualifications from any reference to where they were achieved, but would at least minimize the human judgement required for assessing learning. It was this claim to independence from both professional judgement and required attendance at a school, college or university that gave outcomes-based qualifications their claim to be egalitarian.

The advantages of an approach to qualifications based on outcomes apply most readily to vocational qualifications, where in many cases it is important to know that someone is capable of competently carrying out specific tasks. Furthermore, a common definition of outcomes is crucial to the feasibility of a single national framework for all qualifications. However, the implications of an outcomes-based framework are far more problematic in relation to the goals of general education, such as personal intellectual development, which can never be adequately expressed in terms of precisely specified outcomes. At best, pre-specified outcomes are congruent with some of the purposes of low-level qualifications where the skills and knowledge needed are relatively unambiguous and where there is less likelihood of a learner needing to demonstrate new (in the sense of unexpected) knowledge. Furthermore, for beginning and low-level learners, pre-specification of outcomes may actually be an advantage in helping them to establish achievable goals and develop a confidence in their own capacities. On the other hand, detailed pre-specification of outcomes of the kind attempted for NVQs downgrades both the knowledge that may be required for but not expressed in competent performance and the role of the professional judgement of teachers and trainers as assessors of student or trainee learning.[4] It also under-emphasizes the forms of tacit learning that cannot be expressed in terms of outcomes but which learners, especially low-level learners, will need if they are going to progress.

The interest in outcomes-based frameworks has been paralleled by approaches to funding that are linked to the achievement of qualifications[5] and can be understood in relation to attempts to make schools, colleges and other training providers more accountable. The educational implications of a single outcomes-based qualifications framework explain the strong opposition to such a framework on the part of those universities that see their mission as promoting excellence and even encouraging their students, when possible, to go beyond what is known by their teachers.

The second significant development that this chapter takes into account is the growing body of research and experience that suggests that the strategy for reforming vocational education based on outcomes that has been adopted by a number of anglophone[6] countries is not working out as well as its proponents hoped (Young 2005). The approach appears to have a number of unfortunate consequences. The question that I will return to is whether these consequences are best seen as 'teething problems' likely to be associated with any radical innovation, or whether they are an indication that relying on outcomes is based on some fundamentally flawed assumptions about their role in educational reform.

The third issue that is important to bear in mind in any consideration of the role of qualifications in educational reform is that a number of countries, most notably those associated with the Germanic and Nordic traditions of education and training, have remained largely immune from the pressures to develop outcomes-based qualification frameworks of the kind found in the UK and other anglophone countries (Young 2005). The question is whether the former group of countries is right to be sceptical of outcomes-based approaches or whether, as is frequently argued by advocates of UK policy, it is a trend that no country seeking to be competitive in the global market will be able to avoid. There is no doubt that all countries are having to reform their education systems and rethink the role of qualifications in light of global economic changes and the related changes in skill and knowledge demands (Lasonen 1996; Young 2005). In this chapter, I will contrast the anglophone approach that sees a *qualification framework* as the best way of responding to these changes with one that focuses on improving the whole *institutional framework* of a country's education and training system.

The remaining sections of this chapter explore the three trends already referred to by considering the increasingly significant role given to qualifications by governments and the growing interest in what I have referred to as outcomes-based approaches. It then proposes a typology for comparing the approaches to qualification reform adopted by different countries. The major distinction that I make is between countries adopting a primarily 'outcomes-based' approach to qualifications and those using what I shall refer to as a 'process-based' or 'institutional' approach. I will then discuss some of the benefits and problems of each approach. Finally, in considering whether a strategy can be developed that draws on the benefits of each, I will draw on a distinction introduced by Raffe (1992) between the 'intrinsic' and 'institutional' logics of any educational policy. I will take Raffe's conceptualization a step further by distinguishing between the 'macro' and 'micro' aspects of the two types of logic.

Intrinsic logic refers to the claims made for a reform, such as introducing a single qualifications framework, that are independent of the actual contexts in which the reform might be implemented. It is the intrinsic logic of any reform that represents its political rationale and not only tends to set the terms on which it is justified or attacked by its critics, but is the basis of any 'borrowing' of ideas between countries. Intrinsic logics are important because they claim to reflect national aspirations and goals and therefore are closely associated with the political purposes of governments. *Institutional logics*, on the other hand, refer to the social, political and institutional contexts, the divisions, power relations and interests that constitute them and the role that contexts are likely to play in how (and whether) any reform is implemented.

The institutional logic of any educational reform can be separated into its 'macro' and 'micro' aspects. Whereas macro aspects refer to forms of stratification, power relations and institutional hierarchies, micro aspects include the specific practices, patterns of interaction and shared values that are the basis for the credibility and acceptance of a qualification by users. It is the macro aspects of institutional logic that act as the most visible constraints on educational reform. A well known example is how in England, the selective role of secondary education based on social class divisions persisted despite the claims that were made for 'parity of esteem' between different types of secondary schools in the 1944 Education Act (Banks 1954).[7] It is the less visible micro aspects of institutional logic that are the condition for processes like qualification, assessment or even learning to take place at all, let alone gain public credibility.

The experience of those countries that have developed (or are developing) outcomes-based approaches to qualification reform suggests that they tend to share a common notion of their 'intrinsic' logic – what they hope a qualification framework will achieve. However, they appear to have given very little attention to either macro or micro aspects of the institutional logic of such a reform. It does not necessarily follow that we should dismiss outcomes-based approaches to qualifications altogether. They highlight a number of the weaknesses of traditional qualification systems even though they may not themselves offer adequate alternatives. The contrast between the two approaches can, however, shed light on i) the limitations of outcomes-based approaches, ii) the enduring strengths (as well as the weaknesses) of the more traditional models, and iii) the dangers of assuming that qualification reforms on their own, and in particular the introduction of an outcomes-based qualification framework, can play more than a modest role in improving education and training.

Qualification reforms: the context

The main official goals of recent qualification reforms in the UK and other EU and OECD (Organisation for Economic Co-operation and Development) countries have been to improve the flexibility of education and training systems, to widen participation, and to enhance the mobility of learners and potential learners. In furthering these goals, most reforms have emphasized:

- encouraging people to see qualifying as a process that starts in initial education and training and continues throughout their adult lives;
- improving opportunities for people to move between different types of qualifications (especially general and vocational) and between vocational qualifications for different occupational sectors;
- promoting informal learning and the links between informal and formal learning, and improving opportunities for people to use their informal learning to gain recognized qualifications.

These are relatively uncontroversial aims, albeit extremely difficult to realize in practice. However, a number of questions about the link between such aims and the kind of qualification reforms that are either proposed or being implemented, especially in anglophone countries, need to be asked. First, why have governments focused on qualifications as their main instrument to reform their systems of education and training? Second, given that as yet there is only limited experience of implementing outcomes-based qualification frameworks, why has the idea proved so attractive to governments, even in countries that have up to now relied on quite different approaches to the organization of education and training and to the role of qualifications? Third, given the enormous diversity of learning demands in a modern society, is it realistic to envisage common criteria that could be the basis of a single framework for the whole range of qualifications – vocational, professional and general? Fourth, given that some of the most effective education and training systems up to now (for example those in East Asia and parts of continental Europe) have relied on developing learning pathways located in specific, institutional, occupational and academic communities and not on the detailed specification of outcomes, we must ask why an outcomes-based framework that is independent of such institutional contexts is seen as providing the best basis for qualification systems of the future in anglophone countries?

Finally, introducing qualifications frameworks is invariably linked to policies to promote lifelong learning. However, although widely seen as a solution to the problems of globalization, the concept of lifelong learning is itself a highly confusing term, used more rhetorically than analytically (Coffield 1999; Young 1998: Chapter 10). In government policy statements, lifelong learning tends to refer to the importance of individuals taking more responsibility for their own learning (Keep 1998). However, a growing body of research suggests not only that learning is a social rather than an individual process (Lave and Wenger 1991) but that an individual's motivation to learn is largely shaped by whether learning is valued in the workplaces or communities in which they find themselves. It follows that policies to promote lifelong learning need to be as much about creating a demand for learning as about motivating individuals to learn and introducing a structure of qualifications through which learning may be accredited. Furthermore, lifelong learning embraces a number of different policies with very different implications for qualification reform. They include encouraging those leaving school to continue learning, supporting those in work to develop their skills and knowledge, and supporting those without work or in unskilled jobs to get qualifications and improve their prospects for progression.

Why qualifications?

It seems likely that one reason why governments have become so enthusiastic about qualifications in recent decades is that not only are they assumed to motivate learners and potential learners, but they can serve other roles that are just as important, but frequently less explicit aspects of government policy. For example, a greater emphasis on qualifications enables central governments to:

- increase their control of education in areas where it is relatively weak;
- provide simple measurable criteria for allocating funds to institutions;
- make local and regional education and training organizations more accountable;
- provide quantitative measures of the success of government policies.

Two continuing parallels in the development of policy are worth noting. The first is that congruence between the growing interest in qualifications by Conservative governments in the UK from the 1980s and their support for neo-liberal, market-oriented approaches to both the economy and the public sector is equally evident in the policies of the three successive Labour governments. The second is that qualification reform from the 1980s has been given most support in those countries which (i) had weaker traditions of central government involvement in education and training (although undoubtedly true of the UK in the 1980s, this is much less so 20 years later; see Chapter 7), and (ii) most readily endorsed the Reagan–Thatcher neo-Liberal policies (e.g. the UK, Australia and New Zealand).

In the UK case, the Labour governments that followed the general elections in 1997, 2001 and 2005 have continued to use qualifications as an instrument to regulate schools and colleges that are supported by public funds. This emphasis on qualifications as measures of performance has been linked to the freeing of schools and colleges from local government control and forcing them to compete in quasi-markets for students and funds.

There are parallels between qualifications (and the QCA, the body monitoring them) and the bodies that have been created to regulate the new privatized monopolies such as water, gas and electricity. Qualifications offer an ideal regulatory instrument for a reforming government, as they appear to serve a dual purpose. They provide incentives for individual learners[8] and they can be used as mechanisms for making educational institutions accountable. The educational problem, however, is that these purposes can be in conflict with each other. More emphasis on accountability leads to tighter specification of outcomes – a trend in all qualification-led reforms. Promoting learning, however, especially among those with previous experience of school failure, requires teachers and learners to feel the confidence to take risks and learn from them. In other words, it requires qualifications that rely more on professional judgement and are less specified in advance. Furthermore, a greater emphasis on qualifications as outcomes puts pressure on institutions and workplaces to give more time to assessment and less to the teaching and learning activities that might in the longer term lead to more appropriate types of learning, and more people gaining qualifications.

Why an outcomes-based qualification framework?

Qualification arrangements in England and Wales have in the past had a number of features in common with those found in other European countries, which it has long been argued are in need of reform. For example:

- General and vocational qualifications have developed separately with quite distinct systems of assessment and with limited possibilities of progression between them.
- Vocational and professional qualifications are often organized by sectors or occupations independently from each other and there are few opportunities for movement or transfer across sectors.

- Most qualifications are closely linked to specific programmes and periods of study in educational institutions. Access is difficult for those with skills but who cannot attend specific institution-based programmes.
- Qualifications have traditionally been underpinned by 'specialist communities' with shared practices such as trades, crafts and professional organizations in the case of vocational and professional qualifications, and by subject and disciplinary associations in the case of general qualifications. These communities have inevitably set the terms for decisions about who should and should not qualify. Historically these 'specialist communities' have been (and in some cases continue to be) socially exclusive, both generally and in relation to specific disadvantaged groups distinguished by race, class and gender.
- Traditional qualifications have offered only limited forms of access to adult learners who have been expected to retrace the steps of young learners rather than build on their adult experience and knowledge.
- Many occupations and even sectors have been characterized by very few of those employed having any qualifications at all. This has been especially the case in the UK, where a 'licence to practise' or other form of statutory requirement to be qualified has only applied in the case of a small number of occupations. As a result, qualifications have, in many cases, been developed in a largely ad hoc manner by a whole variety of commercial, professional, educational and charitable bodies and with minimum state intervention.

Since the late 1980s, all these features have been seen by governments and other reformers as barriers to increasing opportunities to expand learning, and at odds with the blurring of occupational boundaries, and the flexible and fast-changing skill and knowledge demands of the emerging global economy. A single framework in which all qualifications were located according to a clear set of levels and progression criteria appeared in principle to be a logical way of overcoming these rigidities.

The shift that has been argued for since the late 1980s and the Review of Vocational Qualifications in 1987, albeit not always explicitly and largely in relation to vocational qualifications, is from a qualification system based on *shared practices* and professional judgements to one based on formally explicit *criteria* that are capable of being defined independently of any specific experience or practice.

Support for a change from a qualification system based on 'shared practices' to one based on 'criteria' was rooted in political as much as educational factors. The old 'provider culture' of further education colleges, local employers and the examining bodies was widely discredited among civil servants and within national employer organizations. This view fitted in with the marketizing zeal of the Thatcher governments in the 1980s and with the efficiency drives of successive Labour governments, with their general scepticism towards professional interests and a belief in a more 'user-led' and market-driven education and training system. In the case of vocational qualifications, support for reform was initially tied to the government's determination to break the power of trade unions that they saw as using trade and craft qualifications to perpetuate out-of-date restrictive practices (Raggatt and Williams 1999). The attempt to 'break with the past' has been a familiar feature of qualification reform, and not only associated with the political Right. Similar frameworks have been introduced in Wales and Scotland, strongly supported by the new Left of Centre coalitions leading the Assembly and Parliamentary Executives. Likewise, the symbolic role of a national framework has played an important part in reforms introduced by the post-apartheid government in South Africa (Jansen and Christie 1999).

Last, it has been claimed (Jessup 1991) that a qualification framework is a mechanism for freeing qualifications from their traditional link with educational institutions and formal learning and, that as a consequence, it can provide access to groups who have in the past been excluded by schools and colleges. In principle, at least, a qualifications framework defined in terms of a clear set of outcomes allows anyone who believes that they have acquired the necessary skills and knowledge to become qualified without further study. It is not surprising, therefore, that the idea of a qualification framework has been closely linked to the promotion of informal learning and the broader lifelong learning agenda (DfEE 1998). However, in the UK it is difficult to find examples of significant numbers of people with skills and knowledge that they have acquired informally in the workplace who are formally unqualified. This is in contrast with South Africa, where the legacy of apartheid left considerable numbers of African workers skilled but not formally qualified. In this case, over a decade after the first bill establishing the national qualifications authority (SAQA), it is equally hard to find evidence that substantial numbers of workers have had their informally acquired skills recognized as qualifications (see Chapter 13). It seems likely that in most cases the assessment procedures for converting informal learning into qualifications may be perceived as being as much of a barrier to those denied opportunities for formal learning at school as the existing learning programmes themselves.[9]

The typology: outcomes-based and institution-based approaches to qualifications

Arising from the previous discussion of different national approaches to the reform of qualifications, a typology is proposed that distinguishes between outcomes-based and institution-based approaches. Before discussing the two models it is important to remember that qualification reforms should not be seen in isolation. There are other no less important dimensions on which national approaches to the reform of education and training can vary and that will shape the way in which qualifications operate. These are not the focus of this chapter, but can be seen as elements of the context that shapes the role of qualifications in any society. Examples are:

- the extent to which funding of education training is based primarily on individuals or the performance of organizations;

- the extent to which government of education and training is devolved (for example the role of the *Lande* in Germany might be contrasted with the increasingly centralized system found in England);
- the extent to which the state or the private sector is the main provider and funder of vocational education and training;
- the location of responsibility for assessment (this can be educational institutions, governments, public agencies, private bodies and employer organizations).

Let us consider the main characteristics of the two models. I shall treat them as 'ideal types' or structural trends for identifying some of the problems each gives rise to, and not as descriptions of the approaches of particular countries; all the characteristics of each type will never be found in one country.

Outcomes-based approaches

Outcomes-based approaches to qualifications assume that:

- a single definition of qualifications can be applied to the wide diversity of levels and types of learning that takes place in any society;
- a set of level descriptors can be agreed for extremely diverse types of learning; for example plumbing and business administration (and history and physics if the framework is to apply to both vocational and general qualifications);
- the precise specification of outcomes is possible and becomes the main guarantee of quality.

As a result, outcomes-based qualifications invariably lead to the jargon of over-specification, bureaucratic assessment procedures and the trivializing of learning (Wolf 1995). There is evidence from both New Zealand and South Africa that outcomes-based frameworks have a series of other consequences. For example:

- In prescribing learning outcomes in advance, such frameworks encourage resistance rather than support from high status institutions such as universities (Ensor 2003) and professional bodies, which have traditionally had responsibility for devising learning programmes and awarding qualifications themselves.
- In giving priority to creating flexible pathways and making boundaries permeable, outcomes-based frameworks disregard the posibility that distinct types of qualification (e.g. vocational and academic) and clear boundaries between qualifications for different occupational sectors can have a positive role in promoting particular types of learning (especially higher level learning).
- In emphasizing that there are generic criteria for all qualifications, single frameworks tend to neglect the importance of specific content in both vocational and general subject areas and can lead to a mismatch between

qualifications defined within a framework and the learning needs of specific workplaces.

- As a consequence of their national character, qualification frameworks can appear to replace the need for national leadership of education and training policy. They can therefore over-emphasize the role that qualifications can have in promoting high quality learning, rather than seeing them as one element in a much broader process.

Last, there is as yet very little evidence that the quality and amount of learning has been enhanced in countries that have introduced national frameworks. In the case of NVQs in the UK, the gross numbers achieving vocational qualifications have not changed significantly since they were introduced. What has changed is the proportion gaining NVQs as opposed to other types of vocational qualification. In a still largely voluntarist system such as that found in the UK where in most jobs there is no legal requirement to have a qualification, and in the absence of a broad employer community with a major interest in the provision and use of qualifications, the take-up of qualifications is largely determined by government funding priorities.

Institutional approaches

Institutional approaches to qualifications are less easy to characterize, partly because in many countries they are taken very much for granted and have a long history. Qualifications are not treated as separate instruments of reform but as embedded and accepted features of the wider education and training system. In a case such as Germany, vocational qualifications are linked to vocational colleges, universities for training vocational teachers, syllabuses, assessment methods and learning programmes, and partnerships between employers, trade unions and providers all working within the overall leadership of the *Lande* Ministries, the Federal Minister and the National Body for Vocational Education and Training (BIBB). Qualifications 'on their own' are not used by governments as an independent lever for change. Governments rely on periodic reviews and clear input definitions based on syllabuses and learning programmes, and progression depends on trust in qualifications by peers within the tripartite 'dual' system (trade unions, government and employers), and partnerships created through institutional links (Ertl 2002).

However, in the context of global economic changes, institutional approaches are not without their weaknesses. For example:

- they are based strongly on consensus and exhibit inertia and resistance to change;
- change is difficult because it involves the 'whole system';
- they are slow to adapt to the learning needs of new occupations;
- progression between different sectors and general and vocational qualifications is often difficult.

Discussion

Most industrial countries, such as the members of the OECD, still have largely institution-based systems of qualifications, though a growing number are exploring the scope of outcomes-based approaches. The exceptions appear to be the anglophone countries, a number of which followed England and have developed an outcomes-based route. England is now hesitantly stepping back from an extreme version of the outcomes position initially adopted by the NCVQ (Raggatt and Williams 1999; also see Chapter 9). Despite the European Commission's enthusiasm for an outcomes-based European Qualifications Framework, this remains little more than a set of proposals. Furthermore, there has been little progress, even in countries where an outcomes-based approach has been longer established, towards a single national framework for all qualifications including those awarded by universities. This uncertainty suggests that we need to explore the possibilities of a middle way that is not, like most compromises, the worst of both worlds. Drawing on the earlier distinction between intrinsic and institutional logic, the next section will attempt to chart such a possibility for the future by considering a number of key questions that arise from an analysis of outcomes-based approaches as they have developed in different countries.

Intrinsic and institutional logics of outcomes-based frameworks: a reassessment

The rationale for introducing a single qualifications framework based on learning outcomes can be summarized as follows. First, by doing away with distinct types of qualifications, it fits in with the increased flexibility that is assumed to be a necessary condition of successful modern economies. Second, a single framework can in theory provide learners, throughout their working lives, with the confidence that they can transfer qualifications between sectors and move between jobs and places of study and at the same time accumulate 'credit' towards further qualifications. Third, the clear specification of levels means that, in principle, no one is excluded from obtaining higher-level qualifications, even if they do not have access to a university – nurses can become doctors and craftsmen can become engineers – at least in theory. This is the intrinsic logic of an outcomes-based qualification framework. However, this rationale comes up against what I referred to earlier as the 'macro' and 'micro' aspects of the institutional logic of modern societies. Let us begin by considering the macro aspects.

Macro aspects

First, the global changes towards more flexible economies have not turned out to be as progressive and evenly distributed as predicted by political economists such as Piore and Sabel (1984) and Reich (1991). The majority of people in work still stay in the same field if not the same company or organization for most of their working lives. The new industries of the e-economy with their new learning demands have had much publicity, but quantitatively they create remarkably few jobs. Furthermore, not only has the transformative capacity of the new technologies, at least in the short term, been vastly exaggerated, but some of the most characteristic jobs of the new economy are in call centres and the fast food and security industries, none of which require many higher qualified 'knowledge workers'. In other words, the increasingly mobile and qualified society on which the claims for qualification frameworks are based bears little relationship to the realities of modern economies.

Second, a seamless framework of qualification levels does not of itself guarantee progression or provide a basis for overcoming deep-seated divisions between different types of qualifications. In England there is a five-level vocational qualifications framework. However, (i) the majority of vocational qualifications are awarded at levels one and two, (ii) there are extremely few vocational qualifications at level five, and few of the established professions have shown any interest in including their qualifications within a national framework, and (iii) of the few who obtain vocational qualifications at levels four and five, most have not progressed from lower-level vocational qualifications, but have entered the framework as graduates, having progressed through the institutional route of school and university. These are examples of the inability of a national qualifications framework to fulfil its aims and reflect the influence of what I referred to as the institutional logic of modern societies – in particular, the continued significance of academic/vocational and professional/vocational divisions that can be found to varying extents in every country.

The solution to overcoming these divisions is not primarily to be found through a qualification framework. It will depend on expanding the range of higher-level professional occupations and improving the opportunities for people to progress from vocational to professional qualifications. Chapter 9 suggests that these developments will be inhibited rather than encouraged by extending the role of outcomes-based approaches.

The old links between National and Higher National Certificates and the access they provided to membership of professional bodies is one model that ought not to be forgotten. It was, however, limited by being developed only in a very limited range of occupations and sectors – primarily engineering. A more recent and successful example of new opportunities for progression to professional occupations is through the links that have been established between vocational qualifications for Accountancy Technicians and Professional Accountancy qualifications. The key factor is not the qualifications themselves but the role of the professional body and its involvement in both professional and vocational qualifications.

The future tasks are not just to create new qualification levels within a single framework. They are: (i) to create genuine *occupational* progression pathways in sectors that have had few qualified people in the past in the growing range of service occupations such as care, retailing and hospitality, and (ii) to create new access routes for people without initial qualifications to gain access to occupations such as engineering and banking. An outcomes-based framework could have an important role if such developments were already in place; it cannot not lead them.

Micro aspects

The micro aspects of the institutional logic of qualifications are less visible but no less fundamental in the problems they pose for reformers. They reflect what appears to be almost a sociological law which states that the credibility and currency of a qualification are only partly based on what it records that the person who is qualified can do or knows. Of far greater significance is the trust that society in general and specific users in particular (those with responsibility for selection, recruitment and promotion) have in the qualification. This trust, as mentioned earlier, has in the past been embedded in various forms of community – trade and craft associations, occupational and professional organizations and, in relation to general education, academic subject and disciplinary associations often linked to organizations with high status such as elite schools and universities. These 'communities of trust' have taken time to establish and have developed their own forms of exclusiveness and resistance to change. Not surprisingly, they have been seen by reformers as barriers to increased access and participation. However, the implications of the argument about the micro institutional logic of qualifications are stark. If these traditional communities of trust – and the professions are a good example (see Chapter 10) – are weakened or destroyed (or in the case of many new sectors, do not exist), either as a result of explicit policies (the replacement of old qualifications) or as the unintended consequences of economic change, their function cannot be fulfilled by the specification of outcomes alone (10). If new communities of trust or some equivalent are not created to give substance and add practical experience to criteria, new outcomes-based qualifications, will not gain credibility among users. This analysis may go some way to explaining (i) the persistence of old non-outcomes-based qualifications, and (ii) the phenomenon of academic drift. Academic qualifications still rely on traditional communities of trust such as those linking specialist subject teachers with colleagues in universities and with syllabuses (even if they are now called subject specifications) and have therefore retained their trust and 'currency value' beyond their particular specialist communities.

Relying on qualifications based on old communities of trust is not an adequate solution in the fast-changing and increasingly competitive economic environment that we face today. As has already been noted, not only have they been exclusive and elitist, but they have not always been the basis for responding to new skill and knowledge demands. It was partly these features that led to professions and trade unions being criticized in the 1980s as sources of vested interest, and to superficially more democratic and innovative alternatives being introduced based on clearly specified and 'transparent' criteria. Twenty years later, policy makers have yet to learn that 'transparency' is a chimera, at least if interpreted as trust expressed in terms of criteria. This applies to learners who always have to take on trust, at least at the level of specificities, what they will learn on a programme. It also applies to those whose job is to recruit and select and who have to draw on their experience in making their judgements about someone's suitability; qualifications are never more than part of the data that they can draw on. The traditional communities of trust, still relevant in some sectors, developed over long periods of time; they were not planned. New communities of trust – for example, in care, retail and customer service occupations – can be created, but not by the current strategy of establishing employer-led organizations with the responsibility for developing and imposing National Occupational Standards. In sectors with a long tradition of apprenticeship and college-based programmes, such as engineering, employer-led sectoral organizations can take the lead because the old communities of trust can be built on. However, in sectors that recruit largely unskilled labour and where profits can be made by selling low quality services or low quality products (Keep 1998), little change can be expected, whether or not occupational standards are developed. A quite new and more complex approach is needed that does not rely on employers generating demands for more qualified people. It is likely to involve a new type of leadership role for college and university partnerships within which exemplars of new approaches to service delivery and production are developed that involve innovative employers who see new profit-making possibilities.

The implication of this analysis is not to oppose the establishment of an outcomes-based qualifications framework, but to recognize its relatively modest role in educational reform. An outcomes-based framework will serve little purpose and repeat the mistakes of the past 20 years, unless the much harder tasks are tackled of creating new forms of production and service that require new qualifications and establishing the new communities of trust that will be needed to underpin them. With the demise of old occupational communities, it is by no means clear what the basis of new communities of trust will be or the nature of the respective roles of the various partners involved.

Conclusions

The two approaches to qualification reform that I have discussed in this chapter reflect not only their origins in different historical times, but the very different roles of the state, employer organizations and trade unions in the countries where they have been adopted or replaced. The new circumstances that most countries face today are, however, not so different. A qualifications strategy for the future cannot be based on the 'shared practices' of occupational communities and their links with institutions that in many cases no longer exist. On the other hand, outcomes-based approaches which break with the traditional occupational communities and their links with educational institutions take no account of how the trust on which qualifications rely is actually created and sustained.

The specification of criteria or outcomes is designed to make qualifications 'portable' across different contexts. Many of the critiques of this process have shown how such specification is endless and trivializing. There is no alternative to embedding such criteria that claim context-independence in shared practices as the condition for the trust on which qualifications rely for their credibility. The question becomes: what form might this embedding take when the identifiable occupational communities within which it took place in traditional qualifications no longer exist, or at least exist in only a very few sectors? I conclude this chapter with some suggestions for how this question might be addressed by drawing on some ideas from Jeanne Gamble's research (Gamble 2006). This also provides a way of linking the discussion of qualification reform in this chapter to the debates about knowledge that have been the main theme of this book. The focus here is on vocational qualifications; the approach I would argue is equally applicable to general or academic programmes.

In her recent paper (Gamble 2006) Gamble draws on Bernstein and Sohn-Rethel to make two kinds of distinction between types of knowledge. One is between context-independent and context-dependent knowledge and the other is between two different types of context-independence, which she refers to as principled and procedural. Traditional vocational qualifications relied on context-dependent knowledge located within occupational communities of trust. Gamble points out that in the specific case of cabinet makers (although potentially generalizeable to other crafts and trades), the context-dependent knowledge associated with the different tasks involved in making a cabinet are held together by a vision of the whole – the making of a complete cabinet. The vision of the whole is context-independent – a form of vertical discourse in Bernstein's language. At the same time it is tacit, and neither codified nor codifiable; it is in the head of the master cabinet maker and each successful apprentice. Despite its strengths, being un-codifiable and with its theory implicit, it cannot be a model for future qualifications. It is, however, important, not only in itself and in indicating why the outcomes-based model was and is doomed to fail, but in indicating the conditions for the development of future qualifications. Because the outcomes-based model rejects the idea of *theory* (codifiable context-independent knowledge) and *vision* (un-codifiable context-independent knowledge embedded in particular communities), the relationship between the whole (the qualification) and the parts (the specific outcomes) is arbitrary. As Barnett (2006) argues and I discuss in detail in Chapter 9, the outcomes-based model cannot be the basis for future vocational qualifications. At best the learner acquires procedural knowledge (codified, context-independent but not conceptually based) to make certain types of routine links between tasks. However, procedural knowledge provides no basis for the person gaining the qualification either to understand the relationship between the whole and the parts or to progress by taking his or her context-independent 'procedural' knowledge to new contexts and new levels of generality. Outcomes-based qualifications claim to be 'portable' and to enable the person who has achieved the qualification to move beyond the context in which they are located. However, if such claims are to be realized, the embedding has to involve principled knowledge – in other words concepts that are both systematically related to each other (as in a theory) and embedded in practices or contexts which give meaning to the theory; criteria on their own are not adequate. In policy terms the implications of these suggestions would of course involve a complete rethink and reorganization of existing relationships (and the creation of such relationships where they are lacking, as often is the case in England) between professions, universities, colleges, employers and awarding bodies that would be specific for each sector.

9   Conceptualizing vocational knowledge

Introduction

Critical commentaries on the system of vocational education in England that have been followed by reforms can be traced back to the late nineteenth century. However, since the end of the Second World War and especially since the early 1980s, both criticisms and proposals for reform have recurred with ever increasing frequency. At the same time, the focus of reforms has varied widely from institutions and curricula to, more recently, national agencies and qualifications. Where responsibility for failure is placed has also varied. In the 1980s, governments blamed trade unions, who were seen as blocking changes that appeared to weaken their bargaining power (Raggatt and Williams 1999); at the same time they also criticized the further education colleges for their ignorance of industrial realities and their academic conservatism. Social scientists, on the other hand, have tended to blame employers for weaknesses in the provision of vocational education and training (VET). Too many, they argue, take a short-term view of the costs and benefits of training. However, they have also located the weaknesses of our system of VET in its wider social and political context (e.g. Finegold and Soskice 1988). Some point to the anti-industrial and elitist culture that has pervaded English governing classes and its tendency to value knowledge as a mark of status rather than as an instrument of economic transformation (Weiner 1981). Others have highlighted the peculiarly voluntarist role of the state that emerged in England in the nineteenth century (Green 1990) and is reflected in the continued reluctance of governments of both Left and Right to extend either the legal obligations on employers to guarantee training or the range of occupations that require some form of 'licence to practise'.

Reforms of VET have of course related highly selectively to these various critiques. In the past decades the focus has been almost entirely on the supply side of the 'VET market'. However, two major issues have been given little attention. The first, now increasingly acknowledged by researchers if not by government, is the lack of employer demand for improved skills and knowledge and the dependence of demand on the dominant forms of work organization and product strategy adopted in different sectors. The second, less acknowledged, issue is the question of vocational knowledge and the VET curriculum. It is the latter which is the concern of this chapter. The chapter seeks to locate a number of policy issues concerning the control and content of vocational education within the theoretical framework developed in earlier chapters. It argues that in contrast to the centrality of the curriculum in school policy debates, the question as to what knowledge those on VET programmes should acquire has been of marginal interest or at best treated superficially even within the research community.

The chapter distinguishes between three approaches to knowledge in proposals for the reform of VET, which have broadly followed each other historically. It argues that, in different ways, each avoids fundamental epistemological issues that need to be addressed if an adequate concept of vocational knowledge is to be developed. In order to tackle the question of vocational knowledge, the chapter distinguishes between the two main social theories of knowledge: social constructivism and social realism. It argues that while social constructivism provides an important critical perspective on VET knowledge policy, it is unable to deal with the question of vocational knowledge itself. The chapter then outlines two key contributions to a social realist approach to knowledge that were introduced in Chapters 3 and 4 of this book: Durkheim's early distinction between the 'sacred' and the 'profane' and Bernstein's distinction between vertical and horizontal 'knowledge structures'. It argues that these distinctions, together with a recognition of the importance of conceptualizing the relations between knowledge and power, provide a necessary basis for conceptualizing vocational knowledge. The chapter concludes by suggesting some possible implications of the analysis for debates about the future of VET.

Knowledge and the vocational curriculum: three approaches

The inadequate knowledge and skills that are acquired by many of those taking a vocational course – even those who succeed in achieving a qualification – have been recognized since the decision in the late 1880s to establish the City and Guilds of London Institute (CGLI) as the first major attempt to promote and organize VET on a national scale (Gay 2000). The latest examples of this issue being recognized are in the proposals for introducing technical certificates as part of the reform of modern apprenticeships and the more recent (non-)vocational diplomas for 14-year-olds. Three distinct approaches to vocational knowledge can be identified which have followed each other historically. I shall refer to them as knowledge-based, standards-based and connective approaches.

The knowledge-based approach was launched in the late nineteenth century in response to a now familiar anxiety that our industries were becoming less and less competitive with those in other countries, especially Germany (Donnelly 1993). The reformers recognized that skills and knowledge needed in the new science-based sectors such as engineering, chemicals and the new electrical industries could not be developed on the basis of traditional work-based apprenticeships. Employees in craft and technician occupations in these emerging industrial sectors needed access to knowledge of the sciences on which these industries were based and which they could not acquire 'on the job'. It was logical therefore that the major focus of the new curricula and examinations launched by the CGLI was on the physics, chemistry and mathematics relevant to the different industrial sectors. Two significant features of this emerging vocational curriculum were to survive in somewhat modified form for almost a century. These were:

- It explicitly excluded the application of knowledge in workplaces or any form of 'trade knowledge'. This was partly because there are intrinsic difficulties in developing and assessing curricula that focus on the application of knowledge. However, of even greater significance was that the application of knowledge is always likely to involve the 'trade secrets' of individual companies. As a result, learning how to apply the new scientific knowledge in specific workplace contexts was left to the apprentices and individual employers.
- It assumed that the natural sciences were important for their specific content and because they provided the appropriate body of reliable, objective knowledge needed by apprentices. However, the natural sciences, and the tendency to assume that such knowledge could be treated as given, objective and reliable, were also seen as a model for non-science-based fields, such as business studies, which expanded from the 1960s and have since come to dominate the vocational curriculum of further education (FE) colleges.

It was not until the late 1970s and early 1980s that the assumptions of this knowledge-based approach to the vocational curriculum began to be seriously challenged. In retrospect, a number of developments appear to have been behind this challenge. They were:

- The number of those employed in those science-based industries where there was a relatively clear link between the science content of the vocational curriculum and its role in the different industrial processes was steadily declining.
- There was a growing concern about the absence of qualifications among the majority of the workforce and a recognition that this might account for the inability of our industries to compete with the emerging Asian economies.
- The possibility was increasingly recognized that the traditional knowledge-based vocational curriculum acted as a barrier to successful learning for the new cohorts of young people entering FE colleges or work-based training programmes, many of whom had achieved very little in the school curriculum.
- There was an emerging belief, shared increasingly by governments and employer organizations, that the knowledge-based approach to the vocational curriculum concentrated too much on what existing college lecturers knew. As a result, it had lost contact with the main purpose of vocational education – developing workplace competence.

In giving primacy to bodies of knowledge in the form of subjects, the knowledge-based approach was seen by its critics in government in the 1980s as providing a rationale for the continuing control of the vocational curriculum by the educational establishment in colleges. These criticisms extended to a highly negative view of any off-the-job component of programmes of vocational education and what became described as a 'provider-based' approach to the vocational curriculum. The alternative proposed was what I refer to as the standards-based approach. This involved a number of assumptions. The most important, which continue to remain highly influential, were that:

- the vocational curriculum needed to be controlled by the key users (the employers), not the providers (FE colleges);
- the skills and knowledge needed by employees in workplaces had to determine all provision for off-the-job learning in colleges;
- vocational qualifications needed to give priority to the assessment of competence, or what can be learned in the workplace, not the knowledge acquired off-the-job in colleges;
- the traditional provider-based vocational curriculum that was based on bodies of knowledge organized and selected for teaching needed to be reformed. It was seen as stressing what students or trainees needed to know and not paying enough attention to what they would need to do when they were at work.

It was argued by key civil servants in the Employment Department at the time that the best way of establishing a vocational curriculum that gave priority to employer needs was not to base it on the expertise of vocational subject specialists in the colleges but to derive it from National Occupational Standards agreed to by employers. The standards would be established by employers in the different sectors, organized into what were initially known as Lead Industry Bodies. These ideas were widely shared by the government and employer organizations such as the Confederation of British Industry (CBI), as well as the National Council for Vocational Qualifications (NCVQ), which was established in 1987. They represented a completely new approach to vocational education in which (at least in theory) outcomes replaced the curriculum, and workplace assessors replaced teachers. In practice it proved unpopular with most employers, and completely unworkable by FE college lecturers who found themselves having to use the standards to construct a curriculum.

The premise of the late-nineteenth-century reformers had been that as industrial change was primarily knowledge-led, or more specifically science- and engineering-led, it was appropriate that the relevant sciences should be the core of the vocational curriculum. The reformers of the 1980s noticed an unintended outcome of the expansion, in the twentieth century, of the college-based component of vocational programmes. This was the emergence of a tension between changes in the learning demanded by employers and the relative lack of change in the college-based curriculum; each appeared to be based on a very different form of specialization. Changes in the demand for workplace skills were being expressed in the increasing differentiation of skills and knowledge needed in different workplaces together with a growing awareness of the importance of generic skills common to a wide range of occupations. In so far as there had been changes in the college curriculum, they were expressed in the proliferation of new subjects that were not necessarily congruent with changes in the organization of work but were in response to changes in student demand. In theory this educational specialization was meant to complement changes in the learning demands of workplaces. However, in practice it appeared to have a kind of logic of its own, reflecting the wider trend of academic drift associated with all educational institutions, even those with specific vocational purposes.

The standards-based approach to the vocational curriculum on which the new National Vocational Qualifications (NVQs) were based was seen as a way of countering what the reformers saw as the academic drift of most college-based vocational courses. Using a method known as functional analysis that was developed by occupational psychologists concerned with job design, the standards-based approach began by identifying and stating curriculum outcomes in terms of competences or what an employee would be expected to do, not what he or she needed to know. Knowledge came second and was only important in so far as (in NCVQ's language) it underpinned performance. In the early days of NCVQ, the standards-based approach was developed in an extreme form, and assumed that all vocational knowledge was implicit in competent workplace performance. It followed that there was no need to consider knowledge separately at all. If someone was assessed as performing competently it was assumed that they must have the adequate (underpinning) knowledge. This position was later modified when it was recognized that in many cases there was knowledge that employees needed that could not necessarily be acquired in workplaces or identified by observing performance. The need to assess knowledge separately led to attempts to provide criteria based on the occupational standards for identifying what became known as underpinning knowledge and understanding (UKU).

A major concern of NCVQ consultants such as Mansfield and Mitchell (1996), who were given the responsibility for developing the criteria for UKU, was to avoid allowing the traditional syllabus-based approach to knowledge to return. It was assumed that if this happened the vocational curriculum would be reclaimed by the colleges, and the NCVQ's mission, to disseminate an outcomes-based approach and the belief that occupational competence could be acquired 'on-the-job', would be undermined. What emerged therefore was a tension between two distinct approaches to knowledge. One was college-based and expressed in terms of subjects and disciplines. This approach was based on the idea that knowledge is produced by researchers (mostly based in the universities) and that subjects are developed from research-based knowledge by school and college subject specialists with their links to subject teaching associations. The traditional vocational variant of this 'academic' approach to knowledge consisted of developing curricula related to broad occupational fields such as business and administration rather than academic subjects or disciplines; it was based on links between vocational teachers in colleges, professional bodies and university faculties in applied fields such as engineering and business studies. At the higher levels of fields like law, medicine and engineering these approaches to the vocational and the professional curriculum became virtually indistinguishable; both had strong roots in the universities and links with professional bodies. The three crucial features shared by both the academic and professional/vocational variants of the college-based approach to the curriculum were (i) they provided clear progression routes between lower levels (e.g. A-levels and National Certificate courses) and higher levels (degrees, Higher National Certificates and professional qualifications), (ii) they depended for their validity on the understandings and values shared within different communities of specialists, and (iii) they maintained quality by relying on a combination of established external examinations and trust within the specialist communities; they did not rely on any formally explicit criteria or specification of outcomes.

The standards-based approach to vocational knowledge rejected the knowledge-based approach as being exclusive and backward looking. It aimed to replace examined syllabuses agreed by groups of specialists with criteria for national standards common to all fields (and, in principle, all subjects) defined in terms of outcomes at five levels and specified by separate employer-led sectoral bodies.

There were attempts in the early 1990s to develop a systematic methodology for deriving knowledge criteria from standards and hence to provide an explicit alternative to the older knowledge-based approach. However, they were discontinued by the mid-1990s before NCVQ was merged into the Qualifications and Curriculum Authority (QCA). Despite much criticism, the QCA retained the standards-based approach to vocational qualifications but relaxed its rigidities. Vocational qualifications are now required to be 'influenced by' rather than 'derived from' occupational standards. Despite this official 'loosening up' which reflected a recognition that the standards-based approach had failed to provide criteria for vocational knowledge, its basic assumptions remain and continue to influence the most recent reforms, such as the proposal that technical certificates should be incorporated into modern apprenticeships as a way of strengthening off-the-job learning. The idea that employer-led bodies (now Sector Skills Councils) should take the lead in developing the vocational curriculum has been retained despite the reality that in many sectors employers are reluctant to take on such a role and frequently lack the necessary expertise. As a consequence, little advantage has been taken of the more flexible approach to standards. What has emerged is considerable diversity between sectors and a largely ad hoc approach to specifying underpinning knowledge. This can take the form of lists of topics which either amount to little more than what anyone would know after a few weeks in a workplace (as in the case of sectors like retail and distribution) or involve a combination of everyday workplace facts (what tools are needed or where to find them) together with some scientific or highly technical topics with little idea as to the depth in which they should be studied. Not surprisingly, some sectors, such as accountancy, electrical installation, and engineering, in which the acquisition of off-the-job knowledge is vital, resisted the excesses of the standards-based approach. Furthermore, not only did the standards-based model fail to take off at higher levels, but the demand for more traditional types of knowledge-based vocational courses has continued to grow.

The limitations of the standards-based approach with its emphasis on accrediting workplace competences is at least implicitly recognized in the recent proposals for technical certificates. Technical certificates are an attempt to reinstate the importance of off-the-job learning in work-based programmes such as modern apprenticeships. They aim to strengthen the knowledge-based component of apprenticeships at the same time as enhancing its relevance to the demands of workplaces. Although not entirely new, it does imply a much greater emphasis on off-the-job learning and its links with on-the-job learning; it is for these reasons that I refer to technical certificates as embodying a connective approach to vocational knowledge (some of the problems with this concept are discussed in Chapter 11). In contrast to the knowledge-based approach initiated at the end of the nineteenth century, technical certificates stress the importance of the knowledge acquired at work, but in contrast to the standards-based approach, they explicitly recognize that the knowledge acquired at work is often inadequate on its own, especially in knowledge-intensive work places. While proposals for technical certificates emphasize the importance of systematically organized off-the-job learning for apprentices, the responsibility for identifying this knowledge remains the responsibility of the employer bodies who were funded by the government to develop course outlines and rationales for off-the-job learning. However, technical certificates still retain a number of problematic features of the previous standards-based model. First, despite the failure to develop a methodology in the early 1990s, technical certificates still rely on the idea that underpinning knowledge and understanding (UKU) can be generated from occupational standards. Second, technical certificates are still based on a 'competing interests' view of vocational knowledge. In other words, it is assumed that the key issue is not the content of the vocational curriculum, but who controls it – employer-led bodies or educationists. The employer-led bodies are advised to consult and negotiate with college-based vocational curriculum specialists in their development of course outlines, but are under no obligation to do so. It is not surprising that technical certificates have made no significant contribution to improving the quality of vocational education.

VET reforms and concepts of vocational knowledge

The account of attempts to reform the vocational curriculum in the previous section suggested that although each reform arose from a recognition of problems with existing provision, there remained issues with which each was unable to deal. In this section of the chapter I want to consider the different meanings given to vocational knowledge that are implicit but not explicitly discussed in the reforms and the critiques that led to them. My argument is that in their attempts to develop a distinct vocational curriculum, each approach avoids the issue of how vocational knowledge can be distinguished from school or academic knowledge on the one hand, and from the skills and knowledge that can be acquired in the course of work on the other. The knowledge-based approach recognized the crucial role of science in a vocational curriculum geared to the new science-based industries, but failed to consider how apprentices could be supported to recontextualize this newly acquired knowledge in the workplace. As a result it became the inevitable victim of academic drift; many technical curricula were little more than inferior versions of similar academic curricula.

The standards-based approach tried to relate vocational knowledge to workplace practice by claiming to be able to derive it from outcomes-based analyses of different occupational roles. However, this not only failed to lead to a practical methodology, it also neglected the extent to which only some of the knowledge relevant to particular workplaces has its origins in those workplaces. The connective approach associated with technical certificates is an explicit attempt to bring these earlier approaches together by making links between off-the-job and on-the-job learning. However, it relies on a connection between off-the-job and on-the-job learning without any understanding of either what knowledge is acquired in the two types of learning or how they might be 'connected'. Furthermore, the connective approach fails to acknowledge that there may be fundamental differences between these types of knowledge and how they relate to differences between the codified knowledge of subjects and disciplines and implicit and sometimes tacit knowledge acquired in workplaces.

If there are important differences in content, structure and purpose between off-the-job and on-the-job knowledge, there are likely to be problems either in attempting to rely on one type as in the knowledge-based approach, or in collapsing these types of knowledge as in some way both derivable from occupational standards. Both approaches mask crucial epistemological differences between types of knowledge, and assume that the only differences that are relevant to the vocational curriculum are around the question of control (whether it is employers or educationists who decide) – not content. The idea of 'connecting' off- and on-the-job knowledge and grounding the connection in national occupational standards as implied by the proposals for technical certificates does little more than avoid the issue. It will be the nature of the connections between the codified knowledge of the college-based curriculum and the tacit and often un-codifiable knowledge that is acquired in workplaces that is the basis for what is distinctive about vocational knowledge. However, in order to be clearer about what such connections might involve, we need a more rigorous way of differentiating between types of knowledge. The next section, therefore, takes a step back from specific curriculum issues, and considers different sociological approaches to knowledge that might provide a framework for addressing this issue.

Sociology and vocational knowledge

The importance of the sociology of knowledge for the issues of concern to VET reformers (and indeed those involved in education policy more generally) is that in its premise it captures what Muller (2000) refers to as the fundamental *sociality* of knowledge. It rejects the view that knowledge is either intrinsically 'in the mind' (idealism) or in the world (materialism) or in any sense given; all knowledge, it asserts, in that it is produced by human beings, is inescapably social in origin. The sociality of knowledge refers not only to how it is shaped by external societal influences, but also to the fact that all our categories, theories, concepts and symbols are inescapably social in origin. It is useful to distinguish between two aspects of this sociality of knowledge, which have led to two very different sociologies of knowledge that I have referred to in earlier chapters as social constructivism and social realism.

By social constructivism I refer to that tradition of social theory which has a long and varied history since Hegel and Marx in the nineteenth century and the American pragmatists in the early twentieth century. It takes its most familiar contemporary form in the variety of perspectives often referred to as postmodernism.

Social constructivism argues that all knowledge is the product of social practices; knowledge is therefore inescapably from a standpoint or a perspective. No knowledge in this view is privileged or, in any strong sense, objective. It follows that the specialized, codified or discipline-based knowledge associated with the college curriculum (and any off-the-job learning) is in principle no different from everyday common sense (or on-the-job) knowledge – it is just some other people's knowledge. There is a somewhat ironic link between the epistemological reductionism of social constructivism (see Chapter 2) and what might be called the behaviourist reductionism of the standards approach discussed earlier in this chapter; both in effect do away with knowledge as something distinctive in its own terms.

There are two interpretations of the very general principle of social constructivism that have important implications for the case of vocational knowledge. They might loosely be described as those that focus on the interests underlying all knowledge and those that focus on knowledge production and acquisition as a process. The first 'interest-based' interpretation of social constructivism has its intellectual roots in Marx's theory of ideology. Whereas Marx was concerned with class interests, the approach has been generalized more recently to refer to any social group – by feminists to include women and by multiculturalists or postcolonialists to include different ethnic groups. Interest-based approaches to knowledge have an important critical role in reminding vocational educators that any selection of knowledge may be an expression of a social interest or embody a particular set of power relations. The vocational curriculum is always likely to be in some part a power struggle between employers, educators and the state. The second 'process-based' versions of social constructivism can be traced back to the pragmatism and symbolic interactionism of social theorists such as Dewey and George Herbert Mead. Their strength is the emphasis they give to the contextual or situated character of knowledge. Knowledge for them is always produced or acquired 'in a context' – it is never entirely context-free. Given the importance of learning on the job in vocational education, it is not surprising that process-based approaches have been taken up by VET researchers and lie at the heart of the few attempts to conceptualize vocational knowledge (Billett 1997).

The problem with these interpretations of social constructivism is that they are at best partial perspectives. The interest-based approach on its own can lead to a reductionist view of all knowledge as power relations; hence the only question this leads to is who has the power? In the case of vocational knowledge, is it employers, the state or the colleges? The problem with process-based approaches is that they fail to distinguish between the 'degree of situatedness' of different types of knowledge. For example, the 'knowledge' needed by a receptionist or a call centre operator is almost entirely *situated* or related to a specific context, whereas the knowledge needed by an engineer or accountant is not. Although this context-specificity is a feature of the knowledge required for all jobs, many jobs also require knowledge involving theoretical ideas shared by a 'community of specialists' that are not tied to specific contexts; such knowledge enables those who have acquired it to move beyond specific situations – in this case workplaces. In focusing only on either the interests or practices involved in the processes of acquisition and production of knowledge, knowledge can easily be reduced to or equated with the interests or practices of groups of knowers; as a result, content becomes arbitrary (at least in theory). Thus social constructivism, while rhetorically powerful both in exposing the power relations that are embedded in all knowledge and in cautioning researchers to be sensitive to particular contexts, is limited in what it can say directly about the vocational curriculum, where the differentiation of knowledge is the crucial issue.

Social realist approaches to knowledge stress that although all knowledge is historical and social in origins, it is its particular social origins that give it its objectivity. It is this objectivity that enables knowledge to transcend the conditions of its production. It follows that the task of social theory is to identify these conditions. Furthermore, social realist approaches address epistemological issues that are involved in the differentiation of knowledge with which social constructivism does not (and in my view cannot) engage. Partly as a result of an unwillingness to recognize the social realist argument, decisions about the VET curriculum have been left to a combination of tradition and pragmatism. I turn therefore to brief accounts of two leading exponents of social realist approaches, Emile Durkheim and Basil Bernstein, already discussed in Chapters 3 and 4.

Durkheim's social realist approach

A social realist approach to knowledge can be traced back to the French sociologist, Emile Durkheim, who began his research in the last decade of the nineteenth century. He wanted to emphasize the 'sociality' of knowledge, but in contrast to social constructivism, stressed the differences not the similarities between different types of knowledge, and explored the different types of social organization associated with them. Durkheim's ideas were based on contemporary studies of religion in primitive societies (Durkheim 1995). His starting point was a distinction between profane and sacred orders of meaning that he found in every society that he studied. The profane refers to people's response to their everyday world – it is practical, immediate and particular (with similarities to 'on-the-job' learning, in the terms of this chapter). He distinguished the profane from the sacred world of religion that he saw as invented, arbitrary and conceptual; the sacred was a collective product of a society, and not related directly to any real world problem. Originally exemplified by religion, the sacred for Durkheim became the paradigm for all the other kinds of conceptual knowledge including science, philosophy and mathematics, which, for him, were equally social and removed from the everyday world. In relation to the issues that are of concern in this chapter, the sacred has parallels with 'off-the-job' learning that is not constrained by the immediacy of practical problems or getting the job done.

Muller (2000) makes the important point that for Durkheim, the sacred, whether exemplified in religion or science, is an order of meaning characterized by what he refers to as the 'faculty of realization'. This for Durkheim has two aspects: (i) the ability to predict, to project beyond the present and to conceive of alternatives, and (ii) the ability to make connections. In its modern form, this is one of the capabilities identified by Reich (1991) as needed by those he refers to as the symbolic analysts of today's knowledge economies.

Both these aspects of knowledge are frequently neglected in vocational curricula and even in general education. It follows that Durkheim's analysis provides an explanation for the problems of the standards-based approach to knowledge that collapses the distinction between the sacred and the profane and inevitably denies learners opportunities to either generalize or envisage alternatives. Furthermore, his analysis also suggests why achieving 'parity of esteem' between academic and vocational learning is so difficult and why attempts to 'vocationalize' general education have been open to the charge that they are little more than forms of social control.

The sacred and the profane as two distinct orders of meaning are for Durkheim inevitably in tension. However, he emphasizes the differences between the two; he is not implying a judgement about one type of meaning being superior to the other. Everyday activity such as work would be impossible on the basis of the sacred alone. Likewise, workplaces restricted to the profane would preclude the possibility of envisaging alternatives and leave the organization of work where it was in pre-industrial societies. Durkheim is making an argument for specialization; in other words, he is emphasizing the distinctive roles of both orders of meaning.

There are two further lessons for vocational education that can be drawn from Durkheim's distinction between the sacred and the profane. The first is that they are not just distinctions between orders of meaning or forms of knowledge; they are also different forms of social organization. Second, by distinguishing between their distinct roles and purposes, Durkheim provides a way of avoiding a simplistic opposition between the two that has characterized many arguments about the VET curriculum. He is asserting that there are different types of knowledge with different purposes that are based on different forms of social organization. One cannot be reduced to the other. It follows that they are not interchangeable, or in competition with each other; they are complementary.

There are, however, some problems with Durkheim's analysis, which reflect his assumption that modern societies have evolved in a linear fashion from earlier societies. The first is that in complex modern societies, the sacred and the profane are no longer homogeneous categories; each pervades the other as in the case of the embedding of science in work. Second, as a result of extrapolating from small-scale undifferentiated societies with little stratification,

Durkheim plays down the extent to which the different orders of meaning are unequally distributed and themselves become stratified. The theoretical problem that this leads to is that relations of power are marginalized in Durkheim's analysis. Despite his insistence that the sacred and the profane only differentiate between different orders of meaning, in practice they become the basis of divisions between academic and vocational qualifications and more generally between mental and manual labour. Third, as Muller (2000) points out, the sacred and the profane are never as distinct as Durkheim portrays them. They are, in Max Weber's terms, ideal not descriptive types, and always enmeshed to some extent in each other. This dichotomizing leads Durkheim to take for granted the problem of crossing the boundaries between different types of knowledge – an issue that is fundamental to the vocational curriculum in explicating the relationship between off-the-job and on-the-job learning. Bernstein's last work (Bernstein 2000) develops Durkheim's social realist approach to knowledge in his distinction between vertical and horizontal knowledge structures. I turn next to a brief discussion of Bernstein's ideas.

Bernstein's vertical and horizontal knowledge structures

Bernstein reconceptualized Durkheim's distinction between sacred and profane orders of meaning by distinguishing between vertical and horizontal discourses. Horizontal discourses are, for Bernstein, local, segmental and context-bound. In contrast, vertical discourses are general, explicit and coherent. They are expressed in either hierarchically organized bodies of knowledge such as the natural sciences or in bodies of knowledge that are segmentally organized into specialized languages, as in the case of the humanities and the social sciences. Work-based or on-the-job knowledge can be seen as a form of horizontal discourse; it embodies no explicit principles for transferring meanings across 'segments' (whether these are sites or occupational sectors) except by analogy that one segment or occupation is 'similar' to another. Furthermore, on-the-job knowledge is usually acquired experientially without relying on any overt pedagogic intervention or following any explicit rules or sequences. In contrast, vertical discourse is expressed in bodies of codified knowledge. It is typically acquired 'off-the-job' and, for Bernstein, in accordance with the principles of recontextualization and strict rules of distribution associated with specific subjects and academic disciplines.

Bernstein argues that horizontal discourses cannot generate vertical knowledge because they embody no principles of recontextualization; by this he means the rules for making explicit the grounds for an explanation. In other words, if we accept, with Bernstein, that one criterion of vertical knowledge is whether it embodies a principle of recontextualization, it is important to distinguish between vertical knowledge and common sense, practical or everyday knowledge. Put simply, whereas there are rules that govern both the production and acquisition of vertical knowledge, this is not the case with horizontal knowledge.

Bernstein's distinction between horizontal and vertical discourses explains the inability of the standards-based approach to vocational knowledge discussed earlier to generate any systematic methodology. It fails to recognize that one kind of knowledge (vertical) cannot be derived from the other (horizontal). The horizontal or tacit cannot be made explicit because it is its tacitness – its immediacy in relation to everyday or working life – that gives it its power. Similarly it is not possible to apply vertical knowledge directly to specific everyday workplace realities where knowledge is needed that is sufficiently flexible to deal with immediate practical problems.

Bernstein argues that vertical discourse can be expressed in the form of two distinct types of knowledge structure, and again he invokes the vertical/horizontal distinction. Vertical knowledge structures are pyramidical and expressed in their purest form in the physical sciences in which knowledge growth involves ever higher levels of generalization and abstraction. Horizontal knowledge structures, on the other hand (Bernstein's examples are the social sciences), involve a number of non-comparable specialized languages but without any overarching principles for linking them. The growth of horizontal knowledge, for Bernstein, consists of the development of new specialized languages. For Bernstein, both these types of knowledge structure are expressions of vertical discourse. Both have explicit principles of recontextualization, and those who have acquired them can provide the grounds of their explanations in terms of a shared set of rules.

Bernstein's analysis highlights the extent to which previous debates about vocational knowledge have limited their focus to the different interests of those defining what is to count as vocational knowledge and not considered the different types of knowledge themselves. These debates have been about whether it should be the employers, as the standards-based approach claims, or the educators (in line with the knowledge-based approach) who should define what is to count as vocational knowledge. Boreham (2002) suggests that reforms within the dual system of apprenticeship in Germany provide an example of how the two sets of interests are combined; it represents an interesting attempt to develop the kind of connective approach referred to earlier. Bernstein's theory, on the other hand, suggests that all such approaches neglect questions of the internal structuring, contents and purposes of the different forms of knowledge and what implications these questions may have for how knowledge is acquired. The importance of Bernstein's theory for conceptualizing vocational knowledge is found in his concept of recontextualization and the pedagogic strategies to which it points. Brier (2002) and Gamble (2006), in slightly different ways, draw on his ideas to develop the useful distinction between *principled* or generalizing and *procedural* or particularizing pedagogic strategies. The former refer to explanations and the latter to the location of specific instances. Distinguishing between types of pedagogic strategy raises questions about how the two kinds of strategy relate to each other, the different kinds of explanation and procedure that may be found in vocational education programmes, and how they may be expressed in differences between occupational sectors.

Bernstein, like Durkheim, tends to favour dichotomous categories. However, he develops his dichotomies by what Abbott (2000) and later Moore and Muller (2002) refer to as fractal divisions. He is able therefore to conceive of vertical knowledge structures including elements of horizontality and vice versa. One of the limitations of his analysis for the concerns of this chapter is that he gives almost all his attention to varieties of vertical knowledge – in particular the differences between the social and natural sciences. Any attempt to conceptualize vocational knowledge requires equal attention to the differentiation of horizontal discourses and knowledge structures across different occupational sectors and types of work.

Bernstein's distinctions can be applied to a number of trends in recent VET curriculum policy. For example, foundation degrees and technical certificates are attempts to increase the knowledge component of work-based programmes; however, by failing to distinguish between types of knowledge, they may well reproduce the problems that they were designed to overcome. Vocational GCSEs and vocational A-levels, on the other hand, seek to incorporate practical workplace knowledge into the vertical structures of the school curriculum. However, as Brier (2002) points out, the inclusion of everyday practical knowledge into the school or college curriculum does not necessarily promote access to vertical knowledge; it can reduce the vocational curriculum to little more than a strategy for improving the students' functioning as employees.

Conclusions

In this chapter I have argued that debates about the reform of vocational education have invariably neglected the question of vocational knowledge. I have suggested that there are approaches in the sociology of knowledge that are relevant to the reconceptualization that is necessary. I draw on the relationship between power and knowledge that is made explicit by social constructivist approaches and the focus on the differentiation of knowledge that arises from the social realist approach developed by Durkheim and Bernstein. Whereas Durkheim's distinction between sacred and profane provides a way of analysing the differences between theoretical and everyday (or workplace) knowledge, Bernstein's analysis allows distinctions to be made between types of theoretical knowledge and types of everyday knowledge, as well as the problems of bridging the gap between them through the process of recontextualization. His analysis highlights the weakness of attempts to base vocational knowledge on national occupational standards. By treating all knowledge as potentially explicit and vertical, the standards-based approach fails to recognize the fundamental differences between theoretical and everyday or workplace knowledge. As a result, vocational programmes that rely on the standards-based approach deny learners access to the rules governing the production of knowledge by the scientific and professional communities. Greater clarity about what knowledge is to be acquired by students on vocational programmes is crucial to wider debates about more effective vocational education and any possibilities of a move towards parity of esteem with general education. The argument of this chapter is that the sociology of knowledge developed by Durkheim and Bernstein offers a powerful way of beginning to tackle such questions.

10 Professional knowledge and the question of identity: an analytical framework

Introduction

Across a range of professions, but also in university research, traditional assumptions about the production and acquisition of knowledge are being challenged by increasingly global economic and political forces (Freidson 2001). This, of course, has always been true up to a point – but it is the extent and form of this questioning that is new. This includes its links with political and economic developments, the challenge to the idea that professions have a distinctive knowledge base, and even the very idea of a distinct group of occupations being set apart as professions.

The focus of these challenges is on opening up, to users and clients, the 'black box' of professional and expert knowledge. They are sometimes expressed in fiscal or regulatory attempts to reduce professional autonomy, but also in attempts within professions such as accountancy to respond to the new circumstances in which they find themselves when they experience a clash of loyalties between their profession and their employer's interests. On a national level, the traditional models of professional knowledge, and their close association with disciplinary knowledge acquired in universities, are also under challenge.

This questioning of the traditional assumptions about the knowledge base of professions and academic researchers' work parallels and has been given powerful ideological support by the various forms of postmodernism and social constructivism that have been fashionable in the social sciences and the humanities. As was argued in Chapter 2, these theories see professional knowledge (but curiously not their own) as little more than a masquerade for protecting privileges. Ideology critiques of this kind are not new, and have long been familiar within Marxism and the Frankfurt School of critical theory. What is new is that, unlike Marxism and critical theory, which had a strong, albeit contentious notion of knowledge and truth, postmodernists reject the very idea that there could be a hierarchy of truth and reliable knowledge. Such ideas are of course the very basis of the professions' claims to a special status in society.

Without such an idea of truth, I argued in Chapter 2, neither knowledge, science nor the idea of a profession would be possible. These arguments raise a number of questions which have recurred throughout this book. However, they have a special significance for members of the professions when questions about knowledge and epistemology can have their sharpest implications. I will mention two of these questions which, albeit somewhat indirectly, the rest of this chapter will seek to address.

1   Are these challenges an indication of the end of disciplinary-based profes-
    sional expertise as we came to know it in the twentieth century and of the
    university as the main institution in which future professionals increasingly
    acquire at least the foundations of their knowledge?
2   If so, is the market, or more broadly some definition of user-needs, an ade-
    quate mechanism for deciding whether to trust specialist knowledge in fields
    as diverse as engineering, medicine and accountancy, or do we have to fall
    back, for such decisions, on politics?

We can, as I do, reject the claims of postmodern theory, and point to the inade-
quacy of markets and user needs as criteria, but we cannot so easily reject the
forces of globalization and the attempts of governments to control and shape them
through regulation.

My argument is that while traditional models of professional knowledge have
often been conservative and resistant to change, and in many cases associated
with indefensible aspects of gender, class and racial privilege, current attempts to
open up the black box of professionalism fail to address both the nature of and
basis for the authority of different types of specialist knowledge and the conditions for their acquisition and production.

What I propose is to draw on some of the less well known ideas of Basil
Bernstein. He offers, I think, although sometimes in highly aphoristic and elliptical
form, a set of concepts that help us to address the implications of the challenges to
professional knowledge, as well as linking them to the broader issues concerning
knowledge and education with which this book has been concerned.

There are three aspects of Bernstein's approach that I think are particularly
helpful in this context. They are:

1   his conceptualization of the relationship between the organization of knowl-
    edge and the formation of social, and more specifically, learner and
    professional identities;
2   his insistence on the importance of the structure of knowledge relations (not
    knowledge contents). These knowledge relations are, for him, invariably
    boundary relations;
3   his account of the changing forms of boundary relations. He traces the suc-
    cessive emergence of knowledge relations that he refers to as singulars,
    regions and generic modes.

Bernstein's focus on knowledge relations sets him apart from much philosophy of
education which, until it started to claim that questions of epistemology could be
reduced to different forms of social practice (Hirst 1983), was concerned with the
logical divisions between different forms of knowledge. It also separates him

from sociologists of knowledge such as Mannheim and Bourdieu who concentrated on the social interests underlying different claims to knowledge and, in Bourdieu's case, different intellectual fields.

Knowledge relations, singulars and identity

The starting point of Bernstein's sociology of knowledge was the conditions that encourage the formation of identities associated with 'inwardness' and the 'inner dedication to knowing'. This is important because, arguably, it is precisely these characteristics that have, albeit in idealized form, defined the scholar and the professional and which now are under most challenge from economic pressures associated with marketization, as well as from government policies which attempt to diminish the autonomy of professionals and direct their activities towards politically defined goals.

The paradigm type of knowledge structure which gives rise to 'inner dedication' was what Bernstein referred to as 'singulars'. He defined singulars as: 'Knowledge structures whose creators have appropriated a space to give themselves a unique name, a specialised discrete discourse with its own intellectual field of text, practices, rules of entry examinations and licences to practice' (Bernstein 2000: 52).

For Bernstein, singulars are a theoretical concept. They refer to strongly bounded entities 'oriented to their own development' which engender identities, celebrate purity of categories and partake (in Durkheim's sociological sense) of the 'sacred'. They generate strong inner commitments, centred in the perceived intrinsic value of the specific knowledge domain.

He identified the key structural conditions for singulars as well as their implications for establishing identities in the following terms:

> Their [singulars'] sense of the sacred ... does not arise so much out of an ethic of knowledge for its own sake, but is more a function of socialisation into subject loyalty: for it is the subject which becomes the lynchpin of identity. Any attempt to weaken [boundaries] between subjects or change classification strength ... may be felt as a threat to one's identity and may be experienced as a pollution endangering the sacred.
>
> (Bernstein 2000: 54–55; my additions in brackets)

He also emphasized the association of singulars with sacredness (again in the Durkheimian sense) and inner dedication: 'the sacred face [of singulars] sets them apart, legitimises their otherness and creates dedicated identities with no reference other than to their calling' (Bernstein 2000: 54). Bernstein also insisted that it was the structuring of knowledge relations that determined the formation of specialized identities. For example:

> the form taken by educational practices depends almost entirely upon the relation between these categories ... . The speciality of each category is created,

maintained and reproduced only if the relations between the categories are preserved [in other words] the insulation between categories.

(Bernstein 2000; my addition in brackets)

However, he provides the elements of a historical as well as a structural account of the sources of inwardness. For this he draws on Durkheim's account of the medieval curriculum of the University of Paris (Durkheim 1977). For Durkheim, it was important that the Trivium (logic, grammar and rhetoric) with its focus on 'the word' preceded the Quadrivium (arithmetic, geometry, astronomy and music) which focused on 'the world'.

Bernstein suggests that the abstractness of this curriculum may have been associated with certain unique characteristics of the Christian religion. Only Christianity, he argues, is uniquely and necessarily abstract. This is a consequence of the dislocation it sees between our inner and our outer selves and how Christianity seeks to resolve it. For Bernstein, Christianity was a religion in which faith was not assured but had to be won and re-won, creating a need for 'theology and then more theology'. As a consequence, in Christianity the word as a 'knowledge relation' takes precedence over the act as doing in the world. It follows, therefore, that 'the Trivium ... constituted a particular form of consciousness ... the valid true inner self, as a necessary precondition that our understanding of the world is valid' (Bernstein 2000: 83).

It is precisely in this pedagogic sequencing (the 'word' preceding the 'world') in which inwardness and commitment shape the terms of practical engagement with the world that Bernstein argues 'we can find the origins of the professions'. He does not elaborate on this. However, its meaning seems clear. Professional commitment and its accompanying sense of dedication originates, at least in part, in the separation of 'word' and 'world'. In the next section, I want to trace the implications of this claim about origins of the professions for the current crisis in professional knowledge by drawing on Bernstein's three concepts of knowledge relations.

From singulars to regions

Bernstein developed his concept of 'regions' as a counterpart as well as a precursor to the idea of 'singulars' already referred to. As approaches to knowledge, regions can be seen as at the opposite end of the spectrum from singulars. They are knowledge structures in which a number of singulars are brought together within an integrating framework. Unlike singulars which face inwards, Bernstein sees regions as facing outwards towards various 'fields of practice' in the world. He refers to medicine and architecture as examples of 'classical regions', institutionalized within universities in the nineteenth century; contemporary regions, he suggests, might include business studies, media studies and journalism.

Bernstein's discussion of the significance of regions is mainly concerned with the possible consequences of what he refers to as the 'regionalization' of knowledge (i.e. the proliferation of regions) within higher education. He contrasts the nineteenth century, when singulars were the modal form of knowledge structure, with the twentieth century, when knowledge became progressively 'regionalized' as higher education managers have been coerced into restructuring courses to meet the perceived demands of students, employers and government. He saw regions, whether classical or new, as being increasingly dependent on the rapidly changing requirements of external fields of practice to which they are linked and that this has led, as he puts it, to a kind of 'flexibilization of the self', and a readiness on the part of professionals and even scholars to respond to whatever the exigencies of markets require in reshaping their intellectual fields. The implications of this regionalization for the central issue of identity he saw as profound:

> Identities ... are what they are, and what they will become, as a consequence of the projection of ... knowledge as a practice in some context .... The future of the context will regulate identity and the volatility of the context will control the nature of the regionalization and thus the projected identity.
>
> (Bernstein 2000: 55)

Thus he depicts a progressive loss of control of regions by members of the professions through a weakening of the tension between singulars and different fields of practice. This is a development that was given a much more benign twist by Gibbons and his colleagues (Gibbons *et al.* 1994) and their idea of the shift from Mode 1 to Mode 2 knowledge.

There are a number of implications of this analysis which are worth exploring. They relate first to certain of the classical singulars and regions where the contemporary reconstruction of the intellectual fields and the associated identity changes may have been most far reaching – and potentially most traumatic – both for those involved and for society generally. Second, Bernstein implies that the 'regionalization of knowledge' in which, in his language, the word and the world are held in tension with each other, is itself under threat from the forces of marketization. This threat is associated with the emergence of a new mode of knowledge relation which he refers to as genericism. The next section focuses on the latter point.

The emergence of genericism

Bernstein notes that from the 1980s, when regionalization was beginning to take hold in universities, a new mode of pedagogic discourse was emerging, initially at pre-university level. It was this that he referred to as generic – here I shall refer to it as genericism. He lists its features as follows:

- it arose outside of and independently of the formal curriculum;
- it was directed primarily towards extra-educational experiences;
- it initially appeared in further education, not in universities;
- it was linked to the perceived demands of the market, and to improving people's 'flexibility' for employment;
- it was based on what was assumed to be common to a widening range of occupations, tasks and jobs.

Since Bernstein published the first version of his paper in 1996, generic models have been extended far beyond their origins in low-level work-based schemes and pre-vocational education; since 2000, they have even been found in doctoral programmes. Typically, they are expressed by such terms as key and core skills, thinking skills, problem solving and teamwork. They are assumed to apply to all subjects, all regions and all fields of practice. Bernstein argues that they are not 'simply economic procedures of acquisition but are based on a new concept of work and life ... which might be called short termism' (2000: 58).

Generic knowledge relations such as key skills have been invoked in successive White Papers since the early 1990s, most noticeably in the way they refer to lifelong learning and not just schools, colleges and universities and to learning and skills rather than education. As Bernstein puts it, genericism assumes we are in a world in which 'life experiences cannot be based on stable expectations of the future and one's location in it. It follows that a vital new ability must be developed' (2000: 59). This he refers to as 'trainability', or the ability, in coping with the new requirements of work and life, to adapt to and profit from continuous pedagogic opportunities. The concept of trainability, which has much in common with the more familiar term 'learning to learn', emphasizes the capacities people need if they are to be open to the ever changing contingencies of the market. This ability to 'learn how to learn' is usually seen as something unequivocally positive and to be encouraged. Bernstein, however, comments that there seems 'to be an emptiness in the concept of trainability, an emptiness which makes the concept self-referential and therefore self excluding ... . If the concept is empty how does the actor recognise her/himself and others?' (2000: 59).

Bernstein's answer is that the recognition that is the basis of identity comes increasingly from the 'the materialities of consumption'. In other words, 'it is the products of the market that relay signifiers whereby temporary stabilities are constructed' (2000).

Bernstein concludes his brief discussion of the implications of the generic mode with the comment that as it is extended from its origins in manual work: 'the concept of trainability is institutionalised as *the fundamental pedagogic objective...*' (2000; my italics). It reproduces imaginary concepts of work and life which abstract such experiences from the power relations of their lived conditions and negate the possibilities of understanding and criticism. In relation to the earlier analysis, identities have moved in Bernstein's account from the strong boundaries and 'inwardness' associated with singulars via the tension between the 'inwardness' and 'outwardness' associated with regions to a situation where identities are increasingly defined externally by the market.

Conclusions

I began by outlining some of the current challenges facing the professions. They relate, I suggested, to their autonomy, to their knowledge base, to the validity of any ethical view of their calling, and of course to the privileges associated with professional expertise. I also suggested that these challenges are related to a broader set of epistemological questions about the nature of knowledge and claims to objectivity and truth which are raised by economic changes and government responses to them and by certain trends in social theory, which are discussed elsewhere in this book.

I then turned to Basil Bernstein's ideas. I showed how he locates the idea of a profession, and more broadly the idea of knowledge, in the dislocation between our inner relationship with our self and our outer relationship with the world, which together constitute our identity as social beings and members of society and, more specifically for some, as members of professions.

I described how Bernstein analyses changes in the way identities are shaped by knowledge relations in terms of three modes of knowledge relation (he also refers to them as modes of pedagogic discourse): singulars, regions and genericism. I then discussed the emergence of regionalization and genericism as the dominant knowledge relations of recent decades.

For Bernstein, singulars, though primarily inward looking and therefore, as he puts it, with a tendency to narcissism, have, like coins, two faces – one turned inward to the idea of a professional calling, and the other outward to the materiality of survival and economic gain. This dual conceptualization of singulars is crucial to avoiding the two opposing tendencies in debates about professions – a sense of self-justification and a cynicism which sees them as no more than an ideology of privilege. In contrast, Bernstein's analysis has potential for exploring the actual situation facing members of professions. Regions, as combinations of singulars, also face two ways in a tension between singulars and fields of practice; however, this tension is increasingly influenced by the external worlds of practice. The generic mode, on the other hand, and its associated concept of trainability Bernstein sees as essentially empty – it has no inwardness, only an ability to respond to every new pedagogic initiative. Followed to its logical conclusion, genericism implies the end of professions as we know them.

From the point of view of the professions, this appears to be a deeply pessimistic and almost deterministic analysis. In a poignant comment, which links the argument about the end of professions to the instrumentalizing of knowledge, Bernstein notes that:

> there is a new concept of knowledge [emerging] and its relation to those who use it and create it ... . Knowledge after nearly one thousand years is divorced from inwardness and literally dehumanised ... what is at stake is the very concept of education itself.
>
> (Bernstein 2000: 86; my addition in brackets)

In pointing to the divorce of knowledge from inwardness, Bernstein is not only warning about the progressive disappearance of the conditions for knowledge or professionalism as we know them. He is also making a prophetic observation about the consequences of allowing the enthusiasm for mobile learning and the supposed educational potential of the internet to go unchallenged (Selwyn and Young 2007).

The charge of determinism and pessimism in Bernstein's analysis has a point, but in my view it is too one-dimensional. He is worried that 'marketization' is undermining the conditions for professionalism and more broadly for knowledge itself. However, on its own, this overstates his structuralism, and neglects the extent to which he also stresses the importance of the specific historical conditions in which professionalism emerged.

I earlier referred to Bernstein's argument that medieval Christianity required 'theology and always more theology' and that faith had to be 'won and re-won'. By analogy, although marketization undermines the conditions for knowledge and professionalism, it is also the professionalism that produces the new knowledge that markets rely on; markets do not create knowledge or products on their own. It follows, therefore, that just as faith had to be won and re-won, so, likewise, the conditions for professionalism and the production of knowledge – their autonomy, and more deeply, the necessity of putting the 'word' before the 'world' – have to be constantly recreated; this is what professionalism means. The necessity of putting the 'word' before the 'world' remains, even though the circumstances within which it will be realized have changed. The agenda that we inherit from Bernstein is to explore how the conditions for professionalism and the creation of new knowledge can be created in the circumstances of our time.

11 Academic/vocational divisions in post-compulsory education and the problem of knowledge

Introduction

Academic/vocational divisions are a feature of all education systems and have a history that goes back far beyond the beginnings of mass public education. My interest in the issue arose nearly 20 years ago when I was involved in establishing the Post 16 Education Centre at the Institute of Education. However, it is not insignificant that it was at a time when UK policy makers were beginning to consider whether such divisions, at least in the form that they took in England, were barriers to improving the level of skills and knowledge in the workforce as a whole, rather than a structure that had to be taken for granted.

In the five years from 1986, the Post 16 Education Centre was funded by the government's Employment Department within the Technical and Vocational Education Initiative that was designed to promote a more vocationally relevant curriculum in schools and colleges. Bearing in mind that the Post 16 Education Centre was based in that most academic of educational institutions, a university, and in a school of education that had few links with the world of work, we were confronted very directly with the reality of the academic/vocational divide. The question that we asked from the beginning was whether this divide was in some sense an inevitable characteristic of modern societies or whether some form of unified (or integrated) system was possible. The theme of this chapter is how, in the past 20 years, I have come to rethink my understanding of what might be involved in trying to develop a unified curriculum and system of qualifications that would replace a system that is based on the traditional divisions between academic and vocational learning.

I was one of the co-authors of the IPPR report *A British Baccalaureate* (Finegold *et al.* 1990) that was published in 1990. Significantly, in relation to the claims that the report made, it was subtitled *Ending the Division Between Education and Training*. In that report we argued, on economic, sociological, political and educational grounds, for the phasing out of a curriculum and a qualification system based on academic/vocational divisions. Instead, we made proposals for a unified post-16 curriculum and qualification system. Seventeen years later, I continue to identify with the broad political vision of a more equal educational system that informed the IPPR report. However, I argue that if we are to progress towards the vision that was expressed in the IPPR report, the grounds for introducing a unified system in the short term need to be questioned. The chapter begins with a brief discussion of the economic, political and societal issues underlying what became known as the 'unification debate', and goes on to concentrate on the specifically educational issues which during the 1990s received less attention.

My approach to the issue of overcoming academic and vocational divisions draws on the theoretical issues in the sociology of educational knowledge that were discussed in Part 1 of this book. Until working on the original version of this chapter for a conference in the Netherlands, these two very different strands of my own work in curriculum policy and sociology of education had remained largely separate. I shall try to show how the debate between social constructivist and social realist approaches to knowledge that has been a central theme of this book is directly relevant to the debate about overcoming academic/vocational divisions. Although a social realist approach is critical of the claims made for unification, I argue that it provides a more reliable basis for improving both general (academic) and vocational education and, in the longer term, fulfilling the broader goals of the IPPR report.

Making connections between the sociology of education and educational policy debates proved harder than I had expected. Relating 'theory' and 'practice' (or policy) is never straightforward. Not only is a neat or easy fit between them never possible, but any attempt at a neat fit leads inevitably to an over-instrumental role for theoretically based research which can easily play down its critical element (see Chapter 7). I pointed out in Chapter 4 that some researchers such as Yrjo Engestrom, the Finnish socio-cultural theorist, take the view that the theory/practice distinction is itself becoming outdated by global economic changes and that we must move towards the integrated idea of 'theoretically grounded practice' (Engestrom 2004). In Chapter 7, I argued the counter view that the blurring of the distinction between theoretical and practical knowledge inhibits the development of theory and makes the engagement with policy by researchers increasingly vulnerable to political and economic exigencies. If, in the long run, theory is to inform practice and policy, it needs its own space. The mistake that I certainly made in the 1970s was to suggest how the world (I had a more limited focus on the curriculum) could be changed before I had an adequate theory of what a curriculum involves.

The rest of the chapter is divided into a number of sections. First I give a brief account of post-16 education policy in England since the 1990s, followed by a summary of earlier arguments about the question of knowledge in the sociology of education. After making the case for a social realist theory of knowledge I go on to explore the relevance of the theory for debates about the post-16 curriculum. Next I critically examine the concepts of connectivity and connective specialization which were, implicitly or explicitly, the underlying principles of the argument for a unified curriculum. After linking the argument in the chapter with Chapter 9 and its implications for the vocational curriculum, I conclude by commenting on the wider implications of the 'unification' debate and my response to it in this chapter.

Post-16 education policy in England since the 1990s

From the late 1980s I, along with many others involved in post-compulsory education in the UK, endorsed the view that divisions between academic and vocational qualifications were both inefficient and unjust, and perpetuated what had become known as a 'low skills equilibrium' in workplaces and in education and training (Finegold and Soskice 1988). This view was taken up in the IPPR report that I have already referred to, in a series of research projects and publications undertaken jointly with colleagues in Scotland (Raffe *et al.* 2007), and in my book *The Curriculum of the Future* (Young 1998). That book focused on the form that a unified curriculum should take, which was no longer based on separate school subjects for general education and national occupational standards for vocational education. I, along with others (Young 1998; Young and Spours 1998), developed the idea that a unified 'Curriculum of the future' should be based on the principle of *connective specialization* – an idea to which I will return later in this chapter.

Attempts to reform the post-16 (and more recently, the post-14) curriculum in England have taken on a curiously cyclical character since 1990. Given that it was published by a then relatively unknown left-of-centre think tank, the IPPR Report *A British Baccalaureate* that appeared in 1990 was unexpectedly influential, and not only within the educational community. It was not surprising, therefore, that the Conservative Government of the time should, a year later and not long before the general election, feel it necessary to publish their own White Paper, *Education and Training for the Twenty-first Century* (HMSO 1991). This firmly rejected a unification strategy, and reaffirmed that future provision would be based on distinct academic (A-levels) and vocational pathways. Over a decade later, history almost repeated itself. The difference was the political affiliation and position of the key actors involved. Proposals for a unified curriculum and a phasing out of separate academic and vocational pathways came in 2004, not from the Left, but from a committee set up by the government (and chaired by the former Chief Inspector of Schools, Mike Tomlinson). The Tomlinson Working Group reported in 2004 (Tomlinson 2004), and proposed that academic and vocational qualifications should, over a ten-year period, be phased out and replaced by a single four-level diploma within which *all* students in the 14–19 age group would take combinations of a single set of core and specialist modules. In 2005, the Labour Government rejected these proposals and, in its own White Paper, decided that separate academic and vocational qualifications and pathways would be retained; the latter became known as specialist diplomas, although the term specialist has since been dropped. We are therefore virtually back to 1991 (or maybe we never really moved!), when the Conservative Government of the time made very similar proposals for continuing a tripartite system of post-compulsory education and training.

My intention in this chapter is not to take sides between the government and Tomlinson. The question that I want to ask is: were those of us who supported the change to a unified system in the 1990s just naive idealists or, if not, what went wrong? Was it our economic analysis, that the new global economy needed a new national education system, that was flawed? Was it our political analysis that assumed that there was genuine popular support for the phasing out of A-levels and the change to a unified system of upper secondary education that was wrong? Were we right in assuming that this reform would be seen as the logical completion of the comprehensive vision for secondary education that was launched by an earlier Labour Government in 1965? Or was it that our sociological analysis of the role of education in the wider society was flawed? Important though they are, I shall only discuss these issues briefly in this chapter.

The economic basis of unification

The economic case for unification and overcoming academic/vocational divisions was based on the progressive interpretation of changes that were taking place in capitalist economies globally that I referred to in relation to post-apartheid South Africa in Chapter 7. However, the predictions in the 1980s of changes in mass production and the weakening of the old divisions between mental and manual labour and knowledge and skill turned out to be at best over-optimistic. Mass production was moving from Europe, and new kinds of jobs were being created, but not all of them were 'high-skill' or 'knowledge based'; thus new divisions were also emerging. Furthermore, the evidence suggested that significant changes in production relations demanded a very particular set of conditions not typical of this country (Payne 2000). There was at least an implicit assumption among the 'unifiers' in publications such as *The British Baccalaureate* that economic change was 'on our side', or at least that it could itself be driven by educational change. Reflecting on the experience of the past 17 years, associating progressive educational possibilities with economic developments seems hard to justify.

The political support for unification

Whereas the decision to establish comprehensive secondary education and abolish grammar schools and the eleven-plus selection test in England in the 1960s had widespread popular support, extending these reforms to the post-compulsory phase of secondary education posed much more complex issues. The numbers taking A-levels expanded from 3 per cent of each cohort when they were launched in 1951 to over 40 per cent of each cohort five decades later. Those of us who in the 1990s supported the abolition of A-levels, or with the Tomlinson Report a decade later, a more modest phasing out, did not fully take into account that their expansion, which had never been the result of an explicit policy, might itself lead to a widening of popular support for them. Seventeen years after the IPPR Report *A British Baccalaureate* (Finegold *et al.* 1990), A-levels can no longer adequately be described as elitist. Catering for nearly half of each cohort, they have themselves become part of a mass and, in some ways, less elitist system. As a result it was not surprising that the Labour Government, whatever the personal views of individual members of the Cabinet, resisted pressures to phase them out. When the Government decided to reject the Tomlinson recommendations and retain A-levels in 2005, there was much opposition from the education community, but no sense that it would be an issue for the mass of voters. Nothing since has contradicted that view.

The societal basis of a unified curriculum

It is almost a sociological truism, all too easily forgotten by some of us in the early 1990s, that like all educational structures, academic/vocational divisions have their origins in the division of labour in society and not in the education system alone. Only a society without a division of labour – and this means either a utopia or the primitive communism described by Marx – could have an education system without academic/vocational divisions. The best evidence for this is from the two countries, Scotland and Sweden, that have unified their provision of post-16 education – Scotland through reforming its qualification system and Sweden by creating comprehensive upper secondary schools. In each case, though other benefits of unification have been noted, academic/vocational divisions as a feature of the curriculum have remained largely unchallenged (Raffe *et al.* 2007).

In this chapter, I intend to concentrate on the educational issues raised by proposals for unifying the curriculum and, in particular, the approach to unification that was adopted in *A British Baccalaureate* (Finegold *et al.* 1990), developed in my book (Young 1998) and reflected, albeit indirectly, in the recent Tomlinson Report proposals. I shall argue that these proposals, and unification strategies more generally, neglect questions of the differentiation of knowledge (and learning) that must remain fundamental to any genuine reform of post-compulsory education. In order to make this argument, I turn to the issues about the question of knowledge that were discussed in Part 1.

The sociology of education and the problem of knowledge

The broad lines of the argument will be familiar to those who have followed the arguments in the early chapters of this book. In 1971, *Knowledge and Control* (Young 1971) was published and became associated with a much wider reorientation of the sociology of education, towards questions of knowledge and the curriculum, and away from its previous focus on the distribution of educational opportunities. What became known as the 'new sociology of education' recognized that it was the process of cultural transmission that lay at the heart of the specific role of formal education and schooling in modern societies. It followed that a key issue for sociologists was the *discontinuity* between the common culture of educational or school knowledge and the differentiated culture that students acquire in their homes, peer groups and communities and bring to school. Engaging with this discontinuity might be defined as 'the pedagogic problem' for teachers as well as the central problem for the sociology of education. The social class basis of this cultural discontinuity in England was first analysed by Bernstein in his work on language codes and educability (Bernstein

1971) and by Bourdieu with his concept of cultural capital (Bourdieu and Passeron 1977). Whereas most empirical research derived, at least implicity, from the ideas of Bernstein and Bourdieu, it tended to focus narrowly on the social factors influencing the differential attainment of children from different social classes. In contrast the 'new sociology of education', which developed from the same concern with cultural transmission, pointed in the opposite direction towards the socially distributed effects of the school curriculum.

Research in the sociology of the curriculum that developed in the 1970s (e.g. Young and Whitty 1977) was largely, if not always explicitly, based on a *social constructivist* approach to knowledge. This saw all knowledge, including the curriculum, as an expression of social activities, interests and purposes. As applied to the curriculum the theoretical role of sociology took on the form of an ideology critique. It aimed to demonstrate how all forms of knowledge selection and organization in the curriculum were representations of particular world views and expressions of particular power relations and interests. The assumption was that this type of critical analysis could be the basis for an alternative curriculum which reflected a wider set of interests and not just those of specialists and or of those currently in positions of power. The curriculum, in other words, was seen as a site of political struggle. There have been many examples since the beginning of mass education that illustrate the truth of this argument – from the exclusion of geology from the school curriculum on religious grounds in the nineteenth century to the current debates about the inclusion of creationism as an alternative to Darwin's theory of evolution in school biology.

The philosophical problem with social constructivism, as was pointed out at the time (Pring 1972), is that it is fundamentally relativist, with all the contradictions that such a position involves. A related point of considerable educational significance is that social constructivist epistemologies are based on an *undifferentiated concept of knowledge.* In concentrating on its social basis, social constructivism treats all knowledge – opinions, beliefs, science and school subjects – as basically the same, from a sociological perspective. All knowledge is an expression of social interests and therefore comes from a particular standpoint. Social constructivism cannot therefore provide any grounds for why some forms of knowledge and not others should be included in the curriculum. From such a perspective, the curriculum is no more than a positioning device, promoting the interests and advantages of some groups rather than others – which may be male, white or middle class.

Recognizing the limitations of social constructivist approaches is not to deny that all curricula have ideological elements. Rather it is to distinguish the social constructivist critique of educational knowledge from social theories of knowledge such as Durkheim's, which recognize the differentiation of knowledge as their starting point. In simple terms, the social realist argument is that social constructivism rejects one of the most basic assumptions of what might be regarded as 'educational common sense'. Educational common sense, as understood here, assumes that a major purpose of formal education is to enable students to acquire knowledge that: (i) is not accessible to most people in their everyday lives, and (ii) enables those who acquire it to move beyond their experience and gain some understanding of the social and natural worlds of which they are a part. These claims for formal education do not assume that it is always success-ful or is successful with all learners – far from it. However, they are the basis, if not always articulated, on which parents in industrial countries keep their chil-dren longer and longer in full-time education, and parents in poor countries make great sacrifices to send their children to school for even a few years. It is also of course one reason why employers recruit graduates, and why graduates are likely to earn more than non-graduates.

The logic of the argument that begins with the differentiation of knowledge from experience is completely at odds with social constructivism, which treats knowledge as *undifferentiated*. If the differentiation thesis is accepted, it follows that the curriculum must recognize this differentiation, even if political and other interests as well as global changes will inevitably shape how this differentiation is expressed. The differentiation thesis does not deny the social constructivist point that all knowledge is social in origin, but it points to a further claim that the dif-ferences between types of knowledge and their different powers and capacities are no less social or fundamental. Knowledge based on experience alone provides only a very limited basis on which to generalize and can easily degenerate into mere opinion or prejudice.

As has been argued elsewhere in this book, a very different sociology of knowledge follows from the assumption that knowledge is differentiated; I have referred to it as social realism. Unlike social constructivism, which treats only the social basis of knowledge as real and objective, social realism treats both the social basis of knowledge and the knowledge itself as real. It follows that instead of concentrating solely on ideology critique, a social realist approach to the cur-riculum seeks to identify the social conditions that might be necessary if objective knowledge is to be acquired. It is an approach to knowledge that has been much neglected until recently in the sociology of education, and by educationalists gen-erally. The next section outlines Durkheim's approach to knowledge discussed earlier, and its implications for the unification debate which is the main topic of this chapter. The chapter extends the argument by drawing on Bernstein's more fully fledged theory of the curriculum.

Social realist approaches to the curriculum

Social realist approaches that treat knowledge as differentiated have a long his-tory that can be traced back to the French sociologist Emile Durkheim, writing a century ago (his work was discussed in some detail in Chapters 3 and 4). It was Durkheim who first identified, in even the most primitive societies, the social ori-gins of the capacity of human beings to differentiate, categorize and classify. In his famous studies on religion (Durkheim 1995; Durkheim and Mauss 1970), Durkheim found that even in these societies distinctions were made between the foundations of knowledge (ideas such as logic and cause) that were general to the whole society and relatively fixed and the practical knowledge that members of those societies developed in response to their survival needs and was necessarily always changing. It was this social differentiation of types of knowledge that Durkheim saw as the basis for all distinctions between 'theoretical' and 'everyday' knowledge in modern societies; and this was the reason why he referred to the religions of those early societies as 'proto-sciences'.

In modern societies that are based on a complex division of intellectual labour and specialization of knowledge, the groups which form the social basis for the objectivity of knowledge are not 'societies' in Durkheim's sense but 'communities of specialists'. The boundaries between knowledge communities have a similar role in establishing social identities to the boundaries between clans that Durkheim identified in primitive societies. It was the contradictory but potentially socially 'disintegrating' effects of this specialization of knowledge creating communities and the absence of any overarching values that particularly concerned Durkheim. The pedagogic implications of the same developments were addressed by Bernstein in his well known analysis of 'collection' and 'integrated' curricula (Bernstein 1971).

It was context-independence as a truth criterion that Durkheim identified as the characteristic which, both in its primitive (sacred) form as religion and in its modern form as science, distinguishes knowledge from the everyday context-dependent understandings that we acquire through experience. The properties of context-independent knowledge are that (i) it can provide a basis for generalizations and explanations that go beyond specific cases (hence its paradigm case is the natural sciences), and (ii) it allows those who acquire it to develop the capacity to imagine alternatives.

From a Durkheimian perspective, the curriculum necessarily must involve access to context-independent knowledge. The questions that follow in relation to the debate about the post-16 curriculum are:

- What are the conditions for the acquisition of context-independent knowledge?
- How, if at all, are these conditions realized within a unified curriculum?

Bernstein and the post-16 curriculum

It was the English sociologist of education, Basil Bernstein, who developed the educational implications of Durkheim's ideas (Bernstein 1971, 2000). Like Durkheim, Bernstein emphasized the crucial link between knowledge and social identity (between what we know and who we are), and that identities are forged by boundaries between domains of knowledge and between knowledge and everyday experience. He introduced the concepts of *classification* and *framing* to describe how these two types of boundary can vary. As he expresses it, classifications and frames can be either *strong* or *weak*. Two implications follow the links that he makes between the identity of the learner and the acquisition of knowledge. First, it follows that the primary conditions for the acquisition and production of knowledge will be strong classification and strong framing. Second, we cannot avoid the reality that historical forms of strong classification and framing are found in the disciplines in universities and in the subjects in the school curriculum, nor can we ignore the socially distributive effects that they have had.

If Bernstein's theory is right, this can explain the resistance to unification and the persistence of academic/vocational divisions in all societies. Unless an alternative basis for learner identity is developed, unification is likely to generate a weakening of both teacher and student identities. A possible consequence of unification might be increased participation but with no parallel expansion of the acquisition of knowledge. This conclusion suggests a number of questions relevant to the unification of the post-16 curriculum.

1   How far are the principles of strong classification and strong framing at odds with the educational implications of global economic changes that emphasize a blurring of boundaries and the need for greater flexibility and openness to change?
2   If curriculum principles and economic pressures are at odds, should curriculum policy resist the pressure to blur knowledge boundaries, or should it adapt?
3   Is the *principle* of strong classification and framing no more than a historical legacy of early nineteenth-century modernization, and therefore potentially of decreasing relevance in the twenty-first century? Or is it the *form* that strong classification and framing has taken – namely the existing disciplines and subjects – that is the historical legacy?

If we accept the latter argument, the curriculum question becomes:

4   What are the twenty-first-century forms of strong classification and framing that support the link between identity and the acquisition of knowledge that Bernstein argues is so important, and what are the implications of this conclusion for such policies as widening participation?

Answers to these questions are sometimes seen as political. The argument in this chapter is that they will also depend on the view held about the specificity of formal education and its boundaries as conditions for knowledge acquisition.

I want to bear these questions in mind in returning to the debate about the unification of the post-16 curriculum that was referred to earlier in the chapter.

Social realist theory and the unification debate in post-16 education

The idea of a unified curriculum based on the principle of 'connective specialization' was developed, somewhat differently but on the same broad principles in Finegold *et al.* (1990), Young (1998), and Tomlinson (2004). A common theme in these texts was that a unified curriculum should involve four main elements:

- a single set of levels within which all modules would be located;
- subject and occupational field specifications which would be expressed as a single set of modules capable of being combined in different ways;
- rules of combination guiding student choice and the grouping of modules;
- a common core of 'connective' knowledge and skills that would be compulsory for all students.

These four elements of a unified post-16 curriculum were underpinned by the principle of connectivity (or connective specialization) which applied to each of the elements. In light of the arguments in the previous section, the problem is whether the principle of connective specialization can be the basis for developing the knowledge/identity link that Bernstein saw as crucial to learning and the acquisition of knowledge, and whether the links between modules, core and rules of combination can be an adequate basis for forging the learner identities that have traditionally been associated with subjects and occupational fields. If the idea of connective specialization cannot provide such a basis, a unified curriculum is likely to create problems, both for progression to higher levels of learning, and as the conditions for enhancing student motivation and wider participation.

It is possible to trace the origins of the concepts of connectivity and connective specialization in a number of ways. First, they can be seen as ways of expressing how digital technologies are creating possibilities for new kinds of 'horizontal' or non-hierarchical relationships between peers (Castells 1998). The new user-created web-based innovations such as MySpace and YouTube, and the recent enthusiasm for 'Mobile Learning' are good examples of these possibilities; what is more in question is in what sense they can claim to have any pedagogic potential (Young 2007). Second, connective specialization can be seen as an innovative way of addressing the dis-integrative tendencies identified long ago by Durkheim as a potential consequence of specialization and growth of the intellectual division of labour in modern societies. Durkheim identified corporatism, the professions and new forms of occupational association as possible sources of integration in modern societies in his time. However, by the 1990s these possibilities seemed too top-down and rigid to warrant development. Connectivity appeared to address the problem of integration in a more bottom-up and democratic way which had more affinity with the times. In its 'pure' form, modularization assumes that students have the capacity (and the right) to construct their own curriculum from some form of modular bank. The idea of connective specialization appeared to present a way of overcoming the potential fragmentation that this can lead to. It at least addresses, albeit without being specific, the neglect in modular curricula of the sequencing and coherence that are important features of all learning that is linked to the acquisition of knowledge. Some of the arguments for connective specialization were developed in *The Curriculum of the Future* (Young 1998).

From the social realist perspective developed in this book, the identity-generating possibilities of a curriculum based on connective specialization are unconvincing. In order to explore why this might be so, it is necessary to consider further the social basis of the concept of connectivity, and to ask whether they can provide the basis for:

1   replacing the rules and practices associated with subjects, disciplines and specialized occupational fields that have in the past provided the link between the knowledge to be acquired in the curriculum and the identities of teachers and students;
2   the links between the different modules that a student chooses and the rules for combining them;
3   the basis for what was referred to as 'core' or 'connective' knowledge and skills that might claim to be the twenty-first-century version of general education.

Bernstein does not discuss the idea of 'connectivity' as such. However, it has many similarities with the ideas of trainability and 'learning to learn' which he does discuss. In his analysis, both can be seen as forms of genericism (see Chapter 10) which have, as he puts it, 'an emptiness which makes the concept self-referential' (Bernstein 2000). Like other forms of genericism such as the fashionable notion of 'learning to learn', connectivity is explicitly not related to any specific body of knowledge. It follows that the concept is empty of knowledge content and, if we follow Bernstein's argument, 'the learner (or the teacher) will not be able to recognize her/himself and others in it' (Bernstein 2000; my addition in brackets); in other words it cannot be the basis for learner identities. The absence of any specific content associated with the concept of connective specialization suggests that while it may be an educational aspiration, it cannot be the basis for replacing subjects and disciplines in a modern curriculum. Connectivity is best seen as a loose but suggestive organizational metaphor that mirrors the kind of development in industry and commerce mapped out by writers such as Robert Reich (1991). It no doubt has links with developments in electronics and neuroscience, where it has a much more theoretically precise meaning. Not being located in a social theory of knowledge and its acquisition, they can have only a very limited value as a curriculum concept. Connective specialists operating as some form of curriculum coordinators would have an organizational and management base but no knowledge base for connecting modules from different domains or for developing a connective core. For similar reasons, the concept of connective specialization can do no more than point to the problems faced by students trying to relate theoretical to practical learning. On the other hand, without some overarching concept, the outcome of curriculum unification will inevitably be modular fragmentation for all but the few, and, most likely, new but less explicit divisions.

An alternative approach to the post-compulsory curriculum from a social realist approach to knowledge is begin with specialists in academic subjects and occupational fields (like engineering and business studies) and the scope they have for extending the role of their specialist knowledge. This might involve them collaborating with other specialists to develop new cross-disciplinary forms of specialization. Such an approach suggests that *innovation within specialist fields by specialists* rather than modularization and new forms of genericism are likely to be more reliable sources of curriculum innovation.

Implications for the vocational curriculum

In the previous section I argued that two implications follow from the social realist idea that knowledge is differentiated. The first is that unification, at least on the basis of connective specialization, is a misconceived approach to the reform of the post-16 curriculum. The second is that subject-based innovation will be the most reliable source of reform in the academic curriculum. The remaining issue that follows from a rejection of the unified model is a reconsideration of the vocational curriculum. This is discussed in some detail in Chapter 9, so I will only consider it briefly here insofar as it arises from the discussion of unification.

As I argued in Chapter 9, the vocational curriculum always has (or should have) two purposes: providing access to the (disciplinary) knowledge that is transforming work, and acquiring job-specific skills and knowledge. The former purpose relies on context-independent knowledge, whereas the latter will be context-specific and related to specific sectors and workplaces. It follows that there are specific curriculum and pedagogic issues that need to be addressed in relation to the vocational curriculum that are avoided by a unified model based on connective specialization. They are expressed by Barnett (2006) in the concept 'dual recontextualization'. This term refers to two processes. One is the *professional or vocational recontextualization* of disciplinary knowledge for occupationally specific purposes; examples are physics for physiotherapy or for engineering. This is undertaken by the respective professions involved. The second process is the *pedagogic recontextualization* of professional knowledge for pedagogic purposes. This refers to the sequencing and pacing of professional knowledge for different groups and levels of learners in ways that take account of the knowledge that students already have and the knowledge that they acquire that is specific to particular workplaces. Both these processes are deeply under-researched in comparison to the parallel process of recontextualizing disciplinary knowledge for pedagogic purposes within the general or academic curriculum.

Conclusions

In this chapter I have drawn on the social realist approach to knowledge developed in Part 1 of this book to argue that the unification of academic/vocational programmes that I and others argued for in the 1990s in England, and that was broadly accepted by the Tomlinson Report on 14–19 education in 2004, was misconceived as a basis for reforming the post-16 curriculum. The government alternative of retaining A-levels and establishing so-called specialist (vocational) diplomas, which I have not considered in this chapter, merely repeats past mistakes, and will inevitably leave vocational education as the low status, low quality alternative for those who are not accepted on A-level programmes (Weelahan 2007). Neither option offers an adequate basis for reforming either the general or the vocational curriculum.

In England there has been a strong political movement for unification within the education community since the early 1990s. It has been, I would argue, a 'coded' attempt to reduce or remove inequalities through educational reform. However, this movement, with which I was actively involved throughout the 1990s, forgot two important truths – one from sociology, and one from the approach to the curriculum developed in this book. From sociology it forgot that, as Bernstein once put it, 'education cannot compensate for society'. In the case under discussion in this chapter, academic/vocational divisions, which have their roots in the wider social divisions between mental and manual labour, cannot be overcome by a unified curriculum or qualification system. In the circumstances of this country, such a move could even exaggerate such divisions. From the perspective on the curriculum developed in this book, the 'unifiers' forgot that no reform, such as the combination of modularization and connectivity that neglects the centrality of the knowledge that it enables students to acquire, and the conditions that make that possible, will be viable educationally.

In terms of promoting greater social and educational equality, my argument is that the unification agenda has been a digression from the two major educational tasks that continue to face those of us involved in post-16 education in England. The first is the reform of the A-level-based curriculum that is now followed by nearly half of each cohort. Despite the recent expansion of the numbers of subjects taken, at least by a few, it remains one of the narrowest curricula for the age group in the world. The second and even more important task is the serious improvement of the knowledge base of the vocational programmes that are offered as alternatives to A-levels. When substantial progress has been made on each of these problems, and particularly when designers of vocational programmes take the question of knowledge seriously, academic/vocational divisions will as a consequence be less significant, and the issue of unification will be more straightforward.

12 Further education and training (FET) college teachers in South Africa and England

A knowledge-based profession of the future?

Introduction

This chapter is based on a paper first presented to a conference held in Pretoria for further education and training (FET) college principals and organized by the South African Department of Education and the Human Sciences Resources Council. However, as I hope the chapter will illustrate, although the circumstances and history of South Africa are in many ways unique, the issues facing those trying to reform further education are not (Young and Gamble 2006). A number of policy developments affecting FET colleges in South Africa, and the problems that they give rise to, have significant parallels with the situation in England. Furthermore, they raise many of the questions about the role of knowledge in vocational education that have been discussed in more theoretical terms in earlier chapters.

Apart from acting as an illustration of the importance of comparative studies, my reason for including this chapter is that it highlights the extent to which epistemological issues are not just questions of relevance to the curriculum issues but equally to the professional development of those who design and deliver the curriculum – in this case, the college teachers. In much of the literature, especially on professional development, these issues are rarely discussed.

There are a number of reasons why the future of the FET colleges in South Africa and those who teach in them is taking on a new importance, and these reasons have some parallels with the recent Foster and Leitch Reports in this country. First, a highly diverse range of colleges which had a history in the racial divisions of the apartheid era have been merged into a smaller number of large multi-site and multi-racial institutions. Second, there has been a substantial increase in funding for FET colleges (reflected in the Minister of Finance's Re-Capitalization Fund). Third, the colleges have been given a highly ambitious set of new goals by the Government. They include:

- access and widening participation;
- lifelong learning;
- contributing to national human resource development goals, especially for intermediate knowledge and skills;

- urban and rural renewal;
- the creation of a new citizenry.

The last of these goals is undoubtedly the most ambitious of them all.

Fourth, and of specific importance for this chapter, there is a further development that could have important implications for the colleges, which has no direct parallels in the UK. It is the publication of a curriculum policy and subject guidelines for the new National Certificate (Vocational) that will, by 2008, replace the old technical (NATED) certificates as the main qualification offered by FET colleges.

The new FET college curriculum

The publication of a new curriculum and subject guidelines for the National Certificate (Vocational) marks an important shift in policy on the part of the Department of Education. Since the election of South Africa's first democratic government in 1994, and prior to the new FET curriculum becoming national policy, it had been widely assumed that a new curriculum for the colleges was not necessary. As in the case of National Vocational Qualifications (NVQs) that were launched in the UK in 1987, it was assumed that colleges would be able to 'design down' their curriculum from national qualifications expressed in the form of unit standards (or outcomes).

In contrast with the outcomes-based qualifications designed within a framework developed by the South African Qualifications Authority (see Chapter 8 for an account of similar developments in the UK), where knowledge content is implicit and left up to teachers, the new curriculum policy is explicit in specifying the specialist knowledge associated with each occupational field to which the new certificate relates. It also makes clear that the acquisition of this knowledge will be assessed by a substantial component of external examinations.

It is worth stating the significance of the term 'curriculum' as it is expressed in the Department of Education's policy documents. It refers to the specification and sequencing, in terms of content, of the knowledge and skills that a learner is expected to have acquired if she/he is to be awarded a National Certificate (Vocational) in one of the 13 occupational fields. In South Africa, this represents a shift from an *outcomes-based* approach to vocational education, which blurs the distinction between qualifications and curriculum, to a *syllabus-based* approach, which recognizes the importance of the distinction. Much painful experience and wasting of resources, in the UK and elsewhere as well as in South Africa, has demonstrated that the 'designing down' approach, from outcomes or standards to a curriculum, is impossible. All that outcomes or standards on their own can lead to are largely arbitrary lists of topics, not a curriculum (see the chapters by Barnett and Allais in Young and Gamble (2006) for illustrations of this argument).

An important consequence of the publication of the new programmes for the National Certificate is that they reassert and redefine the distinctive vocational role of the FET colleges, and move beyond the increasingly circular debate in South Africa as to whether the FET colleges should develop vocational or occupational programmes, or both. This debate echoes the debate in the UK about the relative merits and purposes of National Vocational (occupational) Qualifications and General National Vocational Qualifications.

Several observations are worth making on the vocational/occupational distinction. First, to restate the point made in Chapter 9, for any country that is striving to be successful in the emerging knowledge economy, all vocational education programmes must 'face both ways' – towards the world of work and towards access to disciplinary knowledge. They must be vocational and develop employment-related knowledge and skills in specific occupational fields. They must also be educational in the sense of providing opportunities for both young people and older workers to acquire knowledge to which they may not have access in the workplace, and which will support their progress to further and higher education.

As the number of occupations that do not require discipline-based knowledge as well as skills acquired at work are becoming fewer, it follows that these two goals need to underpin all programmes offered by FET colleges. In effect, this means that the vocational/occupational distinction loses its meaning. Why then does it persist? There are three possibilities that are worth examining.

First, it is sometimes claimed that occupational qualifications defined in terms of job-related skills or competences will relate more directly to immediate employer needs. However, the skill (in the narrow sense of practical or manual skill) needs of different employers are highly specific, subject to change, and often better provided and, if necessary, assessed by the employers themselves. If, however, the definition of skill is broader, and is seen as having intellectual as well as practical aspects, the basis for the occupational/vocational distinction disappears. All modern vocational programmes, whether broadly defined or designed as preparation for specific occupations, must include both practical and theoretical knowledge and must involve college-based study as well as work experience.

A second possibility is that the vocational/occupational distinction is a legacy of a former era when in some occupational fields, especially the crafts, it was possible to acquire specific occupational competences in workplaces, sometimes supported by college-based programmes. In the UK, attempts have been made to reinvent a distinct occupational route through new-style apprenticeships and what are known as foundation (in effect two-year) degrees; both have some parallels with what in South Africa are known as Learnerships. In the UK the new apprenticeships have had, at best, mixed results, varying in quality enormously across sectors.

A third possibility is that a strong emphasis on the knowledge base of vocational programmes, as in the policy and guidelines for the new National Certificate (Vocational), will come up against a lack of teachers in the colleges with the appropriate specialist vocational knowledge. This may well be the reality in many colleges in South Africa, as it is in England. However, offering narrower, skill-based, occupationally specific programmes in colleges does not seem to be a solution. FE colleges in South Africa, as in other countries, will never be able to offer skills training that is geared to specific workplaces. Such skills, where they are needed, are better offered in the workplace. The problem in South Africa, as in England, is still a lack of demand among employers for higher qualified employees.

As has frequently been argued by Keep and others (Keep 2006), improving employer demand will require changes in industrial policy and in employer attitudes to productivity, rather than just changes in what colleges offer. The colleges, I argue, in South Africa and in rather different circumstances in the UK, have to concentrate on their distinctive role as institutions for vocational education. In South Africa the terms for this role are set out clearly in the new curriculum policy.

The Department of Education's subject guidelines for the new National Vocational Certificate are consistent with this view of the major vocational role of the FET colleges. It follows that, from a college perspective, the vocational/occupational distinction is of no relevance.

The remainder of this chapter is concerned with the conditions for developing, among existing and future FET college staff, in both their initial training and further professional development, the knowledge and skills that they will need in delivering the new curriculum.

The professional development of FET college teachers: a history of neglect[1]

In the UK and in South Africa there are a number of reasons why the professional education and development of FET college staff have been and still are neglected. The most important are detailed below.

- The generally low status of FET colleges: this may partly account for why, in South Africa and until recently in the UK, universities have been reluctant to offer programmes for future teachers in the colleges.
- The absence of links between FET colleges and universities: this absence of FET college/university links underpins the lack of knowledge and experience of FET colleges among university-based teacher educators and educational researchers and university teachers more generally.
- FET college recruitment policies: in the absence in South Africa of well defined programmes of initial training for future teachers in FET colleges, staff tend to be recruited from the schools and sometimes directly from industry.
- The inflexibility of block release programmes: the block release legacy in South Africa has meant that industrial experience has been given greater importance than specialist pedagogic knowledge as the primary qualification for an FET college lecturer, especially in technical fields.
- The assumption that qualifications can be adequately defined in terms of their outcomes: in outcomes-driven systems of vocational education, like that associated with NVQs and GNVQs in the UK, and similar qualifications approved by SAQA (South African Qualifications Authority) that have, until the new policy, shaped the FET college curriculum, the emphasis is placed on teachers as assessors, rather than on the need to enhance their pedagogic and curriculum knowledge.

Reasserting the 'vocational education' role of FET colleges

The argument of this chapter has been that the new curriculum policy in South Africa places a premium on the reassertion of the vocational education role of colleges. Apart from the different age distribution of their students, it is this vocational role that distinguishes colleges from schools (except for the small number of technical schools) in South Africa, as in the UK. In many European countries where academic/vocational divisions are less shaped by social class differences, the equivalent institutions to South Africa's FET colleges and the UK's FE Colleges are known as vocational colleges.

Although the vocational role of colleges is not new, the meaning of vocational education has changed radically since the early block-release programmes that were tied largely to engineering apprenticeships. First, vocational education is increasingly pre-employment and full time, rather than supporting employment and part time. Second, the dual purposes of vocational education are beginning to be recognized (see Chapter 9). These are the acquisition of occupationally related knowledge and skills, and the acquisition of knowledge as a basis for progression to higher education or new occupations. The growing emphasis on the second of these two purposes of vocational education arises from changes in the global economy that are affecting all countries. Traditional occupations are disappearing faster, and new knowledge-based occupations, in which both knowledge and skills have a much shorter 'shelf life', are increasingly common. Third, the range of occupations for which colleges now prepare students has broadened significantly.

The implication of this redefinition of vocational education is that FET college teachers need to be specialists in a number of senses. First, they must be specialists in areas of knowledge related to specific occupational fields such as construction, financial services, tourism, electronics, etc. It follows that it is increasingly likely that they will be graduates in a technological or other professional field of knowledge. Second, they will not just have graduated in a specialist field such as electronics or finance; they will have gained experience in using their knowledge in a number of specific workplaces. This means that prior to becoming an FET college teacher, they will have had some industrial or commercial experience linked to their prior studies. Third, they will be specialist vocational teachers in particular areas of the curriculum. This means that they will need to be familiar not only with the content and philosophy of the new curriculum and how it may need to change, but also with its implications for teaching, learning and assessment in their specialist field. For example, teaching marketing or business administration raises quite different pedagogic and assessment issues to teaching plumbing or electrical installation. It is this specialist pedagogic knowledge that college teachers will need to acquire, either before they join the staff of a college or, at least in the next few years, as part of their professional development.

This outline of the professional needs of FET college teachers, if the aims of the new curriculum are to be realized, raises profound issues for educational policy makers. The next section of the chapter explores some of these issues, and examines a number of possible models for professional development.

Models for the professional education of FET college lecturers

The previous section outlined the combination of subject and pedagogic knowledge that FET lecturers will need if they are to deliver the new curriculum. This section considers how and where that knowledge might be acquired, both in initial training and in further professional development. It draws on the UK experience and considers four possible models and their advantages and disadvantages.

The National Institute model

A number of European and other countries have established a National Institute for Vocational Education, with responsibility both for the vocational curriculum and for the training and professional development of vocational teachers. Such an institute has the advantage of consolidating national expertise, and appears to work well in countries with a well developed vocational curriculum, and where the level of expertise in vocational pedagogy is relatively high, as in the case of a number of former East European Communist countries. Establishing such an institute in South Africa would, however, depend on recruiting from the small existing pool of professional expertise in the colleges and universities. With limited expertise, it would be difficult for such an institute to establish a professional as opposed to a bureaucratic relationship with FET colleges and their staff. Furthermore, it would continue to separate vocational education and vocational teachers from the rest of the educational community, and would do little to encourage the development of research in vocational education in the universities.

The college-based model

This model has parallels with school-based initial teacher training. Individual FET colleges, and groups of colleges, would be encouraged to develop programmes in vocational pedagogy through which their existing and future staff would obtain their professional development. The advantage of this model is that, as in the case of many professions, it gives responsibility to colleges and their staff for their own professional development. However, it has two important disadvantages. First, with a substantially new curriculum, few FET colleges are likely to have the appropriate expertise and, if so, only in some vocational fields. Second, it would mean that, as in the UK, where there are many examples of the model in use, those training to become FET teachers would continue to be cut off from the rest of the education community, and would have few opportunities for progression to higher level professional studies. Furthermore, as in the case of the National Institute model, it would do little to encourage research in vocational education in the universities, or to promote university/college links.

The university-based model

The university-based model, which has expanded considerably in the UK in the past decade, is based on existing models for the university-based professional development of school teachers, and begins with the advantage of having access to the pedagogic expertise of university education departments. It assumes that future FET college teachers will have specialist qualifications in a professional or vocational field, and would then complete a further diploma at a university, which would focus on developing the pedagogic knowledge and skills that they would need in order to teach the new vocational curriculum.

The problem with the model is that few academics in university education departments in South Africa (as was and to some extent still is the case in the UK) have *vocational* pedagogic expertise or experience of FET colleges. Academics in university education departments are either specialists in educational studies or in one of the subjects of the school curriculum. In the UK, courses for those preparing to teach in FE colleges tend to be generic rather than vocationally specific, and therefore leave their students relatively unprepared for their new role. Furthermore, opportunities for FET lecturers to progress to higher degrees in aspects of their specialist field are likely to be limited.

The university/college partnership model

This model is a modification of the previously discussed university-based model that aims to take account of its strengths and weaknesses. The model has been widely adopted in the UK, where it has usually involved a partnership between a university education department and a group of colleges. A typical division of labour between the institutions has been that the university education department specializes in the broad professional educational issues involved in becoming a teacher, and the colleges are responsible for developing the student's specialist vocational pedagogy.

The major problem with how the model has been developed in the UK has been that FET colleges rarely have the resources and expertise in vocational pedagogy to take on the role prescribed for them. As a result, the students do not have the opportunity to develop their specialist vocational pedagogy. Furthermore, the division of labour between colleges and universities does not encourage research and development in specialist fields of vocational pedagogy.[2]

A recent Ofsted Inspection Report[3] highlighted major weaknesses in all FE teacher training provision in the UK that, if repeated in South Africa, would profoundly limit the ability of the FET colleges to deliver the new curriculum. A key weakness identified by Ofsted was the absence in even the best university/college partnership programmes of any systematic approach to specialist vocational pedagogy. In the UK, very little attention is given to developing the specialist vocational knowledge and skills of future college teachers. The assumption of university/college partnership programmes that the Ofsted Inspection Report calls into question is that FET lecturers can rely on a combination of generic pedagogic knowledge acquired in the university and the ad hoc vocationally specific skills that they pick up during their teaching practice in colleges.

Options for the professional development of FET college teachers in South Africa

My conclusion from an examination of the four models is that while the university/college partnership model offers the best possibilities for professional development of college teachers, the form it has taken in the UK needs significant modifications if it is to prepare them to deliver the new South African vocational curriculum. In this section I will suggest two possible ways in which the university/college partnership model might be modified to take into account the importance of future college teachers developing their specialist vocational pedagogic knowledge and skills. Both their relevance and the difficulties in introducing them are, I would argue, as applicable to the UK as to South Africa.

The first possibility would involve a research-based university with strong departments in professional fields such as engineering, IT, agriculture and law, as well as in education. Programmes for FET college teachers would need to include staff not only from the university's education department and the colleges, but also from departments in a range of specialist professional fields. At least in theory, such programmes would not only strengthen the specialist knowledge base of FET teacher education curriculum; it would also help establish vocational education as a cross-disciplinary field for applied educational research and higher degrees in the universities involved. The major problem is that in both South Africa and the UK, there is virtually no experience or history of departments such as engineering and other technical and commercial fields being involved in the preparation of college teachers. This lack of a tradition of inter-departmental collaboration is likely to be compounded by the way universities are funded, for both teaching and research. A collaborative initiative between several departments would probably require a substantial source of funds from outside the university. Another possible explanation for the absence of any involvement by other professional departments in teacher education is the strength of boundaries between disciplinary fields in the university, as well as, no doubt, the historically low status of the FET curriculum as a field for research and teaching in both countries.

A slightly different and possibly more feasible option would be to establish partnerships between colleges and the 'new' universities in the UK,[4] and the universities of technology and comprehensive universities in South Africa. Several of the latter, which arose from mergers of the former technikons (polytechnics), have education departments and departments in a range of applied professional areas such as management, IT, agriculture and engineering that cover many if not all of the 13 fields of curriculum for the new National Certificate (Vocational). They are likely to be less resistant than the research-based universities to cross-departmental collaboration.

Conclusions

I have argued that if colleges are to deliver the new National Certificate (Vocational) curriculum, they must not only be familiar with the new curriculum and its pedagogic demands, but must also be clear about the new meaning of the vocational role of colleges. Second, I have argued that if the new curriculum is to become a reality, systematic attention needs to be given to the professional development of FET college teaching staff. Third, by contrasting the strengths and weaknesses of a number of different models, I have suggested two possible approaches through which FET college lecturers might become, as the title of the chapter suggests, members of a knowledge-based profession. I am aware that such proposals have considerable resource implications, at which I have only hinted. They would also require a change of attitudes, especially within universities, but no doubt within the colleges as well. If there is a positive lesson from the UK experience to draw on, it is that university prejudices about further education are at least reduced when new funding opportunities become available.

Reflecting on the immense barriers that are likely to face any attempt to implement the relatively modest proposals made in this chapter for the reform of the training of FET college teachers in South Africa and in England raises a more theoretical point. The likely difficulties facing the proposed reforms highlight the contrast between the UK and South Africa and a country like Germany. A number of the most prestigious German universities have longstanding faculties of vocational education, undertaking research into vocational pedagogy in specialist fields such as electronics, manufacturing technology and business administration, and offering programmes in vocational education up to doctorate level. A comparative/historical study of the 'peculiarities' of the English tradition of the liberal university, which in many ways South Africa has inherited, would go some way to explain such sharp divergences between countries that are in other ways at similar stages of development.

13 Experience as knowledge?

The case of the recognition of prior learning (RPL)

Introduction

This chapter is concerned with an issue that lies at the heart of this book – the boundaries between everyday or experiential learning and formal education. An earlier version was written as a contribution to a book entitled *Re-theorising the Recognition of Prior Learning* (Andersson and Harris 2006). For a sociologist who has not worked in the field of adult education, and has only been very marginally involved in RPL itself, I found the collection of papers refreshing and provocative even when I disagreed with some of the arguments. Many of the papers give insights into the dilemmas and difficulties faced by RPL practitioners in a range of different countries. However, they also provide concrete and specific ways of raising the much broader educational issues concerned with learning, knowledge and pedagogic authority which other chapters of this book have tried to address.

Andersson and Harris's book is far from typical of most publications on RPL and adult education that I have come across. The difference is exemplified in a number of ways. First, the book locates its discussion of RPL in a critique of the philosophies of experientialism, constructivism and progressivism that have dominated adult education as a field of educational studies. As a result, the book reminds readers of the narrow and insulated intellectual world that adult educators have been a part of and have tended to take for granted. Second, it demonstrates that RPL, like most apparently quite specific educational practices, can also be a lens, or perhaps more accurately, a specific case, which can illustrate questions about the purposes and practices of education more generally. Third, the book argues that like progressivism and learner-centred pedagogies, RPL did not become popular with policy makers just because of the educational goals associated with it. Although RPL, especially in the USA and South Africa, has been associated with political movements for social justice, redistribution and redress, it is economic forces and the need to maximize the human capital within the workforce that have led governments to support the recognition and accreditation of informal learning as a relatively low-cost basis for fast-track routes into higher education for adults.

Fourth, despite recognizing the potential of RPL and the wider provision of adult education for promoting social justice, the book does not treat them as moral and political goods that are almost beyond criticism except within very limited parameters. Fifth, most RPL practice assumes the equivalence of experiential and formal learning; the only problem that frequently appears to follow is how this equivalence is demonstrated and accredited. The book calls into question the issue of equivalence, and presents RPL as a complex and often contradictory set of practices at the interface between formal education and people's everyday experience. Operating at this interface, the example of RPL reminds us of the inequalities and distributive effects of both formal education and people's everyday experience, and forces us to ask when and under what circumstances the former can overcome or merely affirm the inequalities of the latter.

In challenging the educational hierarchy between formal and informal knowledge, RPL is unequivocally an example of the application of 'standpoint theory' that was discussed in Chapter 2. In other words, it is a claim to knowledge based on the experience of the claimant rather than on the knowledge itself. This is an understandable position to take for those who have been excluded from access to academic knowledge. It is less clear that such debunking of formal knowledge by RPL practitioners, themselves often based in universities and with university degrees, is in the interests of those who have been excluded.

RPL is also a challenge to what I have in an earlier chapter referred to as the 'educational common sense' that assumes that formal education has some kind of monopoly in providing access to the powerful knowledge that is unavailable from everyday experience.

There is a contradiction that lies at the heart of the RPL project that is highlighted in Andersson and Harris's book. First, there is a tension between the *recognition* of how someone has learned from experience and whether such recognition requires assessment and *accreditation*. If recognizing that valuable learning can be based on experience is the main goal of RPL, this goal could be undermined by a strategy which (i) seeks to accredit that learning, and (ii) seeks to demonstrate by accreditation that learning from experience is, or can be, of equal value to formal academic learning. The intrinsic value of the learning acquired through experience is in effect denied. Furthermore, there is evidence (Grugulis 2003) that the process of accreditation itself can destroy what is specific to learning from experience, or can undermine the learner's confidence in the learning they have gained from experience. Finally, if 'parity of esteem' between formal and experiential learning is the basic assumption of RPL, why would RPL practitioners want the latter to be an access route to higher education?

The counter view derived from the arguments in this book is that 'parity of esteem' is an inappropriate goal where real differences between types of learning are involved and that it can lead to the undervaluing of both. On the other hand, starting from the differences between formal and experiential learning and the knowledge that can be acquired in each case is not the same as arguing that one is better than the other in some absolute sense. Two conclusions follow. First, they have different but non-reducible purposes. Second, each can be a resource for the other but is not replaceable by it. A useful distinction that follows from this argument for differences rather than parity is between two strategies: *RPL for access* and *RPL for credit* that leads to qualifications. There is evidence from a number of countries that access courses which build on experience (RPL for access) have provided important new routes for adults into higher education (Gallagher 2006); there is far less evidence that RPL-based qualifications on their own (RPL for credit) bring similar benefits or are ever treated as equivalent to qualifications obtained through courses of study.

An important advantage of focusing on a specific set of practices such as RPL is that issues such as the confrontation between adult experience and specialist or academic knowledge which are often debated within educational theory are considered in the very practical contexts faced by those involved. This is in sharp contrast to much debate about the politics of educational research, when such issues tend to be raised in highly abstract ways that are very difficult to relate to any specific educational practice. This is as true of the rather esoteric debates about postmodernism in educational research as it is of the more overtly political debates such as those concerned with the work of the Italian Marxist and educational theorist, Antonio Gramsci. To paraphrase Harold Entwistle's argument, 'in order to be a political radical, do you, like Gramsci, have to be an educational conservative?'(Entwistle 1979). Whether or not one accepts Entwistle's interpretation of Gramsci as an educational conservative, RPL forces one to ask what exactly such categories as 'radical' and 'conservative' might mean in educational terms. Is RPL a way of opening access to academic knowledge, or of undermining it, and which of these are radical? Is it a way of opening up higher education to a wider range of people's experience? If so, why would one want to do this and in what sense could it still be claimed to be higher? Or more radically, is RPL the beginning of a new 'transformative' pedagogy and curriculum that integrates theory (or specialist knowledge) and experience, or is it even the beginning of the end of specialized institutions for learning? In the remaining part of this chapter, I want, albeit indirectly, to address these questions by considering a number of issues which I think RPL forces us to consider. These issues concern the role of knowledge, specialization, politics, authority and qualifications.

RPL and knowledge

A core dilemma for RPL practitioners which has up to now gone largely unrecognized is the discrepancy between the codified knowledge that can be acquired through formal education and the experiential knowledge that RPL practitioners seek to accredit. Recognizing prior experiential learning as a pedagogic strategy cannot be an educational goal in itself; it can only be a step towards providing access to knowledge that takes learners beyond their experience. The question of the relationship between knowledge and experience is as old as education itself. It is both an epistemological issue (where does 'true' knowledge come from?) and a pedagogic issue (how do we enable learners to acquire knowledge that takes them beyond their experience?). RPL dramatizes these issues; it is not a short cut to resolving them. I have referred to the approach to these issues proposed in this book as social realism: it stresses the externality of knowledge that is separate from the processes of knowing and learning. However, realist approaches have a tendency to equate knowledge with natural science and to accept an unresolved dualism between knowledge and the world and, therefore, theory from practice. It follows that while such a realist theory can suggest the basis for a curriculum which distinguishes theoretical and everyday knowledge, it is not an adequate basis for a pedagogy which seeks to overcome such a separation. As a consequence, a curriculum policy based on social realism can appear to differ little from one derived from an a-social and ultimately conservative epistemology. Chapters 3 and 4 attempted to overcome the problem of dualism between mind and world by recognizing the pre-conceptual nature of the external world and therefore, in Vygotsky's terms, the embeddedness of theoretical concepts in the everyday world. However, by not addressing the disembeddedness as well as the embeddedness of both theoretical and everyday concepts, interpretations of Vygotsky easily slip into a sophisticated form of relativism. Further research on the relationship between 'recognition' and accreditation in RPL practice could make a valuable contribution to the these difficult issues as well as to the viability of RPL itself as a pedagogic strategy.

RPL and specialization

Most RPL practitioners seek to challenge what they see as the dominance of specialist (or academic) knowledge and, by implication, the dominance of specialist educational institutions. They appear ambivalent about whether RPL should provide a more inclusive access route to specialist educational institutions or an opportunity to undermine their dominance. From the point of view adopted in this book, the issue for RPL practitioners is clear. Specialization in education as in other fields has been a crucial factor in the modernization of societies and in the improvement of people's quality of life. This process has, however, also created barriers and boundaries which at the same time have helped preserve inequalities and privileges. One of the positive outcomes of RPL strategies is that they can force educational gatekeepers to be more explicit about the grounds of their pedagogic practice and the purposes of the boundaries that they seek to defend. It may be that boundaries are defended because programmes are oversubscribed; this then becomes a political issue concerning the distribution of resources rather than a pedagogic issue. On the other hand, defence of academic boundaries may be a form of inertia or occupational conservatism, which needs to be challenged. However, it is also possible that certain students are excluded on the grounds that they lack the prior specialist knowledge to benefit from a particular programme. In such cases excluding some students maybe a positive step in their further learning and a basis for genuine opportunities for others; in such cases, exclusion needs to be defended.

RPL and politics

Most RPL programmes have arisen from concerns about social justice and the lack of educational opportunities experienced by many adults (Harris 2006).

The dilemma that this can pose for all teachers, but is often starker for RPL practitioners, is where broader political issues end, and where issues that are specific to education begin. Not so long ago, the phrase 'the personal is the political' was popular on the Left, and played an important role in broadening definitions of 'the political', especially in relation to gender relations. However, the only societies where the personal and the political have actually been fused, such as Stalinist Russia and Nazi Germany, have been highly authoritarian and left very little space for the personal or the political. Learning is a social process but this does not mean that it can be treated as solely a political process. It is public policies about learning and those they support and those they neglect that make learning political. RPL practitioners have to resist the over-politicization of learning, and the potential of the language of radical politics to mask the necessary conditions for teaching and learning.

RPL and qualifications

Policies for RPL have developed in parallel with the growing interest on the part of governments in expanding the numbers of people gaining qualifications (see Harris 2006 and Chapter 8 in this book). RPL appeals to governments as a cheap way of enabling adults with considerable life and work experience to gain qualifications without attending school or college. From the point of view of the adults, RPL provides an opportunity to have their existing skills and knowledge officially recognized. The idea that some people may be 'qualified' in the sense of being capable and knowledgeable, even though they lack any formal qualifications, is important. However, it does not necessarily follow that they should be persuaded to have their experience formally accredited. The assumption that adults always stand to benefit if the knowledge and skills that they have acquired during their life is accredited as a qualification neglects what can happen to learning and experience when it is transformed into a qualification by an RPL process. It may be that the strengths it had in being unaccredited (and by definition not formalized) may be lost in the RPL process. On the other hand, the knowledge acquired in completing the accreditation process may have little to do with the practice that the qualification claims to refer to (Grugulis 2003).

Conclusions

The general point I have tried to make in this chapter is that RPL is not only a practice that needs retheorizing, as Andersson and Harris's (2006) book asserts. It is a practice that offers the possibility of new theorizing. Questions about knowledge, authority, qualifications and different types of learning have recurred in this book. Too easily they are treated as the 'givens' of formal education. If RPL can be freed from its largely rhetorical role as *the* radical strategy for overcoming inequalities among adults, it can be seen to offer a unique and very concrete set of contexts for exploring the fundamental differences between lived experience and theoretical knowledge, and the pedagogic strategies that might be developed to bridge them.

14 The knowledge question and the future of education in South Africa

Introduction

This chapter began as a response to Elana Michelson's (2004) critique of Joe Muller's book *Reclaiming Knowledge* (2000), and in particular his approach to knowledge, and its implications for the future of South African education. I have two related purposes in revising the paper for this book. The first is that despite being located in the South African context, Muller's book raises much more general issues and, as will have been apparent in Chapters 3, 5 and 7, have much influenced my own thinking. Furthermore, it is not insignificant that I have included our joint paper for the recent World Congress of Sociology as the final chapter of this book. Second, the example of educational reform in South Africa, while interesting in itself and as an example of a country in 'political transition',[1] illustrates the extent to which apparently abstract and academic debates about knowledge are not just the luxuries of intellectuals in countries with relatively well developed educational systems; they have a real significance for what happens in thousands of school classrooms.

The chapter begins by providing a brief account of the political and educational context in which the arguments about knowledge arose in South Africa. As I suggested in Chapter 12, it is a particularly important time for the issue of knowledge to be at the centre of educational debates in South Africa. The Minister is in her second year of office, the senior officials in the Department of Education are all still relatively new, and the impact of the newly established Quality Assurance and Qualifications Authority for general and further education, UMALUSI, is only beginning to be felt in the schools, colleges and provincial departments of education. None of this new educational leadership was associated with the policies on curriculum and qualifications that have had such a checkered and contested history in South Africa since 1994 (see Chapter 7). Furthermore, there appears to be a new willingness within national government, and among those working in education at other levels, to question ideas that were previously taken for granted. The three most significant examples in relation to policies that were largely accepted after 1994 are (i) that the curriculum can be based on outcomes or standards, (ii) that educational policy should be driven by qualifications, and (iii) that education and training can be seamlessly 'integrated'.[2]

With the benefit of the growing distance in time from the apartheid era, albeit with the awareness of its continued legacy of inequalities, it has become more possible to recognize its evils without assuming that all educational provision in that period must be dismissed as irredeemably racist. Three examples will illustrate this point. First, by 1990, the apprenticeship system, although originally reserved for white workers, was beginning to be opened up to Africans. Second, the 'matric' examination, despite excluding the majority of (but certainly not all) Africans, was a tried and trusted system that was not so different from the examinations systems found in other countries. Third, the newly elected democratic government inherited a tradition of good quality technical education in the colleges, which were beginning to become more diverse in their intake. The outcomes of Government policies in a number of areas show signs that the goal of achieving a more just and fair system does not always or necessarily mean a completely different system.

In this context, the role of educational research and theory takes on a new significance, not as perhaps was assumed in the period leading up to democracy (1990–1994), by providing new policy proposals, but as I argued in Chapter 7, by providing intellectual spaces within which alternative policies and their possible consequences can be evaluated and debated. The disagreements between Michelson and Muller which are the main theme of this chapter provide an excellent illustration of why such spaces are necessary.

In the post-1994 period in South Africa, there was an understandable attempt to establish a new and different system, completely free from the legacy of apartheid. Not only were words changed – students became learners and teachers became educators – but those elements of the previous system such as a curriculum with prescribed content and an inspection system which had taken explicitly authoritarian and oppressive forms under apartheid were rejected in principle as inescapably racist. At the same time, policy makers were left with the question of what kind of new system was needed that could provide real opportunities for the many and not just the few. A single system that did away with the previous 18 racially based departments was an obvious first step. However, in setting out the principles on which the new provincial departments should develop, the policy makers went further. They wanted not only to reject racial discrimination, but to reject any divisions between types of learners and types of learning. It followed logically that credit should be given to all the previously unrecognized skills and experiences that had been acquired by those (mostly, but not only Africans) who had previously been denied formal education. It appeared equally obvious (at least to some) that a single qualifications framework and a curriculum expressed in terms of outcomes would be the most effective method for achieving a more equal system.

Not surprisingly, policy makers looking for alternatives turned to a range of overseas models untainted by apartheid. They drew on ideas about qualifications from the UK and New Zealand, and an outcomes-based approach to the school curriculum from the USA.[3] The result of such policies, as has been increasingly widely accepted in South Africa (Jansen and Christie 1999), was confusion among teachers trying to devise lesson plans on the basis of outcomes, and a bureaucratic and jargonized qualifications system (Allais 2003). The new policies shared a scepticism about any forms of educational tradition or authority associated with the past, such as that of school subject specialists, and about the idea of disciplined or systematic knowledge that was not located in practice, or could not be shown to be directly relevant to some practical outcome. They also shared an uncritical faith in (i) the capacities of individual learners when freed from any external constraints (Muller 2000), (ii) the possibility of stating formal criteria that could be reliably used to map (and therefore assess) individual performance, and (iii) the possibility that any educational goal could be broken up into 'units' of learning activity and 'put together' again by the learner.

It was in part to challenge this orthodoxy that the essays Muller brought together in *Reclaiming Knowledge* were written. In my view it is his (and others') theoretical work, some important empirical research, and the practical experience of many teachers and lecturers of the non-viability of a curriculum and qualifications system based on such assumptions, that has led to the present rethinking among policy makers. Michelson's paper can be seen, at least in part, as a defence of the post-1994 innovations. That, then, is the context, theoretical and practical, in which I want to locate my discussion of the disagreements between Michelson and Muller.

Both Muller's book and Michelson's critique are engaged primarily in theoretical debates; they are not pitched at the level of specific policies. Muller does discuss important issues such as the NQF and literacy policy, but primarily to illustrate the relevance of his theory. Michelson's primary target is Muller's defence of the boundaries between formal and informal knowledge as an inescapable basis for the curriculum; she sees a focus on the defence of boundaries as inhibiting the task of addressing what to her are the more important questions about how such boundaries can be overcome. Muller's target is 'social constructivism', not as Michelson sees it – from her New York university base, as 'the vast and scholarly literature ... which has consistently distinguished itself from the kind of epistemological relativism that holds all accounts of the world as equally valid' (Michelson 2004) – but as an ideology with lived material consequences in South Africa (and, although usually with less acute consequences, elsewhere). In a sense, therefore, her critique is beside the point, and passes his arguments by. It does not matter that many social constructivists may be, as she claims, nuanced in how far they will push the socially constructed nature of knowledge. Nor does it matter that not all constructivists would agree with Harry Collins when he wrote that 'the natural world has a small or non-existent role in the construction of scientific knowledge' (Collins 1981).

The point that Durkheim made about pragmatism, which was developed earlier and is taken further in the final chapter of this book, is relevant here. As an ideology or even as a set of ideas, social constructivism was undoubtedly progressive in its origins. However, there is much evidence that it can have deeply conservative consequences in practice (Muller 2000), as, for example, Gramsci showed in his account of the Gentile reforms in post First World War Italy (Gramsci 1971). Donna Haraway may, as quoted by Michelson, combine in one sentence the 'radical historical contingency of all knowledge claims' with a 'no-nonsense commitment to faithful accounts of a "real" world'; however, such a combination of opposites would be impossible if she was a curriculum developer, teacher or policy maker. Furthermore, some knowledge claims, such as Euclid's axiom that parallel lines do not meet, are not *historically or socially contingent* except in very specific conditions in outer space, and these are conditions of which physicists have very precise knowledge.

My concern, in relation to educational policies in South Africa, is that the ideology of social contructivism, partly through its superficial radicalism and partly though its association with progressive political movements, is in danger of taking on a kind of political correctness. For example, the new National Qualifications Framework is defended uncritically by some as a 'social construct' created by the democratic movement. The inclusion of indigenous knowledge in the curriculum specifications for school science can be similarly justified. In the end, such political correctness is doing no favours to the cultural importance of indigenous knowledge in the new South Africa, let alone to the opportunities for school students to learn what science is about and why it is important.

Michelson devotes nearly half of her paper to challenging Muller's use of Valerie Walkerdine's research (Walkerdine 1988) to support his case for rejecting informal or experiential knowledge as the basis of the curriculum. This is not the place to go into their competing interpretations of Walkerdine's text in any detail. My own view is that Walkerdine and Muller are not as much at odds on the role of informal knowledge as Michelson would suppose. Michelson collapses the categories of curriculum and pedagogy, and whereas pedagogy is Walkerdine's primary concern, Muller's is the curriculum. Pedagogy has to start with the learner (and his or her everyday knowledge) as well as the curriculum. The curriculum, however, with which Muller is concerned, is about educational purposes; it must start with (formal) knowledge that is to be acquired. Walkerdine, as both Muller and Michelson recognize, accepts this when she writes that 'the existence of exclusive domains of discursive activity [such as mathematics] is a *sine qua non* [for the curriculum]' (Walkerdine quoted in Michelson (2004); my additions in brackets). Without such an assumption about school knowledge, it is unclear how either teachers or students would know where they were going or what they were trying to teach or learn. A major problem with trying to base a curriculum on outcomes (what in South Africa is known as OBE, or outcomes-based education) is that it assumes that the idea of a syllabus is a relic of apartheid to be done away with. As a result, in effect, OBE does away with any idea of a curriculum at all.

A further strand of Michelson's critique of Muller's ideas is what she sees as his over-emphasis on the idea of knowledge boundaries. She focuses specifically on his interpretation of Bernstein's concepts of classification and framing. First, she claims that whereas Bernstein uses the idea of boundary for progressive purposes, in Muller's hands it leads to 'far more conservative conclusions'. Bernstein is a notoriously elusive writer, but I know no textual basis for the distinction that she seeks to make. For example, in some of his earlier papers Bernstein warns against the seductions of progressive pedagogy and integrated curricula as strategies for promoting greater equality (Bernstein 1971, 1990). It is not clear if

Michelson has actually read much of Bernstein's work. My conclusion is that she failed to recognize the analytical character of both Bernstein's and Muller's distinctions. For example, for Bernstein, vertical and horizontal knowledge structures do not describe different types of knowledge. Verticality refers to features found to a different degree in all claims to knowledge; it is, in Max Weber's sense of the term, an 'ideal type'. The important point, which Michelson avoids, is the range of empirical inquiries (ironically, several are referenced by her and deal with her own specialist field of experiential learning (see Andersson and Harris 2006)) that Bernstein's theory has generated.

A final strand of Michelson's critique of Muller that I want to consider is her claim that his book can be seen as an expression of 'South African exceptionalism'. Her argument is not only that South African history is unique, but that

> the attention to epistemological dualisms in the literature of experiential learning and the preoccupation with gate-keeping are a specifically South African phenomenon. They are not present in the extensive international literature that has come out of the US, Canada, Britain, Australia, and New Zealand, ... [this] attention to gate-keeping and the insistence on the purity of knowledge-domains may also reflect a defensiveness that is a product of the historical moment in which South African academics find themselves, in which the movement for a more just South Africa in which, to their credit, many of them participated, has, as it were, moved closer: out of the halls of government and into the classroom in ways they are not fully able to control.
> (quoted in Michelson 2004 from an unpublished thesis)

What is meant by the last sentence is far from clear. It strikes me that it would be easier to find evidence for a quite different explanation of why a number of South African researchers have turned to epistemological critiques of social contructivism. To take one example, they make sense, as Muller demonstrates in his book, of the confusion among teachers that has been generated by an outcomes-based curriculum which leaves them bereft of the resources of a syllabus.

An additional observation on Michelson's argument about South African exceptionalism relates to the substance of Muller's theory itself. She claims that there is no debate about the epistemological basis of experiential learning outside South Africa. This is just plain wrong or, at best, an incredibly narrow reading of the literature that says more about her own insularity in the world of North American adult education than about the issues concerning boundaries and epistemology. Martin Jay offers a possible explanation of this narrowness when he argues that America has always been a 'culture of experience' (see Eagleton 2005).

What, then, are we to make of Michelson's critique of Muller, and where does it leave us? Clearly, Muller's book irritated her and caused her problems. His arguments did not fit well with her idea of what it meant to be a radical intellectual in South Africa. Furthermore, his defence of the educational case for strong knowledge boundaries casts serious doubt on policies which see the recognition of experiential learning, a particular focus of Michelson's work in South Africa, as offering any sort of long term strategy for promoting greater equality (a point that I elaborated on in Chapter 13). On a broader policy level, Michelson offers little beyond a weakly substantiated critique. This serves to confirm the argument made in Chapter 2 of this book that social constructivist approaches to knowledge are in principle unable to go 'beyond critiques'.

Does it matter, then, whether she or Muller is right, or is her paper just another incident in the largely North American 'culture wars' that happens to be a paper published in a South African Journal? It may be that, for Michelson, her paper is best seen in that way. Perhaps she feels that the same 'culture wars' need to be fought in South Africa as well. At no point does one gain any sense that her critique implies any alternative to a knowledge-based model of the curriculum. The last part of this chapter sets out to argue why the differences between Michelson and Muller do matter, and are more than another battle in the 'culture wars' (Sokal 2003). They matter, I suggest, not only theoretically, for those involved in debates about educational knowledge, but also practically, in their implications for education policy both in South Africa and elsewhere.

From the perspective of someone working in the UK, at least, Michelson's combination of political radicalism and a social constructivist epistemology is not unfamiliar. In the UK, as is discussed in Chapter 15, it has invariably led to both political and scientific (in the broad sense of the term) *cul-de-sacs*. Furthermore, at least in the UK, it has been largely irrelevant to educational policy, except to lend support to the typical scepticism about educational research that is all too often shared among policy makers This, however, as I argued in Chapter 7, is far from the situation in South Africa, where academics and administrators are in much closer contact, and where it is far more likely that ideas dreamed up by academics, however naive, will be implemented as policy.

At the beginning of her paper Michelson mentions but does not discuss South African policy developments in the field of education, training and qualifications. One could easily add such examples as the idea of literacies (as opposed to literacy), learner-centred pedagogies and indigenous knowledge referred to earlier. None of these developments has its origins in South Africa. All are informed by the well intentioned but, in my view, fundamentally misguided idea that if education is to be emancipatory and available to all, it must be learner-centred. Learning, according to this view, becomes to be seen as little more than the 'construction of meanings' or 'a conversation' – regardless of what these meanings are, what the conversations are about, or whether they give learners any reliable understanding of the world, or power over it. One unfortunate legacy of apartheid is that many curriculum developers have been enthused by what they have seen as the emancipatory possibilities of social constructivism. This has led them to dismiss any notion of curriculum content being prescribed by specialists, and to see syllabuses as inherently authoritarian, rather than as frameworks that are necessary if genuine intellectual development is to take place.

However 'nuanced' Michelson's 'vast school' of social constructivism may be in their academic writings, it is as slogans that such ideas are interpreted by curriculum developers, especially, but not only, in such a potentially fluid and open context as post-apartheid South Africa. Boundaries between formal and informal knowledge are important in the sense argued for by Muller, not because they are fixed and given distinctions that describe the world, but because they provide a basis for moving beyond the local, the particular and the situated that is most people's non-school experience. As a result of blurring the distinctions between the two types of knowledge, the informal side of the formal/informal dualism has taken on a disproportionate (albeit largely rhetorical) role in education policy in South Africa. Social constructivist ideas provide academic legitimization for such policies. The truth is that despite the good intentions of policy developers, there is growing evidence, both statistical and anecdotal, that the new policies are not working; attainment rates are not improving, and often teachers are confused and do not know what to teach. The argument about knowledge that has been made throughout this book is that this failure is not just because the new curriculum has been poorly implemented and under-resourced, even though both of these things are true. It is because the new curriculum is based on fundamentally mistaken assumptions about knowledge and education. It is these assumptions about the constructedness of knowledge and the mutability of boundaries which divide Muller and Michelson. The merit of her response, however much I disagree with it, is that it brings these epistemological issues and their implications for policy into the arena of public debate about the curriculum.

What Michelson is contesting is, in the broadest terms, not unlike the target of the postmodernists discussed in Chapters 1 and 2 of this book; it is the legacy of the Enlightenment – that set of ideas including those of Newton and the French philosophers of the eighteenth century that have underpinned the processes of industrialization and modernization, the growth of science and technology, and the expansion of schooling in Europe, North America and more recently South East Asia. The question is whether, with whatever variations that reflect its different history, this is also the future for South Africa. And if not, what alternative future might be envisaged? Of course, as Michelson points out, the Enlightenment took place in a historical context in which a new ruling elite, white, middle class and largely male, was emerging. It is also true that one interpretation of the application of reason, expressed as a form of technological rationality, led in different circumstances to the horrors of the Holocaust in twentieth-century Europe. However, as I have argued in earlier chapters, what is distinct about the formal knowledge that can be acquired through schooling – and that therefore needs to be the basis of the curriculum in any country – is (i) the conceptual capacities for envisaging alternatives that it offers to those who acquire it, (ii) the autonomy of the knowledge from the contexts in which it is developed (for example, Chinese students need to learn about Boyle's Law, regardless of the fact that Boyle himself was a representative of an elitist and very English 'gentry' culture), and (iii) it contrasts starkly in conception and organization with the everyday knowledge that learners bring to school. These differences between the knowledge that needs to be the basis of the curriculum and the everyday, local and practical knowledge that people acquire in the course of their lives do not imply that the former is superior in any absolute way. It is superior for certain purposes; for example, such curriculum goals as rigorous criticism, explaining, exploring alternatives and hypothesizing futures. Without formal or theoretical knowledge, such goals are impossible. Equally, there are many things that formal knowledge cannot do.

Knowledge is social, and in a trivial and not-so-trivial sense, we are all social constructivists. Most, but not all, theoretical knowledge that transcends everyday experience has been produced by those who are western European, white, and usually male. It is of course true that this was not always so, and with the rise of China and other South East Asian countries, this distribution of knowledge producers will change. However, in so far as the curriculum is based on such knowledge, it will inevitably prioritize a certain kind of citizen, certain sets of power relations, and not just a certain kind of knowledge. One of the tasks of social theory is to make explicit these links between knowledge and citizenship, and to explore how far one constrains the other.

It is not so much a matter of which side I am on in the debate between Michelson and Muller, although the answer to that question is no doubt clear. There are problems with a social realist approach to the curriculum which some of us are only just beginning to explore. The point of making explicit the differences between Michelson and Muller is that the issues raised are fundamental to the future of education, not only in South Africa but more generally. Michelson is right to remind us (Muller also does so) that all our knowledge is social in origin, and that it does not come as neutral or free of its context. We cannot avoid questions about the origins of theoretical knowledge and the significance of recognizing that it is neither 'in the head' nor 'in the world', but inescapably a product of human beings acting on the world in history. It can be seen as a kind of 'third world' in Popper's sense, that is neither tied to specific contexts, nor as context-free as many claim. Being social, knowledge is always in a sense 'in a context'. What distinguishes theoretical from everyday knowledge is (i) the nature of the context, (ii) the extent to which it enables one to move between contexts, and (iii) its locatedness in specialized communities with their codes and rules for guaranteeing its reliability and generalizeability. The importance of boundaries and the dualisms that an emphasis on boundaries gives rise to is that they are starting points, not end points, for those in education. As Bernstein expressed it, 'enhancement has to do with boundaries and experiencing boundaries as the tension points between the past and possible futures' (Bernstein 2000: Preface). The difficult educational roads from the informal to the formal and back always have to be travelled if learners are to learn and knowledge is to progress. The problem I have with dualisms such as Bernstein's is that while they are unquestionably suggestive, they can focus too much on the distinctiveness of knowledge categories and not enough on their embeddedness in each other. If they were not to some extent embedded, we would never be able to escape from the everyday and think conceptually. Likewise, we might acquire 'theoretical' concepts but never be able to use them. On the other hand, the combination of embeddedness and separateness poses extremely difficult questions for both educational research and policy. How they are resolved in curriculum policies will be one factor determining the educational opportunities that are available to the majority in South Africa and other developing countries.

In a final point, I want to return to the issue of South African 'exceptionalism'. Earlier in this chapter I criticized Michelson's formulation of this issue. My own view, which draws on my experience of visits to South Africa over the past decade and a half, is that it is 'exceptional' but not in the sense Michelson claims. In the context of educational policy, South Africa is 'exceptional', especially as a developing country, in having a number of researchers who are raising basic questions about the links between epistemology and educational policy that are rarely recognized by researchers and policy makers in a country like the UK. We have philosophers of education and some sociologists of education who explore epistemological issues. Quite separately, most educationalists are hell bent on delivering, evaluating or criticizing the latest government policy, whether it is personalized learning, work-based learning or widening participation, but with little or no regard for epistemological issues. Unlike in South Africa, epistemology and policy debates hardly meet. I suspect this difference at least partly reflects the urgency of the situation in South Africa, and the collective will in that country to make democracy succeed for as wide a section of the population as possible. This is one of the positive legacies of the struggle against apartheid. We in the ex-colonizing countries have a lot to learn from them.

Conclusions

This book has argued that improving education relies on a curriculum that is explicitly based on the differentiation of school from non-school knowledge. This chapter has set out to show the relevance of this general thesis about the sociology of school knowledge to the questions facing curriculum policy makers in South Africa. By challenging the American educationalist Elana Michelson's (Michelson 2006) critique of Muller's influential book *Reclaiming Knowledge* (Muller 2000), the chapter lends support to Muller's arguments. It makes the case that real improvement will only be possible if the knowledge base of the new curriculum is expressed in syllabuses generated in association with the specialist knowledge producing communities in the universities and the professional bodies.

Educational reforms in South Africa since 1995 have had an explicitly progressive intent and have been committed to redressing past inequalities. However, by imagining that it is possible to express a curriculum in terms of broad outcomes (what is known in South Africa as OBE) while leaving to individual teachers the responsibility for issues such as the selection and pacing of knowledge, success in expanding admissions has not and could not have been matched by similar improvements in attainment levels.

Part 3

Next steps

15 Truth and truthfulness in the sociology of educational knowledge

(with Johan Muller)

... endless forms most beautiful and most wonderful.

(from the last sentence of Darwin's *The Origin of Species*)

There is only knowledge, period. It is recognizable not by its air of holiness or its emotional appeal but by its capacity to pass the most demanding scrutiny of well-informed people who have no prior investment in confirming it. And a politics of sorts, neither leftist nor rightist, follows from this understanding. If knowledge can be certified only by a process of peer review, we ought to do what we can to foster communities of uncompromised experts. That means actively resisting guru-ism, intellectual cliquishness, guilt-assuaging double standards, and, needless to say, disdain for the very concept of objectivity.

(Crewes 2006: 5)

Introduction

In his book *Truth and Truthfulness* (2002), Bernard Williams identifies the 'commitment to truthfulness' as a central tendency in current social thought that can be traced back to the Enlightenment and now stretches from philosophy and the humanities to 'historical understanding, the social sciences and even to the interpretations of discoveries and research in the natural sciences' (2002: 1). He describes this tendency as 'an eagerness to see through appearances to the real structures and motives that lie behind them' (ibid.). However, he sees this 'commitment to truthfulness' as increasingly paralleled by a no less pervasive 'scepticism about truth itself', 'whether there is such a thing [as truth] ... whether it can be more than relative or subjective or something of that kind' (ibid.). His argument is that the latter inexorably corrodes the former.

The two tendencies, towards truthfulness and against the idea of truth, are not for Williams, as for many, just a contradiction or tension that as sociologists or philosophers we have to live with. Rather he sees an acceptance of the notion of truth as the condition for a serious commitment to truthfulness. This chapter takes Williams's claim as a starting point for re-examining what kind of activities the sociology of knowledge (in educational studies, and more generally) is engaged in, bearing in mind that in most forms it has been an almost paradigmatic case of endorsing a scepticism about the truth.

Williams compares the sociology of knowledge with muck-raking journalism, with which it has some similarities. Both seek truthfulness, but more often are little more than forms of debunking. Muck-raking journalism and some strands of the sociology of knowledge have little doubt about what truth is or where it lies – it is in identifying the corruption of the powerful. This is the basis for the tendency to moral self-righteousness and absolute certainty that we find in some campaigning journalists. Some sociologists of education have tried to resolve the tension between truth and truthfulness in similar ways, often by assuming that their identification with the powerless or with a particular disadvantaged group brings them automatically closer to the truth. Such positions are often referred to as 'standpoint' theories,[1] even if the grounds for claiming that a standpoint can be the basis for a theory are far from clear. Though superficially attractive, such solutions, Williams argues, serve only to deflect us from facing the really difficult questions about knowledge and truth that we cannot avoid if sociology is to offer more than – as some postmodernists claim – a series of stories (Mendick 2006).

Williams also points out that the end of the 'science wars' and the 'culture wars' and the gradual collapse of any credibility that postmodernism had as a social theory (Benson and Stangroom 2006) has not led to a new commitment to exploring the inescapable links between truth and truthfulness. More commonly, he suggests, the outcome has been 'an inert cynicism ... [which] runs the risk of sliding ... through professionalization, to a finally disenchanted careerism' (Williams 2002: 3).

In this chapter we focus largely on the sociology of knowledge as it has developed within educational studies. This is partly because this is the context within which we have worked. However, locating the question of knowledge in educational debates raises more fundamental questions for social theory that are not always recognized. As Durkheim and Vygotsky (and more recently Basil Bernstein) recognized, just as every theory of education implies a theory of society, educational theories always imply a theory of knowledge (see Chapters 2 and 3).

As sociologists of education, we are, as Floud and Halsey (1958) pointed out long ago, creatures of the rise of mass education and the range of attempts to resolve its particular contradictions. As an aspect of modernization, mass education faced and still faces what might be described as the fundamental pedagogic issue: overcoming the discontinuity (sometimes expressed as a conflict) between the formal, codified, theoretical and, at least potentially, universalizing knowledge of the curriculum that students seek to acquire and teachers to transmit, and the informal, local, experiential and everyday knowledge that pupils (or students) bring to school.

When most of the small proportion of each cohort who attended school shared the underlying cultural assumptions of those designing and delivering the formal curriculum, this discontinuity was barely acknowledged. Nor was it seen as a problem, at least by policy makers, in the earlier stages of industrialization when schools prepared the majority for unskilled work and knowledge acquisition was seen as only important for a minority. However, the clash between the democratizing, universalizing goals of mass education and the selection, failure and early leaving that was the reality of schooling for the majority in most countries was never going to remain unnoticed for long. Mass schooling was not achieving the social justice and equality goals set for it by the emerging democratic movements, or fulfilling adequately the growing demand from a globalizing labour market for higher levels of knowledge and skills.

This was the context in the 1960s, when the sociology of education was 're-established'[2] in the UK as a sub-discipline of sociology, and not, as it had tended to be, an aspect of social mobility and stratification studies. At that time, the central problematic of the sociology of education became, and has largely remained, the discontinuity between the culture of the school and its curriculum and the cultures of those coming to school. It was partly as a critique of existing approaches to access and equality, and partly to focus on the deeper cultural and political issues that underpinned the persistence of educational inequalities, that Bourdieu and Bernstein developed their early work on cultural capital, language codes and educability (Bourdieu and Passeron 1977; Bernstein 1971). One outcome of their ideas was that a focus on the sociology of the curriculum emerged as a key element in what became known as the 'new sociology of education' (Young 1971).

Despite starting with the theoretical goal of reorienting the sociology of education towards the question of knowledge, the sociology of the curriculum in the 1970s took on many of the characteristics that Williams identified with muckraking journalism rather than with social science. It knew the truth – the link between power and knowledge – and set out to show how this truth manifested itself in the school curriculum.[3]

It is not our intention to dismiss the new sociology of education's 'commitment to truthfulness' or its attempt to 'go deeper' and explore the links between curriculum organization and the wider distribution of power.[4] Reminding educationalists that the curriculum, and indeed knowledge itself, is not some external given but a product of historical human activities – part of our own history – was an important task at the time and remains so. However, it would be foolish to deny that many of those working in the sociology of the curriculum at the time identified, albeit not always explicitly, with the prevailing scepticism about truth and knowledge itself (Jenks 1977). This led many to question the idea that a curriculum committed to the idea of truth could 'truthfully' be the aim of the sociology of educational knowledge. As a consequence, the 'new' sociology of education that began, in Williams's terms, with a radical commitment to truthfulness, undermined its own project by its rejection of any idea of truth itself.

The aim of this chapter is to reflect on and explore the issues that Williams raises in the particular case of the sociology of education. The next section considers two questions. First, what went wrong with the sociology of knowledge in educational studies and the social constructivist approach with which it was associated? Second, what might be the basis of an alternative to social constructivism that retains a commitment both to truthfulness and to the idea of truth itself? We then begin to suggest how an alternative might be developed by drawing on the work of the French sociologist and educationalist, Emile Durkheim. The issues that Durkheim posed in relation to the rise of pragmatism before the First World War (Durkheim 1983) have extraordinary echoes in the dilemmas posed by the 'new sociology of education' in the 1970s. In going on to revisit Basil Bernstein's development of Durkheim's ideas, we show that despite Durkheim's remarkable insights and the highly original conceptual advances made by Bernstein, both remain trapped in the belief that the natural sciences remain the only model for objective knowledge and knowledge growth. This discussion paves the way for the next section, when we draw on the work of Ernest Cassirer and propose a sociological approach to knowledge in terms of his idea of symbolic forms. Finally we return to our starting point: how far can a social realist approach to knowledge in educational studies that draws on Cassirer's idea of 'symbolic objectivity' come to terms with the tension between truth and truthfulness that was articulated so clearly by Bernard Williams and was left unresolved, even unaddressed, by the 'new' sociology of education of the 1970s?

We started by showing, via Bernard Williams, that if a commitment to truth is paired with a scepticism about truth, the latter inevitably corrodes the former. We end by arguing that sociology of education must realign itself with realism, either of a naturalistic kind (after Durkheim 1983 and perhaps Moore 2004) that relies on the natural sciences for its model of objectivity, or of a formalist kind (after Cassirer and, although less clearly, after Bernstein). Nor need there be that kind of choice. The primary choice, we will argue, is between objectivity and anti-objectivity. There was a time when the idea of objectivity in the social sciences seemed to be aligned with oppression, and the route to an acceptable objectivity politically blocked. The time is ripe, we argue, to consolidate and develop the considerable advances made by current developments in the sociology of education that demonstrate the case of its potential objectivity (Nash 2005).

Social constructivism in the sociology of education: what went wrong?

Our answer to the question 'what went wrong?' begins by accepting the premise that the 'new sociology of education' and its social constructivist assumptions were an important, albeit a seriously flawed, attempt to establish a sociological basis to debates about the curriculum. It undoubtedly represented an advance on the uncritical acceptance in England of the idea of liberal education (Hirst and Peters 1970) and on the technicist tradition of curriculum theorizing prevalent in the USA at the time (Apple 1975). It created considerable interest within educational studies, as well as much opposition; however, it did not provide a reliable basis for an alternative curriculum. Nor did it provide an adequate theory of how, in practice, the curriculum was changing. Why was this so?

First, it is important to recognize the extent to which the sociological approach to knowledge and the curriculum that emerged in the 1970s, and the social constructivist ideas that underpinned it, were neither new nor isolated developments. This was true in two senses. First, despite its claims to novelty at the time, the apparently radical idea that all knowledge is in some sense a product of human activities, and that this leads at least implicitly and sometimes explicitly to scepticism about the possibility of objective knowledge, was not itself new. It can be traced back to the sophists and sceptics in Ancient Greece, and found a new lease of life in Vico's challenge to the emergent hegemony of natural science in the early eighteenth century (Berlin 2000), and it survives to this day among those, like Richard Rorty, whom Bernard Williams refers to as the 'truth deniers' (Williams 2002). It is also true that very similar sets of ideas could be found at the time in every discipline within the social sciences and the humanities. In other words, we are dealing as much with the context of the time as with the content of this supposedly 'new' sociology of education.

If there was anything new about the 'new sociology of education', it was the educational contexts in which the idea of 'social constructivism' was applied, and the particular conclusions that were drawn from the assumption that the educational realities of curriculum and pedagogy were socially constructed and could be changed by teachers – almost at will (Gorbutt 1972). The 'decisionism' this displayed is typical of all cognate constructivisms.

For social constructivists, how we think about the world, our experience, and any notion of 'how the world is', are not differentiated. It follows that the idea that reality itself is socially constructed had two closely related implications as it was interpreted in the sociology of education. First, it provided the basis for challenging any form of givenness or fixity, whether political, social, institutional or cultural. It was assumed that challenging givenness was as applicable to science or knowledge in general as to the social rules, conventions and institutions that had traditionally been studied by sociologists.[5] Second, it was able to treat all forms of givenness as arbitrary and, given different social arrangements, potentially changeable. It followed that in so far as a form of givenness persisted it was assumed to express the interests (political, cultural or economic) of some groups vis-à-vis others. The intellectual battle was between those, the social constructivists, who saw their task as exposing the apparent givenness of reality for 'what it really was' – a mask to obscure the deeper reality of arbitrariness and interests – and those who opposed them by defending as given what was 'in reality' arbitrary. The distinction between 'constructivists' and 'realists' is inevitably an oversimplification.[6] The primary difference between them was that the constructivists claimed that the only reality was that there was no reality beyond our perceptions. What with hindsight is puzzling is the combination of indeterminism (everything is arbitrary) and determinism (everything can be changed) to which this led.

Within the 'broad church' of social constructivism in educational studies, a range of different perspectives were drawn on that had little in common and sometimes directly contradicted each other. At different times, different theorists and traditions were recruited. Within the sociology of education, at least from the early 1970s, the dominant perspectives from which the idea of social constructivism was drawn were the social phenomenology and ethnomethodology of Schutz, Merleau Ponty and Garfinkel, the symbolic interactionsism of Mead and Blumer, the eclectic social constructivism of Berger and Luckman, the cultural anthropology of Robin Horton (and later Clifford Geertz), the neo-Weberian sociology of Pierre Bourdieu and, albeit slightly uneasily, the critical Marxism of the Frankfurt School. For Bourdieu, for example, the unmasking of arbitrariness was sociology's core problematic. What these writers had in common, or were interpreted as having in common, was a form of sociological reductionism. As everything was social, sociological analysis could be applied to and account for anything and everything – even though sociologists often disagreed about what the social was. In the 1980s these theoretical traditions were extended to include (and, for many, were replaced by) discourse and literary theories. The latter drew on writers such as Derrida, Foucault and Lyotard who treated the social as just another text, a discourse, or in the case of the latter, a language game. The reductionist logic, however, was the same.

Education was in a sense a special, or even, one might say, an ideal case for social constructivist ideas. This partly reflected the relative theoretical weakness of educational studies and hence its openness to (or inability to resist) any new theory that came along. However, the sociology of the curriculum and the idea that educational realities were socially constructed had a quite specific appeal in the often authoritarian, bureaucratic and always hierarchical world of schooling. It easily led to challenges to existing forms of school knowledge, subjects and disciplines and their familiar expression in syllabuses (Keddie 1971; Young and Whitty 1977). More fundamentally, social constructivism challenged and exposed what it saw as the arbitrariness of the most basic categories of formal education such as intelligence, ability and attainment (Keddie 1971, 1973) and even of the institution of school itself. If social constructivism could show that all such categories, rules and institutions were arbitrary, this also made them potentially open to change, even if social constructivism could not say how or to what. The links between social constructivist ideas and the political Left, or at least parts of it, were hardly surprising, although more often than not expedient.

Why did these ideas gain such a stranglehold in educational studies, and why later were they so easily criticized and rejected? Did this pattern of initial support but later rejection indicate some flaw in the basic idea of reality being 'socially constructed', or did the idea contain, as Marx said of Hegel, a 'rational kernel' that somehow got lost? Why were these ideas particularly seductive and, as with hindsight we can see, particularly disastrous for educational studies and the sociology of the curriculum in particular?

Two different kinds of response to such questions can be given. One is an external or contextual argument. It is familiar, relatively uncontroversial and can be dealt with briefly. It is relevant only to the extent to which it reminds us of the non-unique aspect of particular intellectual fields and that the sociology of education is no exception. Two kinds of external or contextual factors are worth mentioning that shaped ideas in the sociology of education – one social and one cultural. The first was the massive expansion and democratization of higher education, the parallel expansion and diversification of the social sciences and humanities, and the assumption, at least in educational studies, that these new types of knowledge could be used to transform what was widely recognized as an inefficient and unequal education system. These developments, magnified since the 1980s by globalization and the emphasis on markets in every sphere of life, created a quite new context for intellectual work in education that had considerable affinity with the new, relativist and supposedly more democratic ideas about knowledge. This new context for educational studies brought in new and sometimes already radicalized students and new lecturers and provided fertile ground for a range of cultural changes which all played a role in shaping the sociology of education. These included a much wider critical and, for a time, highly politicized academic climate, an affinity with populist ideas, a sometimes uncritical respect for the cultures of subordinate and minority groups and those from non-western societies, and a parallel scepticism about the academy and all forms of authority, including science and other forms of specialist knowledge. All these developments drew on and were implicitly or explicitly supportive of social constructivist ideas (Benson and Stangroom 2006).

It is the internal issues – developments within the intellectual field of educational studies – that we want to concentrate on in this chapter. From early in the 1970s, social constructivist ideas were challenged, usually by philosophers (e.g. Pring 1972) but sometimes by other sociologists (Gould 1977; Demaine 1981). However, it was relatively easy for the 'new sociologists' to dismiss these critics by labelling them as reactionary,[7] reformist or 'social democratic'[8] (Whitty and Young 1976).

In developing a less superficial response to its critics, social constructivism in educational studies only had two ways to go, at least within the terms it set itself as a radical theory. One direction was towards a politics that linked constructivist ideas to the privileging of subordinate (as opposed to ruling class or official) knowledge. Subordinacy could refer to the working class and be linked to Marxism, to women and be linked to feminism, or to non-white groups and what later became known as postcolonial or subaltern studies. In a response that was quite specific to the sociology of education, identification with subordinacy was linked to a celebration of the culture of those who were rejected by and failed at school. Their language and their resistance to formal learning were seen as at least potentially supportive of a new more radical working-class consciousness (Willis 1977).[9] The other direction for social constructivism was towards postmodern versions of a Nietzschean nihilism and the denial of any possibility of progress, truth or knowledge. Not only were such interpretations of Nietzsche somewhat dubious, as Bernard Williams shows (Williams 2002: Chapter 1), they offered little that was substantive to educational studies beyond a continuing, if largely empty, role for theory (or theorizing, as it became known).[10]

To summarize our argument so far: social constructivism provided teachers and students of education with a superficially attractive but ultimately contradictory set of intellectual tools. On the one hand, it offered the possibility of intellectual emancipation and freedom through education – we, as teachers, students or workers have the epistemological right to develop theories and to criticize and challenge scientists, philosophers and other so-called experts and specialists. Furthermore, in some unspecified way, this so-called freedom was seen as contributing to changing the world. This emancipation from all authoritative forms of knowledge was linked by many to the possibility of achieving a more equal or just world, which for some but not all meant socialism. On the other hand, by undermining any claims to objective knowledge or truth about anything, social constructivism, at least in some of the ways it was (and could legitimately be) interpreted, denies the possibility of any better understanding, let alone of any better world. For obvious reasons, however, this denial tended to be ignored by educational researchers, at least most of the time.

The double-bind that combined emancipation and its impossibility was particularly problematic in education. If not only the selection of knowledge in the curriculum, but even the rankings, reporting and everyday judgements made by teachers about pupils were treated as arbitrary, then continuing to be a teacher (let alone an educational researcher) became deeply problematic, except in 'bad faith'. Furthermore, such ideas have left their mark in today's fashionable language of facilitation, group work and 'teaching is a conversation'. All these pedagogic strategies can be seen as strands of an attempt to suppress hierarchy, or at least render it invisible (Muller 2006). This new 'language of practice' or activity in educational studies, increasingly linked to the 'promise' of e-learning, mobile phones and the internet, is now with us and has close affinities with the language of the market. It is of course supported by many who know little of the original sociological critiques of pedagogic authority.

Why did such ideas persist, and why are they resurrected again and again as if they were new? It is not because they are true, unless a fundamental contradictoriness and the consequent impossibility of knowledge can be the truth. Nor, as in the case of new ideas in physics and chemistry, can it be that the idea of reality being socially constructed is so powerful that it has been used to change the world in ways that no one can deny. At best, social constructivism reminds us that however apparently given and fixed certain ideas or institutions appear to be, they are always the product of actual human activities in history. They do not have their origins solely in the material world external to us, nor can we find their origins, as Descartes thought, in our heads. In Cassirer's terms, as we will see in a later section of this chapter, ideas and institutions are 'expressive'; that is, they are part of social action that is both of the objective social world, but suffused by subjective meanings which frequently push at the bounds of any objective categories. At worst, social constructivism has provided an intellectual legitimacy for criticizing and challenging any institution, any hierarchy, any form of authority and any knowledge as arbitrary. The superficial political correctness and at times the idiocy that this position leads to has been a heavy price to pay for the small 'moment' of emancipation that is expressed in the truth that reality is socially constructed. One response to this latter observation, widely if not always explicitly admitted, has been to reject the enterprise of the sociology of education and more particularly sociology as it is applied to the curriculum. This was the response of the political Right, who labelled it as left-wing ideology (Gould 1977). A more pragmatic and technocratic version of this position has since been adopted by most teacher training programmes and an increasing number of higher degrees in educational studies in the UK today. Programmes of initial teacher education or professional development that include the systematic study of the sociology of education are increasingly rare. This rejection of the sociology of knowledge was also, with rather more justification, the position taken by the group of natural scientists who waged the science wars (Sokal 2003)[11] and who had, by the 1990s, become massively impatient with the patent circularity of constructivism. It is not unlikely that the latter provided the intellectual justification for the policy consequences of the former.

A more positive alternative, in our view, is to begin by remembering something that was too easily forgotten in the heady days of the 1970s, and often still is. That is that sociology itself, like all social life, institutions, knowledge and even science, has a history. We need, it follows, not only to see society and education historically, but to recall the history of sociology and the sociology of education and to recognize that debates within one generation of sociologists always need to be extended to be debates with earlier generations.

The social constructivists were wrong, we have argued. However, as we shall see, like the pragmatists such as James and Dewey at the beginning of the twentieth century, and with whom they had much in common, they were not wholly wrong. They were right to emphasize the socio-historical character of knowledge (and therefore the curriculum) as against the prevalent view of its givenness. Their flaws, we can see in retrospect, were (i) in not spelling out the limits of the theory, and (ii) in giving substance to their opening claim. The theory remained, therefore, largely rhetorical. Let us take one example. It is one thing to claim that such an apparently solid idea like that of a liberal education is a social construct, and therefore no more than an exercise of domination. It is quite another to document liberal education as a historically changing phenomenon – very different for Eliot, Leavis and C.P. Snow from how it had been for Arnold and Newman.

Social constructivism was fundamentally wrong in the conclusions that it drew about knowledge and the curriculum. The social character of knowledge is not a reason for doubting its truth and objectivity, or for seeing curricula as no more than politics by other means. Its social character is (even more truthfully) the only reason that knowledge can claim to truth (and objectivity) (Collins 2000) and therefore for preferring some curriculum principles to others. To begin to see where this idea leads, we will turn to Durkheim's argument in his far too little known lectures published as *Pragmatism and Sociology* (Durkheim 1983).

The remarkable thing about Durkheim's lectures is that in the pragmatism of James (and to a lesser extent, Dewey), Durkheim confronted almost identical problems to those introduced by the sociology of education in the 1970s. He knew that pragmatism was an advance on the rationalism and empiricism of the time, just as social constructivism was an advance on the view of the curriculum and knowledge that treated it as an a-social given. At the same time he also saw that pragmatism's form of 'humanizing' or socializing knowledge and truth, if left unqualified, led to far worse problems than those it claimed to overcome. The next section draws heavily on Durkheim (1983) to suggest a basis for how we might develop an alternative to social constructivism for the sociology of education.

From social constructivism to social realism: some lessons from Durkheim

There are significant but not complete parallels between our engagement in this chapter with the social constructivist ideas that became part of the sociology of education in the 1970s and Durkheim's engagement with the pragmatist ideas that were sweeping French intellectual life 60 years earlier. However, our interest in finding an alternative to social constructivism is somewhat different from Durkheim's concerns about pragmatism. As many writers have commented (most notably Lukes 1972), Durkheim was writing at a time of great social upheaval in France that had been triggered in large part by militant opposition to the powers of the Catholic Church. He saw pragmatism, with its antagonism to any notion of objective rationality and its linking of truth to its consequences, as adding to the disorder and providing no basis for the consensus that for him underpinned any just social order. His primary concern therefore was to develop an objective basis for the moral values that could constitute a new consensus. Ideas of truth and knowledge, were important for Durkheim not primarily for themselves, but on account of their moral role. He saw them as binding people together as members of society. Without denying the moral role of knowledge and truth, our concern is rather different. It is with the intellectual basis of the curriculum and the nature of knowledge, and the way the former was undermined and the latter avoided by the relativist implications of social constructivism.

Both pragmatist and social constructivist approaches to knowledge arose as responses to the weaknesses of existing epistemologies – both rationalist and empiricist. Both the latter led to static and dualist assumptions about knowledge and its relationship to the world. In trying to overcome this dualism and also to 'humanize' knowledge by locating it 'in the world', Durkheim argued that pragmatism (and by implication, social constructivism) treats concepts and the world of experience as part of one seamless reality. In other words, they assume that knowledge is undifferentiated from human experience. In contrast, for Durkheim, the humanness of knowledge can only be located in society and in the necessity of concepts being both 'of the world' (a world that includes both society and the material world) and differentiated from our experience of it. The social was 'objective' for Durkheim at least in part because it excluded the subjectivities of the ego and, for him, the 'profane' world of individual action and experience.

Durkheim agrees with the pragmatists in not treating knowledge or truth as in some way independent of human society and history. However, this does not mean, as James assumed, that truth is subjective – or no different from people's feelings and sensitivities. Truth and knowledge have a givenness, but it is a givenness that is historical and social. We create knowledge, Durkheim argues, just as we create institutions; not in any way but in relation to our history, and on the basis of what former generations have discovered or created.

Perhaps surprisingly for someone so concerned with consensus, it is Durkheim, rather than the pragmatists with their obsession with problem solving, who, by recognizing the tension between knowledge as a social given and this givenness being historically formed, provides the basis for a social theory of innovation. The body of work in the sociology of science inaugurated by Robert Merton (1973) makes this plain. Furthermore, it was in the differentiation between the 'sacred' as an internally consistent world of concepts and the 'profane' as a vague and contradictory continuum of procedures and practices that Durkheim found the social basis of science and the origins of speculative thought (Muller 2000).

Another parallel between pragmatism and social constructivism is exemplified in Durkheim's argument about how pragmatism resorts to an instrumental theory of truth, what he referred to as 'logical utilitarianism'. Knowledge was true for the pragmatists if it satisfied a need. Similarly, social constructivism, although not explicitly concerned with satisfying needs, emphasizes the situatedness of all knowledge, and therefore locates it in practice (hence we have the origins of what became known as 'the practice turn' in social theory). Furthermore, social constructivism has also associated itself with the importance of knowledge 'being socially relevant' – a utilitarianism thinly veiled beneath a moral correctness. As Durkheim pointed out, satisfying a need could never account for the essential impersonality of truth that is not related to any specific individual, standpoint, interest or need.

A related problem with pragmatism for Durkheim was that if the truth can only be verified by its consequences – i.e. a posteriori – it always depends on what may (or may not) happen. As he points out, something cannot logically be judged true on the basis of what may happen; that is like relying on hope or 'wishful thinking', a tendency that has bedevilled much Marxist writing. To claim that because something works, it is true, is to confuse (or blur) two distinct categories – truth and utility. If something is true because it works, this either relies on an implicitly subjective and a priori criterion of 'what works' or it points to the need for a complex consideration of what working means and for whom, and on its own tells us little. Durkheim argued that truth must be a priori – not a priori in the Kantian sense, which makes it rigid and abstracted from human life, but a priori in the social sense – it is prior and it relies on what society has demonstrated to be true. Likewise for social constructivists, knowledge and truth are located in who the knowers are and in their interests.[12] Just as with pragmatism we are left with consequences, so with social constructivism we are left only with interests. In both cases, both truth and knowledge disappear.

Durkheim's strongest objection to pragmatism was that it neglected what he saw as the unique character of truth: its external, constraining, obligatory and, for him, moral force. When applied to social contructivism, Durkheim's insight emphasizes the limits that the social (for him society) imposes on our ability to socially construct reality. It is those limits – the boundaries, as Bernstein would put it – that free us to search for the truth. To paraphrase Durkheim, we feel the pressure of the truth on us; we cannot deny it, even if we do not like it. Satisfying a need or relating to an interest are ultimately subjective criteria and can never be adequate as criteria of truth. Sometimes the truth does exactly the opposite to satisfying a need and does not seem to be in one's interest; however, that does not stop it from being true.

Let us summarize this section so far. We have argued that in his critique of pragmatism Durkheim offers us at least the beginning of an alternative to social constructivism that retains the idea that knowledge has a social basis but does not reduce the idea of 'the social' to interest groups, activities or relations of power. At the same time, in his sacred/profane distinction which underpins the separation of objective concepts from practical subjective reality, and in his recognition of the continuity in modern societies of both mythological and scientific truths, his theory recognizes the crucial importance of the social differentiation of knowledge.

Finally, there remains the issue upon which we touched earlier. For Durkheim, the social is the moral; it is about values. In so far as knowledge (and the curriculum) are social, they too for Durkheim are primarily moral issues. This makes it difficult to use his framework to explore questions of knowledge content and structure that are avoided by the reductionist implications of social constructivism. Is Durkheim right in equating the social with the moral, even when it comes to the question of knowledge? Or can we envisage a non-moral concept of the social? We think the answer to the latter question must be yes; furthermore, a cognitive as well as a moral concept of the social is essential if we are to develop an alternative to social constructivist sociologies of knowledge (Moore and Young 2001; Schmaus 1994).

Durkheim seems to focus more on the shared values on which the objectivity of knowledge depends rather than on the nature of the knowledge itself. A clue to this feature of Durkheim's work may be found in his indebtedness to the Kantian tradition of a priori-ism. In his short book with his nephew Marcel Mauss (Durkheim and Mauss 1970), Durkheim makes clear that it is not knowledge in the sense of what we know about the world with which he is concerned, but the foundations of that knowledge – how it is possible. In other words, he is interested in the social basis of notions such as logic and cause, without which knowledge would not be possible. For Durkheim the objectivity of morality and logic have the same basis: society.

Paul Fauconnet, in his introduction to Durkheim's *Education and Sociology* (Durkheim 1956), offers an interpretation of Durkheim's sociology of education which gives more attention to his intellectual (or cognitive) concerns. In commenting on Durkheim's rejection of pragmatism's utilitarian concept of education, he writes that

> the transmission [of knowledge] through the teacher to the pupil, the assimilation by the child of a subject seemed to him [Durkheim] to *be the condition of real intellectual formation* ... [our emphasis]. One does not recreate science through one's own personal experience, because [science] is social not individual; one learns it.

So much for ideas like 'pupil as scientist' (or theorist) popularized by constructivists (e.g. Driver 1983). Fauconnet continues: 'Forms [of the mind] cannot be transmitted empty. Durkheim, like Comte, thinks that it is necessary to learn about things, to acquire knowledge'.

For us, therefore, despite Durkheim's stress on the moral basis of society, issues of the structure and content of knowledge must lie at the heart of the sociology of the curriculum. Although Fauconnet notes that Durkheim prepared lectures on specialist pedagogies, in mathematics, physics, geography and history, no texts survive. Durkheim leaves us, therefore, with only some very general propositions about the social basis of the foundations of knowledge and its differentiation. However, it is precisely the issue of differentiation, so crucial to a sociology of the curriculum, that the English sociologist Basil Bernstein addressed in his early papers on classification and framing, and in a paper published towards the end of his life, in which he introduces the distinction between vertical and horizontal knowledge structures. It is therefore to Bernstein's ideas that we turn in the next section.

Bernstein's typology of vertical and horizontal knowledges

This section begins with a brief description of Bernstein's ideas on the differentiation of knowledge. He intervened decisively in the discussion about the form of symbolic systems (or knowledge) and set out to delineate the 'internal principles of their construction and their social base' (Bernstein 2000: 155). As is by now well known, he distinguishes between two forms of discourse, horizontal and vertical, and within vertical discourse, between two kinds of knowledge structure, hierarchical and horizontal.

For Bernstein, knowledge structures differ in two ways. The first is in terms of what may be called verticality. Verticality has to do with how theory develops. In hierarchical knowledge structures, it develops through the integration of propositions, towards ever more general sets of propositions. It is this trajectory of development that lends hierarchical knowledge structures their unitary triangular shape. In contrast, horizontal knowledge structures are not unitary but plural; they consist of a series of parallel and incommensurable languages (or sets of concepts). Verticality in horizontal knowledge structures occurs not through integration but through the introduction of a new language (or set of concepts) which constructs a 'fresh perspective, a new set of questions, a new set of connections, and an apparently new problematic, and most importantly a new set of speakers' (Bernstein 2000: 162). Because these 'languages' are incommensurable, they defy incorporation into a more general theory.[13] The level of integration, and the possibility for knowledge progress in the sense of greater generality and hence wider explanatory reach, is thus strictly limited in horizontal knowledge structures.

Before we proceed to discuss grammaticality, the second form of knowledge variation, it is worth making a few observations on verticality. The first is that it artfully incorporates and recapitulates the fierce dispute in the philosophy and sociology of science between the logical positivists and the non-realists. Bernstein is implicitly asserting that the logical positivists (or realists) were right, but only in respect of hierarchical knowledge structures, and that the non-realists (Kuhn and those who followed him) were likewise right, but only in respect of horizontal knowledge structures. In other words, encoded into

Bernstein's principle of verticality are the terms of the debate in the philosophy of science.

Second, we note that horizontal knowledge structures span a surprisingly broad range; they include not only sociology and the humanities but logic and mathematics. The anomaly is that in the latter exemplars of horizontal knowledge structures, we have a form of verticality that is almost equivalent to that obtained in hierarchical knowledge structures. The germane question then becomes not so much what hinders progression in all horizontal knowledge structures, but rather what internal characteristics distinguish those horizontal knowledge structures such as the social sciences that proliferate languages from those like mathematics, where language proliferation is constrained. It was in search of a sociological answer to this question and to provide an alternative to Bourdieu's sociological reductionism (see Bernstein 1996), that Bernstein began by setting out his distinction between vertical and horizontal knowledge structures.

We turn now to the second form of knowledge variation, grammaticality. We have suggested that verticality has to do with how a theory develops internally (what Bernstein later referred to as its internal language of description). In contrast, grammaticality has to do with how a theory deals with the world, or how theoretical statements deal with their empirical predicates (what he later referred to as its external language of description: Bernstein 2000). The stronger the grammaticality of a language, the more stably it is able to generate empirical correlates and the more unambiguous, because it is more restricted, is the field of referents. The weaker the grammaticality, the weaker is the capacity of a theory to stably identify empirical correlates and the more ambiguous, because it is much broader, becomes the field of referents. Thus knowledge structures with weak grammars are deprived of a principal means of generating progress (or new knowledge), namely empirical disconfirmation. As Bernstein puts it, 'Weak powers of empirical descriptions remove a crucial resource for either development or rejection of a particular language and so contribute to its stability as a frozen form' (Bernstein 2000: 167–168).

To summarize, whereas grammaticality determines the capacity of a theory to progress through worldly corroboration, verticality determines the capacity of a theory to progress through explanatory sophistication. Together, we may say that these two criteria determine the capacity a particular knowledge structure has to progress.

However, for all its rigour and suggestiveness, this analysis merely starts the ball rolling, so to speak. What it provides is a survey of the range of variation, but even the charitable must admit that the poles remain clearer than the intermediate zones of the range. This is partly because the precise nature of and relation between verticality and grammaticality is unclear. A plausible surmise could be the following: verticality is a categorical principle; it consigns knowledge structures to either a theory-integrating or a theory-proliferating category. On the other hand, grammaticality is an ordinal principle, constructing a continuum of grammaticality within each category, or perhaps across the entire spectrum. Although at one point Bernstein depicts grammaticality as a feature only of horizontal knowledge structures (Bernstein 2000: 168), at another point he refers to physics, his paradigm of verticality, as having a 'strong grammar' (Bernstein 2000: 163). What this means is that Bernstein at times uses the 'grammar' metaphor to refer to the internal language, though mostly it refers to the external language.

However, even if we grant the surmise, anomalies persist, none more so than in the case of mathematics. In Bernstein's account, mathematics is a horizontal knowledge structure with a strong grammar. However, the principal criterion of strong grammaticality – how the theory deals with the world – doesn't quite fit. As Bernstein (2000: 163) concedes, mathematics does not progress by empirical corroboration, like physics does. It is a deductive system, and its grammar appears to be a purely internal one. This depicts mathematics as a knowledge structure with a strong internal but weak external language of description – the latter categorizing it as similar in type to the social sciences. However, the history of mathematics suggests this picture is far from adequate. As Penrose argues in his remarkable book *The Road to Reality* (Penrose 2006), time and time again, mathematical concepts at extraordinary levels of abstraction (one of his examples is the patterning of prime numbers), and with no apparent relationship to the material world, turn out to be integral to our understanding of both the structure of the universe and the structure of matter (see also Cassirer 1943). Such examples are not evidence of a 'weak external language of description', but maybe of the need for a more developed sense of what grammaticality involves. Perhaps, as Kay O'Halloran (2006) suggests, mathematics is the language the empirical sciences must use to generate verticality in their internal languages. If that is so, then its lack of an external language ceases to be strange.

The difference between sociology and mathematics is strikingly brought out by Moore and Maton's (2001) example of the epistemic continuity displayed in the story of the proof of Fermat's last theorem:

> What is so striking about this story is its sheer scale in historical time and in geographical and cultural space. It tells a story of a mathematician in late-twentieth century England effectively communicating with a French judge at the court of Louis XIV, and through him with Babylonians from three millennia ago. It represents an epistemic community with an extended existence in time and space, a community where the past is present, one in which, when living members die, will be in turn the living concern of future members ...
>
> (Moore and Maton 2001: 172)

Things could not look more different in sociology.[14] On the other hand, mathematics also shares this temporal feature with literature. Gyorgy Markus (2003) has remarked that the 'tradition' in the arts is 'ever expanding' and 'of great depth in time' (2003: 15), a feature he contrasts to science which has a 'short-term' tradition, because it is ever 'evolving' (ibid.). Which knowledge form is nearer to which? Maths and science in one sense; and maths, literature and perhaps sociology in another? The fact is, it is not at all clear which forms comprise the middle of the knowledge range. Is geography closer to physics than to biology, for example, and how would we know? Would we count their respective numbers of languages? It is certainly the case that empirical study would help to shed light on the theory, but it is also likely that the theory stands in need of some elaboration.

Towards a logic of the social and human sciences

As we saw in the previous section, Bernstein develops a language of description for dealing with variations in knowledge structure that provides us with tools for discussing variation that are so far unmatched in sociology, with the possible exception of Randall Collins (Collins 2000). Bernstein's main intent was to develop a way of discussing how different symbolic ensembles become socially distributed. In so doing, he had also to confront the age-old question as to how knowledge progresses. The conciseness of the concepts of verticality and grammaticality have taken us a considerable way towards those goals. And yet, the long shadow of physicalist idealism falls over this attempt, as it does over practically all other attempts in the history of philosophy and social thought. When the chips are down, Bernstein's model for knowledge progression is ineluctably that of physics or, more precisely, as Cassirer expresses it, that of the mathematical sciences of nature. Here the recurrent problem for sociology rears its head again: is there only one ideal form of objectivity, namely that of physics? Or is there another?

Bernstein certainly strives to distinguish the form of progression in hierarchical knowledge structures from that in horizontal knowledge structures. But the difficulty is apparent in the name he gives to the latter. These progress, says Bernstein, by developing parallel theoretical languages, that is, horizontally. It is not hard to see that while this might account for how knowledge elaborates, it cannot account for how it grows. The pathos of this description is sharpened when we consider it in the light of Bernstein's own strenuous attempts to develop a more vertical and robust language of description for sociology. Yet according to his own account of how sociological knowledge develops, his attempt can at best contribute another parallel language. It is not expressly said in these terms, but it is hard to avoid the conclusion that, unless and until sociology can stiffen its vertical spine and develop more powerful worldly corroborations – that is, become more like physics – sociological knowledge will not progress.

We return inevitably to the dilemma that we raised earlier (Muller 2006). We argued that Bernstein characterizes hierarchical knowledge growth in a way that parallels the accounts of the logical positivists, and horizontal knowledge growth after the accounts of Kuhn and the constructivists. This effectively rules out the possibility of growth or progress in the social sciences. We are thus left with a position that is uncomfortably close to the relativism of pragmatism and constructivism, a position with which Bernstein in his larger intents certainly did not align himself. As we saw at the beginning of this chapter, for Bernard Williams the two views – a commitment to verticality or truthfulness on the one hand and scepticism about its realization on the other – do not co-exist happily. The latter must inexorably corrode the former.

At least the outlines for a route out of this impasse can be gleaned from another of Bernstein's favourite sources, Ernst Cassirer (Durkheim being the first). Cassirer wrote in the period between the two world wars, at a time when natural science, especially physics, was at a peak of creative flowering, when the humanities were in something of a decline and when philosophy at least in Germany 'enfeebled and slowly undermined the forces that could have resisted the modern political myths' (Cassirer was referring here to Heidegger's tacit endorsement of Nazism; Cassirer 1943). Whereas mathematics provided a meta-language for organizing the burgeoning knowledge of nature (O'Halloran 2006), philosophy, which had, since Descartes and Kant, played a similar organizing role also for the humanities, had begun to fragment, helped on in no small measure by the range of 'vitalisms' associated with the work of Bergson, Heidegger, Nietzsche and the pragmatists who we discussed earlier in this chapter. For the 'vitalists', as physics and the mathematical world had become severed from Life, and philosophy had been consumed by the arid abstractions of Logic (logical positivism), the consequent aridity was threatening Life itself.

Not only were the humanities internally fragmenting (proliferating parallel languages, in Bernstein's terms), unconstrained by a unifying philosophical meta-language, but they were decisively parting company with the natural sciences. Cassirer, like Hegel and Husserl before him, felt the need to return to first principles, to reassert the unity of man, as both a part of nature and separate from the rest of nature, and therefore the unity of all knowledge, while giving each branch of knowledge its distinctive due.

Cassirer's fundamental gesture was to assert, against the vitalists and the pragmatists, that knowledge, indeed all culture, was fundamentally formal in the sense of being necessarily symbolically mediated. In order to understand a knowledge form one had to understand the logical structure of the symbols that constituted it. Cassirer distinguished, in his four-volume work *The Philosophy of Symbolic Forms* (Cassirer 1996), between three principal forms of knowledge, a threefold division somewhat reminiscent of Bernstein's horizontal discourse, hierarchical and horizontal knowledge structures. But whereas Bernstein distinguished the internal structure of these forms principally in terms of their distributive potential, Cassirer discusses them more fundamentally in terms of their function, as to how each relates a symbol to its object. In the expressive function of symbols (paradigmatically found in mythic thought), the relation is mimetic; there is a unity of symbol and object, and the two are not distinguished. It follows that there can only be different myths, not better myths. In the representational function of symbols (paradigmatically, the case of language), the relation is analogical; there is an absolute disjunction between symbol and object, metaphorically distancing symbol-categories from the world of particulars. In the conceptual function of symbols (paradigmatically the case of science), the relation is properly symbolic (or conceptual); the object is viewed as a construction of the symbol. This frees the symbol-category to be a general case, untied to any one particular or determinate context, and hence able to function as a signifier for the entire class of particulars (Verene 1969: 38). It is only with this disarticulation of symbol-category and particulars that we are able to generate stable conceptual descriptions of the world that are not dependent on any one particular part of it, the condition for any objective description (Habermas 2001: 18). This progressive abstraction of the symbol system from particulars comes with a price: the loss of the 'living body' and an increasing dependence on 'a semanticised nature' (2001: 24). Only the fourth symbolic form, art (the others being myth, language and science) for Cassirer successfully balances freedom and abstraction. The others all, to a greater or lesser extent, pay 'Descartes' price', the loss of immediacy for greater generalizing power (O'Halloran 2006).

We can see more clearly here than we can in the case of Bernstein how Cassirer extrapolates a set of distinctions drawn from a traditional evolutionary account of the history of consciousness to its 'systematic dimensions' (Verene 1969: 44), from an account of stages of development to differences of logical structure. To put this another way, Cassirer's theory of civilization presumes an increasingly sophisticated distancing of symbolic forms from their object domains, the costs mitigated by the reunifying power of the arts.[15] The conceptual extrapolation is identical in each case. We can also see an intriguingly parallel argument to that of Durkheim's, with both deriving the lineaments of scientific thought from that of mythic or, for Durkheim, religious thought. Yet Cassirer was acutely aware of the need to avoid the trap of setting up science (or at least physical science) as the prototype of all knowledge, and likewise of setting up strict logic as the prototype of intelligibility for all forms of the human spirit, as Hegel had done. 'Cassirer regards his philosophy of symbolic forms as an attempt to create a system that overcomes the tendency towards logic inherent in Hegel's system' (Verene 1969: 35).

In the terms developed in this chapter, Cassirer intended his system to provide an account of verticality (general/particular relations) that did not reduce all knowledge progression to the verticality requirements of physics. So where Durkheim had attempted to deal with the pragmatists' 'reduction to scepticism' with a purely conceptual attack on their principal premises, Cassirer attempted to avoid the cognate trap of the cultural pessimism of the vitalists by avoiding the subordination of spirit to logic in philosophy that culminated in the logical positivism from which our contemporary vitalists (constructivists and pragmatists both) are trying to extricate themselves. Cassirer's attempt is based on the differential internal structure of different knowledge forms, as it was for Bernstein and for Durkheim in his *Elementary Forms of Religious Life* (Durkheim 1995). Where Bernstein's account was based on the results of structural difference (pyramids and parallel languages), whose differential distribution he then set out to account for, Cassirer aimed for the principle that constructed the difference by theorizing the differential relation of concept to object in terms of differential objectification.

Cassirer starts by delineating two broad families of scientific concepts. The conceptually organized perception of things is organized into a set of organic forms, which constitute the sciences of nature, and the conceptually organized perception of expressions is organized into a set of symbolic forms, or sciences of culture. Organic forms (or natural concepts) differ from symbolic forms in the form of objectification they effect. In organic forms the object is accounted for entirely – subsumed – by the natural concept via mathematicization; this is a subsumption that can be expressed in formal mathematical terms. The natural concept, expressed ideally as a law, allows for (in theory) the complete deduction of the object. In symbolic forms, or cultural concepts, by contrast, the concept and its properties characterize but do not (cannot precisely) determine the object.

What Cassirer is here setting out as the key logical distinction between the two families of concepts is the subsumptability of particulars by a structural law. As he puts it, 'We understand a science in its logical structure only once we have clarified the manner in which it achieves the subsumption of the particular and the universal' (quoted in the translator's Introduction to Cassirer 2000: xxxv). Where the natural sciences aim for perfect subsumption, leading to a 'unity of being' (of a concept united with a particular), the cultural sciences aim for imperfect subsumption, leading to a 'unity of direction' whereby a concept indicates certain features of the particular but does not exhaust its semantic potential. The idea of 'imperfection' here should not be interpreted as some kind of deficit. Rather, the principal objects of the cultural sciences – expressions – exhibit a freedom that natural objects do not have because cultural objects are always mediated, in ways that natural objects are not, by a certain self-consciousness or reflexiveness. In other words, whereas the natural sciences generate concepts of things, the cultural sciences generate concepts of concepts. This places strict limits on the subsumptability of particulars by concepts claiming universality in the cultural sciences. The result is that descriptions in the cultural sciences can express regularities that have all the lineaments of truth but whose description may not be found in all details in any one particular case. The particular is classified by, but not subordinated to, the universal.

Cassirer's example is of Burkhardt's concept of the 'Renaissance man', which provides a generic description that will not be found in all aspects in any one particular Renaissance man. Bernstein's vertical and horizontal discourses and knowledge structures are themselves examples of such concepts; there are others in sociology, although there are few in the sociology of education.

What we see Cassirer doing here is conceding the first part of the critique that Vico and the vitalists launched against scientific naturalism; namely, that the *mathesis universalis* (or mathematicization) is unable to explain cultural objects. In other words, for Cassirer, scientific naturalism is a special case, not the general case. But a special case of what? Cassirer provides the surprising answer: it is a special case of constituting objectivity. Perfect subsumption is one, but only one, form of constituting objectivity; imperfect subsumption is another. Both aim at the same end, namely, achieving the maximum absorption of the object by the concept, taking account of the particular form of resistance offered by the kind of object in question. Two conclusions follow: cultural objects are not analysable like natural objects; but that does not, in the least respect, absolve the cultural sciences from the obligation to truth, which is to aim for the maximum amount of abstraction or objectification possible under the circumstances consistent with the nature of the objects under study. Durkheim would not have conceded as much to the pragmatists but, curiously, the end result is the same: for both Durkheim and Cassirer, knowledge of the social must be objective in order to be knowledge.

The place of Cassirer in our account should be getting clearer. Whereas Durkheim asserts the objectivity of the social ('social facts'), he does so without showing in his methodological discussions in what way objectivity in 'social facts' might be differently constituted from the way it is in 'natural facts'; the primary and common feature of both for Durkheim is their externality. For this omission – since the discussion on pragmatism clearly shows it to be an omission – he is still, in some ill-informed circles, considered to have been a positivist. Bernstein, on the other hand, displays what Cassirer might have called a 'conceptual formalism' which was not so much wrong as partial, a partiality that he only belatedly situated in a broader methodological framework with his discussion of internal and external languages of description. For his inadvertent imputed omissions he is still regarded, probably in the same ill-informed circles, as a 'structuralist'.

In his fourth study in *The Logic of the Cultural Sciences*, Cassirer (2000) makes perhaps his most daring move, which is to argue that formal and causal explanations are artificially separated, not only in the natural sciences since post-Newtonian science excised Aristotelian formalism,[16] but also in the cultural sciences. Both branches of science need reintegrating, but how could that be understood without a reversion to naturalism? It is this that Cassirer set out to do. Cassirer distinguishes between four forms of analysis that together constitute a general approach to the sciences of culture. The first he calls the 'analysis of work' (as in the 'works of culture'), by which he means a general empirical classification of the object-types to be studied in the cultural sciences. Having isolated the object-types – the different material classes of culture such as art, religion, pedagogy, etc. – a second analysis is called for that he refers to as the 'analysis of form'; that is, a morphology of the different forms in terms of structure and function.[17] Having established the essential formal properties of a cultural form, Cassirer argues that we need next to explore how the contents of these forms vary across social groups and temporal periods. This calls for what he refers to as an 'analysis of cause' – a causal analysis of social and historical variation of formal configurations. Finally, and this mode of analysis can only come at the end, he suggests that we initiate an 'analysis of act', that is, an analysis of dispositions or habitus which constitute the subjective experiences of the cultural forms. What this betokens is a presumptive sequence of analyses that shows how descriptive, conceptual, causal and interpretive moments of analysis can be considered as parts of an overall analytical strategy. There are two points that deserve emphasis. The first is that each moment constitutes an 'objective' analytical move; the second is that 'causal' and 'formal' moments do not belong to organic and symbolic forms respectively. All scientific analysis in the cultural sciences can, in principle, embrace all of these analytical methods. With this, the unity of knowledge is once more preserved.

Crude as this may be, this approach displays Cassirer's cardinal virtue, which is to have demonstrated the essential unity of conceptual inquiry by showing the way out of the impasse that scientific naturalism, the dominant account of unity, had created. At the same time and in the most civil way possible he shows why the constructivist/vitalist alternative turns out to be the 'false sortie' that it is. The truth is that the failure of the natural sciences to deal adequately with cultural phenomena is no reason to reject a science of culture or a social science. In other words, Cassirer provides the outline of a philosophical justification for scientific objectivism in both the natural and social sciences.

Conclusions: the sociology of knowledge in educational studies

Arising from the tension between being truthful and the idea of truth that was identified by the philosopher, Bernard Williams, this chapter has taken four steps in the journey to find an adequate basis for the sociology of knowledge in educational studies (and more generally). First we set out to document the weaknesses of the social constructivist position as it emerged in the 1970s, and which, with few changes, is still with us today (and largely, but not entirely, unchallenged) (Weiss *et al.* 2006; Young 2006). To do this we drew on the remarkable parallels between Durkheim's diagnosis of the weaknesses of pragmatism and the problems that the 1970s social constructivism gave rise to. Our second step was to extend the discussion to Durkheim and establish his two fundamental insights for the sociology of knowledge. The first was that the sociality of knowledge does not undermine its objectivity and the possibility of truth, but is the condition for it. The second is the key role that he gives to differentiation (for him between the sacred and the profane) as the origins of speculative thought and the growth of knowledge. Despite these insights, Durkheim was more concerned with the conditions for the possibility of knowledge – the Kantian question expressed in sociological terms – than with the development of knowledge itself. Furthermore, just as Kant's model of truth was Euclid's geometry, so for Durkheim it was the natural sciences. This limits the extent to which Durkheim's sociology of knowledge can, on its own, provide an adequate alternative to pragmatism and social constructivism.

Our third step was to turn to the work of the leading contemporary Durkheimian, Basil Bernstein, and his highly original analysis of knowledge structures and their variation. Bernstein takes Durkheim's insights further than anyone else. However, he is, like Durkheim, trapped in the assumption that physics represents the model for all knowledge growth. Ironically, this leads to his inability to provide the grounds for the progress that his own theory makes. Our fourth step was to turn to the German philosopher, little known among sociologists, Ernest Cassirer. Rather than classifying different knowledge structures, Cassirer classifies different types of objectivity, according to the relationship that the concepts of knowledge form have to their object. Crucially, this allows sociology to free itself from the trap of comparison with the mathematical sciences at the same time as not thereby renouncing the possibility of objective sociological knowledge; the natural sciences for Cassirer are a special case of objectification, not a model for objectivity itself.

We argue that Cassirer takes us further than Bernstein by theorizing the well-spring of knowledge progression – objectification – in terms of two different forms of subsumption. To put that in plainer terms: while Bernstein, despite his own best efforts, left us with an unsatisfactory account of knowledge progression for sociology, as a kind of lateral sprawl of new languages, Cassirer explains the differential prospects for knowledge growth in sociology in terms of the expressiveness of its object domain. Whereas it could be argued that Bernstein conceded too much to the sceptics in his account of sociological progress in terms solely of horizontal proliferation, not in terms of verticality, Cassirer allows us to reconsider sociology's prospects in terms of a different verticality. In addition, Cassirer's analysis suggests that sociology could be examined in terms of his four modes discussed earlier in this chapter; 'work', 'form', 'cause' and 'act'. His argument is that these modes are equally applicable to all forms of knowledge. We have hardly begun to explore the implications of our journey for the sociology of education. Suffice to say, it would take us far from the well intentioned naiveties of social constructivism.

For sociology in general, it should be clear that it has an embarrassment of riches in terms of Cassirer's fourth mode (the interpretative, where the subjective outweighs the objective) and the first mode (where particularity is weakly subsumed into a generalizing conceptual framework, if at all). Where we remain weak is in the second and third modes, which refer to conceptual and causal analysis. This is manifestly where our best efforts should now be directed.

To return to Williams one last time: in his most artful way, Williams suggests that a commitment to truthfulness shorn from a commitment to truth ends up in a bogus valorization of sincerity, that principle most prized by the image industry. To imagine that sincerity, a commitment to knowing our inner selves, is sustainable without a commensurate commitment to knowing our external world, natural or social, is possibly the central illusion of our age. As Harry Frankfurt puts it in his unexpected and heartening little bestseller, *On Bullshit*,

> The contemporary proliferation of bullshit also has deeper sources, in various forms of scepticism which deny that we can have any reliable access to objective reality ... [which leads to the] pursuit of an alternative ideal of sincerity ... . Our natures are, indeed, elusively insubstantial – notoriously less stable than the natures of other things. And insofar as this is the case, sincerity itself is bullshit.

> (Frankfurt 2005: 64–67)

It is the world beyond bullshit that is the one worth exploring. Further, it is (or should be) the world that education is about. The nature of that world, and the conditions under which it shapes the curriculum, define the project of the sociology of educational knowledge.

Endword

Basil Bernstein: a personal appreciation

I first met Basil Bernstein as an MA student at Essex University in 1966. The effect of his seminars on me and, I am sure, on my fellow students, was electric, and a revelation about what sociology of education might involve. It went far beyond anything we could have found in a book or a journal. We came to his seminars full of enthusiasm for sociological theory (nearly all American, as that was what was mostly available in 1966!) that we imagined could be 'applied' to education. However, Bernstein had quite other ideas; he saw education as a social phenomenon in its own right and as a source of theories about society as well as a source of problems of which to make sense. For him, the task of the sociologist was not to apply theories to education that had been developed elsewhere, but to make explicit the ways in which educational institutions and categories exemplified features of the society of which they were a part. In this way, sociology of education not only offered a fresh and more objective view of educational problems, but could address more fundamental issues about the nature of society. Bernstein saw that who we are and who we become and how societies are made and changed are all influenced in important ways by institutions like the school and the curriculum and by processes like pedagogy and assessment.

I sometimes used to travel to London with Basil after the Essex seminars and on a number of occasions he invited me back to his home in Dulwich. We would talk late into the night in what was both a continuing conversation and, for me, an extended tutorial. It was during these talks that he made two suggestions that were to shape the rest of my professional life. First, he encouraged me to apply for a lectureship in sociology of education at the Institute of Education; something I, only recently a school teacher, had not dreamed of considering. Second, he introduced me to the idea that it was the curriculum – the very stuff of education – that should be at the centre of the sociology of education. The curriculum was the topic of my MA dissertation, and has been at the centre of my research interests ever since.

The story of how my first book, *Knowledge and Control* (Young 1971), came about tells much of Bernstein's generosity to a junior colleague with an academic reputation still to make. He encouraged me to present a paper on the sociology of the curriculum to the 1970 Annual Conference of the British Sociological

Association. When it was clear that the official collection of conference papers was not going to point to the new directions for the sociology of education that he thought were important, it was Bernstein who suggested that I should edit a book that would sharpen the issues. The idea for a book took shape after the conference in the bar of the Russell Hotel in a conversation with Basil and Pierre Bourdieu (who had also spoken at the conference). Bernstein not only encouraged me to edit the book, but helped me to find a publisher, and agreed that his own paper should be included. Furthermore, despite his own strong views, and the fact that he was far from sympathetic to the book's eclectic and (with hindsight) over-relativist approach to knowledge and the curriculum, he made no attempt to influence its content or my editorial role.

Sociology of education in the 1970s was dominated by the debate, which seemed all-important to many of us at the time, between the 'old' and the 'new' sociologies of education. It was Basil Bernstein who pointed out that the debate could be understood not only in its own terms but, sociologically, as an example of generational conflict within the academic community. I was reluctant to see this at the time, and remember being quite upset when his paper making this argument was published in an Open University Reader; it felt almost like a personal attack. It was not until much later, when confronted with the extreme relativism of contemporary postmodernists, that I recognized the full importance of his insight.

The sociology of education would be infinitely poorer without the contributions of Basil Bernstein. Everyone's list of what they find important will vary. For me, after 40 years since meeting him, it was his continued affirmation of the importance of the work of Emile Durkheim, especially at a time when many of us too readily dismissed him as a conservative functionalist. It was from Basil Bernstein, although not always at the time, that I learned about the creative as well as the constraining role of boundaries in the development of new knowledge, and Durkheim's conviction, long before it was 'discovered' by sociologists of science such as Randall Collins, that the social character of knowledge (and therefore, necessarily, the curriculum) did not undermine its objectivity; on the contrary, it is the condition for it.

Basil Bernstein's legacy will continue to be felt in many different intellectual fields. For those of us who met him and worked with him, this legacy will relate as much to him as a person as to his writings. He and I had our differences and sadly we spoke together little in his last years. However, I shall always regard it as a privilege that I was taught by him and worked with him as a colleague. In particular, I shall remember his continuing ability to ask the important educational questions, his scepticism about anything that seemed like an intellectual fashion, and his willingness to take the ideas of others seriously. Finally, there is something that I am sure will stay with many of us: even a decade after he retired and when he was already far from well, Basil Bernstein never thought his job was done; he never gave up tackling the most fundamental educational problems faced by modern societies.

A final thought. Bernstein was an extremely complex person but always, I think, a radical at heart. However, he had the courage as well as the insight to know that even for radicals there are things which it is vital to conserve.

Notes

1 Rescuing the sociology of educational knowledge from the extremes of voice discourse

1 The term 'field positioning strategy' refers to the way that ideas can be used, often by new or marginal members of an intellectual field, to assert their right to be taken seriously vis-à-vis the established figures in the field.
2 Collins (1998) explores this approach in the case of philosophy.
3 The notable exception is of course Durkheim, whose social theory of knowledge is discussed in Chapter 4.
4 Since the initial version of this chapter was published, I have come across an interesting paper by David Pelz (Pelz 1996). He argues that those such as Bloor (1991), who claim that Mannheim showed a 'failure of nerve' in relation to the sociology of the natural sciences, are guilty of, at best, a misrepresentation. Pelz suggests that in excluding the natural sciences and mathematics from the sociology of knowledge, Mannheim was primarily concerned with establishing the 'scientific' status of sociology without requiring the discipline to follow models developed within the natural sciences. He was more agnostic, Pelz says, as to whether, in the longer term, a sociology of scientific knowledge was possible. In this he had more in common with Cassirer (Cassirer 2000), who is discussed in Chapter 15, than I, certainly, would have supposed.
5 I find that a similar problem arises in the work of philosophers of education who seek to find a basis for thinking about education in the idea of 'social practices' (Hirst 1993).
6 In Chapter 5, I partially revise this view. Education is always a fundamentally practical activity. However, it is a highly complex form of practice, with multiple determinants, and it follows, I argue, that there is an important space for theories of education that are not immediately located in practice.
7 Although I still think that the insular/connective distinction between types of specialization continues to offer some insights into the implications of curriculum change, I have become more aware of its weaknesses and, in particular, the extent to which it makes no explicit links to a theory of knowledge. In Chapter 11, I take up this point in developing a critical analysis of the idea of connectivity as a curriculum principle, and explore some of its implications.

2 Knowledge and the curriculum in the sociology of education

1 The debates discussed here refer to the period 1997 to 2000, and many of the specific issues have changed. However, there is no evidence that the underlying assumptions nearly a decade later have changed.
2 This issue is dealt with in some detail in Chapter 11.
3 Three observations are worth making about this account eight years after the paper on which this chapter is based was written. First, although the A-level system still relies

on individual choice, this has been significantly extended by the introduction of a six-module structure. Second, over the period, the steady fall in the number of candidates for the sciences and foreign languages has continued. Third, the expansion of 'staying on' at 16 which continued until the mid-1990s has not continued. The contrast in rates of post-compulsory participation with many other continental European countries suggests a structural feature of English society that has yet to be seriously examined by sociologists.

4 This comment about the periodic table was made with some irony seven years ago. However, the latest QCA proposals for GCSE science suggest that a significant reduction in the content of science syllabuses is turning out to be a disturbingly reliable prediction (see 'Science for the twenty-first century pilot', online. Available at: <http://www.qca.org.uk/10963_1734.html> (accessed 8 February 2007).

5 There are some parallels between this idea of knowledge being 'rarely if ever' monolithic and the arguments of the critical realists such as Roy Bhaskar (Bhaskar 1975) for the stratification or multi-dimensionality of the world (and hence of knowledge).

6 For a useful extension of these ideas by drawing on Knorr-Cetina's concept of an 'epistemic community', see Guile 2006.

7 Notable exceptions are the ASDAN Youth Award and the new Trinity College/Guildhall Community Arts Award supported by the Arts Council. It is, however, worth noting that both are located in relatively marginal parts of the curriculum. The test will be the extent to which they can provide models for mainstream subject areas.

8 Chapter 6 develops this idea.

3 Durkheim, Vygotsky and the curriculum of the future

1 In fact, those supporting hybridity tend to reject the possibility of pedagogic grounds.

2 My point here is not to oppose schools, colleges and universities trying to attract new students, but to question whether this should itself be a *curriculum* criterion.

3 As I note later in the chapter, both Durkheim and Bernstein recognize the issue of knowledge change; however, their discussions are not central to their overall sociology of knowledge.

4 There are indications that Vygotsky (see Vygotsky 1987: 28) was aware of the need to deal specifically with the problem of knowledge in his theory, though it is unclear how he would have tackled it if he had lived longer.

5 This point is developed further in Chapter 4.

6 The social anthropolgist Robin Horton (Horton 1974) argues that Durkheim was somewhat ambivalent as to the extent to which the sacred/profane distinction survived in modern societies of his time.

7 Durkheim did not concern himself either with the role of religion in provoking conflict or with relations between nations in which the role of religion, even in his time, was far from integrative.

8 For example, whether or not they can be represented mathematically (Collins 1998).

9 Some recent interpreters of Kant (e.g. Garnham 2000) have argued that his philosophy was an implicit social theory and that he always saw reason as having to resolve arguments within a community, however abstractly expressed. This strand is most evocatively expressed for Garnham in Kant's view of man's 'a-social sociality'.

10 It follows from Durkheim's argument that capacity for abstract thinking was not an individual capacity unevenly distributed, but a property of being a member of a society.

11 If expressed in the terms Durkheim used for analysing the social division of labour, this stratification of knowledge would be an example of what he referred to as the 'forced' division of labour (Durkheim 1964).

12 In a discussion of Durkheim's analysis of the medieval university, Bernstein writes about the progressive dislocation of the knowing self from the process of knowing the world (see Bernstein 2000 and Chapter 11).

13 As Daniels (2001) points out, there are also similarities with Bernstein's vertical and horizontal knowledge structures.

14 One example is when Vygotsky states that 'philosophically this argument [that logical thought and the need for knowledge of truth itself arises in the interaction between the consciousness of the child and the consciousness of others] is reminiscent of Durkheim' (Vygotsky 1987: 85).

15 This may have been a tactical political decision, given that many Soviet writers at the time saw a reference to Durkheim as a sign of bourgeois revisionism.

16 Vygotsky shared this view of pedagogy with his Marxist contemporary, the Italian Antonio Gramsci, who linked pedagogy to his theory of hegemony.

17 The emergence of organic solidarity which Durkheim identified in his study of the division of labour (Durkheim 1964) was his response to Comte and Marx, who both thought that changes in the division of labour would lead a breakdown of social order. Whereas Marx welcomed this possibility as the conditions for the new society (socialism), Comte argued that it needed to be stopped – if necessary, by an autocratic government.

18 Some of the implications of interpreting Vygotsky's concepts as part of a Marxist theory were indicated in the previous section.

19 'I want to find out how science has to be built ... having learned the whole of Marx's method' (Vygotsky 1987).

20 At the same time, Vygotsky explicitly emphasizes why this is no justification for not teaching grammar (Vygotsky 1987: 100).

21 There is of course a parallel with Marxism as a theory of society. Despite the loss of interest in Marxism, both within left-wing politics and within the academic community since the 1980s, it remains a powerful if increasingly neglected critique of contemporary capitalism. On the other hand, few would still claim that it offers either an adequate theory of social transformation or a basis for generating non-capitalist alternatives.

22 Unless one wants to claim, as Hardt and Negri do in their book *Empire* (Hardt and Negri 2000), that the anti-globalization/anti-capitalist protesters are the successors to Marx's proletariat.

23 The Soviet psychologist L.V. Zankov invoked the authority of Vygotsky in developing the following didactic principles:

- high level of difficulty of the subject matter;
- rapid pace of instruction;
- leading role of theoretical knowledge;
- conscious school work of pupils;
- systematic and aim-targeted development of every pupil in the class.

Peter Gavora (Comenius University, Bratislava) informs me that attempting to introduce these principles nearly crippled the Czechoslovak primary school system between 1970 and 1980.

24 Although Durkheim was sympathetic to the pragmatism of James and Dewey as a kind of sociological philosophy, he was worried about its links with idealist philosophy, which was being popularized in France at the time by Bergson. Durkheim feared that pragmatism with its instrumental idea of truth could be used to undermine the credibility of science (see chapter 15).

25 In using this term I am suggesting no links with the tradition of social realism in art and cinema.

4 'Structure' and 'activity' in Durkheim's and Vygotsky's theories of knowledge

1 The parallels with similar trends in social and educational theory that were discussed in Chapters 1 and 2 are not hard to see.

2 For Durkheim, as Paul Fauconnet says in his introduction to Durkheim's *Education and Sociology*,

> the transmission [of knowledge] through the teacher to the pupil, the assimilation by the child of a subject seemed to him [Durkheim] to be the condition of real intellectual formation ... . Forms [of the mind] cannot be transmitted empty. Durkheim, like Comte, thinks that it is necessary to learn about things, to acquire knowledge.
>
> (Fauconnet's introduction to Durkheim 1956)

Vygotsky expresses the crucial role of knowledge transmission slightly less directly in the way that he links pedagogy to the move from 'everyday' to 'theoretical' concepts.

3 More space in this chapter is given to Durkheim's work than that of Vygotsky. This is for two reasons. First, as a sociologist I am more familiar with Durkheim's work. Second, the issue of knowledge with which I am concerned, although often neglected by sociologists, is at the centre of Durkheim's work and only indirectly addressed by Vygotsky.

4 I am using 'social realist' in the sense that for both writers, knowledge and society are realities that are independent of individual actions and beliefs.

5 Social activity is not used in this chapter in the specific sense that is associated with activity theory, the tradition that specifically derives from Vygotsky's work. Rather 'social activity' is used here in its broader materialist sense, similar to Marx's use of the concepts 'human labour' and 'labour process'. It refers to the ways people in history have engaged in collective activities (initially in the form of hunting and gathering) to appropriate the natural world for their survival needs, and later for the creation of wealth.

6 This point about Vygotsky having a social theory of knowledge is especially significant as it has been largely neglected in the psychologically oriented tradition of activity theory within which his work has been developed.

7 The distinction between types of classifications can be seen as the precursor, as Joe Muller (University of Capetown) pointed out to me, of Bernstein's distinction between vertical and horizontal discourse and knowledge structures (Bernstein 2000).

8 Some, such as Needham (1970) and Worsley (1956), have argued that the 'epistemological priority' that Durkheim assigns to society is the least convincing element of his social theory of knowledge.

9 The following section draws significantly on Worsley's account (Worsley 1956).

10 This issue about the roots of knowledge arises in another context in considering whether, as Roger Penrose (2005) argues, even the most abstract mathematics such as the pattern of the primes appear to have a material as well as a conceptual basis (this point is returned to in Chapter 15).

11 A position not endorsed by more recent research (Derry 2003; 2004).

12 Some would include the work of the French sociologist Pierre Bourdieu. However, my view is that Bourdieu was a sociologist primarily interested in the question of power, even when he wrote specifically about the sociology of science (Bourdieu 1975). Knowledge itself was only a secondary concern for him – or, as he might have put it, just another field within which power struggles are played out.

13 In stressing the weaknesses of Vygotsky's theory as an explanation of the inadequacies of Soviet schools, Davydov may be giving it too much importance when one can find very similar problems in education systems that have hardly heard of Vygotsky's ideas.

5 Curriculum studies and the problem of knowledge: updating the Enlightenment?

1 Successful acquisition is of course a complex social process that involves both a theory of pedagogy and a theory of learning.

2 Is it surprising that employers complain endlessly about the quality of those they recruit? The depressing thing is that governments somehow imagine that the problem

will be solved if employers are given more say over the curriculum. Employers quite legitimately want better qualified recruits; I have never yet heard one who wanted to give serious time to their education.

3 And of course this assumes that learning can somehow be learning for some other reason.

6 Education, knowledge and the role of the state: the 'nationalization' of educational knowledge?

1 Bernstein uses the term 'pedagogized'.
2 Chapter 2 develops this argument.
3 Crouch (2004) uses the term 'commercialization' to refer to similar developments.

7 Rethinking the relationship between the sociology of education and educational policy

1 Bernstein was surprisingly pessimistic about whether sociologists could claim to generate what he termed 'vertical knowledge structures'.
2 The presentations at the round table were the basis for the book I co-edited (Kraak and Young, 2001).
3 This is in no way to dismiss Erik Olin Wright's highly original Realistic Utopias Project at the University of Wisconsin (Madison, USA).
4 This does not mean he is responsible for my formulation.
5 It is important to stress that in this period the sociology of education community was extremely small.
6 Examples are those on the curriculum and on the work of Pierre Bourdieu and Basil Bernstein.
7 This shift was first pointed out for me by Phil Hodkinson in his review (Hodkinson 2000) of my book *The Curriculum of the Future* (Young 1998).

8 Contrasting approaches to qualifications and their role in educational reform

1 Qualifications are increasingly linked closely to funding mechanisms in a modern version of 'payments by results'. The impact of funding on the curriculum needs a discussion of its own which is not explored in this book.
2 NVQs drew on the earlier experience in the USA of competence-based certification and assessment, and more generally on the method of functional analysis developed within occupational psychology (Wolf 1995).
3 For example, apprentices and students might acquire integrity or develop their sense of responsibility.
4 The requirement, which was exemplified in the Training and Development Lead Body (TDLB) standards and insisted on by the NCVQ, was that teachers and trainers could be trained to interpret the criteria in the 'correct' way. It was not surprising that teachers dismissed the standards as de-skilling. The fact that the NCVQ was able to force teachers to engage in what was little more than ritual 'box ticking' merely compounded the problem.
5 A kind of modern equivalent to 'payment by results'.
6 I am thinking of the four 'home' countries in the UK that have adopted somewhat different approaches to qualifications reform, and New Zealand, Australia and South Africa, though somewhat similar reforms based on NVQs are being introduced in Mexico and some Eastern European countries.
7 A similar point was made by later researchers concerning the continuing role of selection based on social class in comprehensive schools.
8 However, as I have heard a number of further education lecturers remark, although more students may have learnt that it is a good thing to get a qualification, they do not always associate this with sustained and disciplined study!

9 An exception is those 'access' courses developed in the 1980s that were designed not to lead to qualification, but provided access to higher level programmes in further or higher education.

10 Questions need to be raised about the old 'communities of trust', especially as the numbers taking sciences and foreign languages in schools and universities decline.

12 Further education and training (FET) college teachers in South Africa and England: a knowledge-based profession of the future?

1 For a full account of this 'history of neglect' see Lucas 2004.

2 For details of the report see: http://image.guardian.co.uk/sys-files/Education/documents/2006/02/06/teachertrain.pdf (accessed 28 February 2007).

3 The nearest examples from the UK experience are the initiatives funded within the Enterprise in Higher Education and Teaching Company/Knowledge Transfer schemes.

4 As far as I am aware, professional development programmes for FE college lecturers based in the new universities in the UK have been based entirely in their education departments.

14 The knowledge question and the future of education in South Africa

1 This issue was discussed in detail in Chapter 12.

2 This issue was discussed in detail in Chapter 12.

3 For a more detailed discussion of these issues see Chapter 7.

15 Truth and truthfulness in the sociology of educational knowledge

1 See Nozaki (2006) and Moore and Muller (1999) for useful discussions of the problems that 'standpoint' theories give rise to.

2 It was of course over half a century since Durkheim made the theoretical case for the sociological study of education (Durkheim 1956). In the UK, Karl Mannheim had been appointed as the first Professor of Sociology of Education in 1946. However, he died within a year, and despite the efforts of those like Jean Floud and A.H. Halsey in the 1950s, it was not until the late 1960s that sociology of education in the UK became a distinct field of research and teaching within educational studies.

3 Perhaps the most sophisticated and influential example of this genre is the work of the American critical curriculum theorist, Michael Apple (1975).

4 One of the authors of this chapter was personally involved in these developments within the sociology of education (Young and Whitty 1977; Whitty and Young 1976).

5 An example of the time is the Reader that I edited by John Beck and colleagues (1977) in which there were chapter headings such as education, rationality, ability and childhood as social constructs. We are not here denying that such categories are and can be usefully seen as social constructs, but that social constructivism in the sociology of education set no limits on what could and could not be constructed in a particular context or over time. As Ian Hacking (2000) noted so perceptively, the idea of anything being a social construct is true at a trivial level; the conceptual issue is in what circumstances is this of more than trivial significance.

6 The terms 'radical' and 'moderate' social constructivism are frequently found in the literature. However, from the point of view of our argument in this chapter, this differentiation misses the point that for even moderate forms of social constructivism, the limits on what can be 'constructed' are always only implicit.

7 Philosophers were easily seen as merely defending their professional interests; an example of what later became generalized as standpoint theorizing!

8 The idea, never given much substance, of 'non reformist reforms' was popular among left educationalists at the time.

9 The idea of 'resistance' took on a life of its own, far removed from Willis's original study, and became elevated to the status of a 'theory' (Giroux 1983).

10 Whereas in North America this 'theorizing' took the overtly political form of the 'critical pedagogy' associated with writers such as Peter McLaren and Henry Giroux, in England a less clearly defined body of 'educational theory' emerged that was exemplified by writers such as Usher and Edwards (1994).

11 For a more measured commentary on these issues, see Haack (1998).

12 This, of course, is the premise of standpoint 'theory' referred to earlier. The kind of difficulties encountered by such an approach to knowledge are well brought out, if unresolved, by Nozaki (2006).

13 This is not to say that such incorporation has not been attempted in a horizontal knowledge structure like sociology. From Max Weber and Talcott Parsons onwards, sociological theory is strewn with largely unsuccessful attempts to integrate diverse sets of concepts into a single conceptual whole.

14 Or could they? Is not an epistemic community within sociology in which 'the past is in the present' assumed when we, in the first decade of the twenty-first century, engage with Durkheim's concept of anomie or Weber's concept of bureaucracy?

15 There are echoes here of Weber's far more pessimistic idea of disenchantment.

16 An excision that some argue is being rectified by 'modern' quantum physics.

17 An example of the kind of analysis that Cassirer is pointing to is Bernstein's famous morphologies of code orientation and pedagogy.

References

Abbott, A. (2000) *Chaos of Disciplines*, Chicago and London: University of Chicago Press.

Alexander, J.C. (1995) *Fin de Siècle Social Theory: Relativism, Reduction and the Problem of Reason*, London: Verso.

Allais, S. (2003) 'The National Qualifications Framework in South Africa: a democratic project trapped in a neo-liberal paradigm?', *Journal of Education and Work* 16 (3): 305–324.

Allais, S. (2006) Problems with qualification reform in senior secondary schools in South Africa, in Young, M. and Gamble, J. (eds) (2006) *Knowledge, Curriculum and Qualifications for South African Further Education*, Pretoria: HSRC Press.

Andersson, P. and Harris, J. (eds) (2006) *Re-theorising the Recognition of Prior Learning*, Leicester: NIACE.

Apple, M. (1975) *Ideology and Curriculum*, London: Routledge and Kegan Paul.

Arnold, M. (1960) *Culture and Anarchy*, Cambridge: Cambridge University Press.

Bakhurst, D. (1995) 'Social being and human essence: an unresolved issue in Soviet philosophy', *Studies in Eastern European Thought* 47: 3–60.

Ballerin, M. (2007) 'What kind of truth? A conversation with Young and Muller's "Truth and Truthfulness"' (unpublished; Department of Education) Bath: University of Bath.

Banks, O. (1954) *Parity and Prestige in English Secondary Education*, London: Routledge and Kegan Paul.

Barnett, M. (2006) 'Vocational knowledge and vocational pedagogy', in Young, M. and Gamble, J. (eds) *Knowledge Curriculum and Qualifications for South African Further Education*, Pretoria: HSRC Press.

Beck, J. (1998) *Morality and Citizenship in Education*, London: Cassell.

Beck, J. and Young, M. (2005) 'The assault on the professions and the restructuring of academic and professional identities: a Bernsteinian analysis', *British Journal of Sociology of Education* 26 (2): 183–198.

Beck, J., Jenks, C., Keddie, N. and Young, M. (eds) (1977) *Worlds Apart: Readings for a Sociology of Education*, London: Collier Macmillan.

Becker, H.S. (1967) 'Whose side are we on?', *Social Problems* 14 (Winter): 239–247.

Benson, O. and Stangroom, J. (2006) *Why Truth Matters*, London: Continuum Books.

Berlin, I. (2000) *Three Critics of the Enlightenment: Vico, Hammann, and Herder*, Princeton: Princeton University Press.

Bernstein, B. (1971) *Class, Codes and Control* (Volume 1), London: Routledge and Kegan Paul.

Bernstein, B. (1990) *Class, Codes and Control* (Volume 4), London: Routledge and Kegan Paul.

Bernstein, B. (1996) *Pedagogy, Symbolic Control and Identity: Theory, Research, Critique*, London: Taylor and Francis.

Bernstein, B. (2000) *Pedagogy, Symbolic Control and Identity: Theory, Research, Critique* (2nd edn), Oxford: Rowman and Littlefield.

Bhaskar, R. (1975) *A Realist Theory of Science*, Leeds: Leeds Books Ltd.

Billett, S. (1997) 'Dispositions, vocational knowledge and development: sources and consequences', *Australian and New Zealand Journal of Vocational Education Research* 5 (1): 1–26.

Bloor, D. (1991) *Knowledge and Social Imagery*, Chicago: Chicago University Press.

Boreham, N. (2002) 'Work process knowledge, curriculum control and the work-based route to vocational qualifications', *British Journal of Educational Studies* 50 (2): 225–237.

Bourdieu, P. (1975) 'The specificity of the scientific field and the social conditions of the progress of reason', in Lemert, C. (ed.) (1981) *French Sociology: Rupture and Renewal Since 1968*, New York: Columbia University Press.

Bourdieu, P. and Passeron, J.-C. (1977) *Reproduction in Education, Society and Culture*, London: Sage.

Bramall, S. (2000) *Why Learn Maths?* London: Institute of Education.

Braverman, H. 1976 *Labour and Monopoly Capital*, Monthly Review Press.

Bridges, D. (2000) 'Back to the Future: the higher education curriculum in the 21st century', *Cambridge Journal of Education*, 3 (1): 37–57.

Brier, M. (2002) 'Horizontal discourse in law and labour law', unpublished paper: South Africa: University of the Western Cape (Education Policy Unit).

Callinicos, A. (1998) *Social Theory: A Historical Introduction*, London and Cambridge: Polity.

Cassirer, E. (1943) 'Newton and Leibniz', *The Philosophical Review* 52 (4): 366–91.

Cassirer, E. (1996: 1923) *The Philosophy of Symbolic Forms: Volume 4, The Metaphysics of Symbolic Forms* (Trans. J.M. Krois), New Haven: Yale University Press.

Cassirer, E. (2000) *The Logic of the Cultural Sciences: Five Studies* (Trans. S.G. Lofts), New Haven: Yale University Press.

Castells, M. (1998) *The Information Age: Economy, Society and Culture*, Oxford: Blackwell.

Christie, F. (2002) *Classroom Discourse Analysis: A Functional Perspective*, London and Sydney: Continuum.

Coffield, F. (1999) 'Breaking the consensus: lifelong learning as social control', *British Educational Research Journal* 25 (4): 479–499.

Collins, H. (1981) 'Stages in the empirical programme of relativism', *Social Studies of Science* 11: 3–10.

Collins, R. (1998) *The Sociology of Philosophies: A Global Theory of Intellectual Change*, Cambridge, MA: The Bellknap Press of Harvard University Press.

Crewes, F. (2006) 'Introducing follies of the wise', online. Available at: <http://www.butter fliesandwheels.com/> (accessed 14 June 2006).

Crouch, C. (2004) *Post-Democracy*, Cambridge: Polity.

Cuvillier, F. (1955) *French Introduction to Durkheim* 1983.

Daniels, H. (2001) *Vygotsky and Pedagogy*, London: RoutledgeFalmer.

Dearing, R. (1996) *Qualifications for 16–19 year olds*, London: Qualifications and Curriculum Authority.

Demaine, J. (1981) *Contemporary Theories in the Sociology of Education*, London: Macmillan.

DfEE (1998) *The Learning Age*, London: Department for Education and Employment.

DfEE (1999) *Learning to Succeed*, London: Department for Education and Employment.

DfES (2003) *The Future of Higher Education*, London: The Stationery Office.

DfES (2005) *Higher Standards, Better Skills For All*, London: The Stationery Office.

Derry, J. (2003) 'Vygotsky and his critics: philosophy and rationality', unpublished PhD thesis: University of London.

Derry, J. (2004) 'The unity of intellect and will: Vygotsky and Spinoza', *Educational Review*, 56 (2): 113–120.

Donnelly, J. (1993) 'The origins of the technical curriculum in England during the 19th and early 20th centuries', in Jenkins, E. (ed.) *School Science and Technology: Some Issues and Perspectives*, Leeds: University of Leeds (Centre for Studies in Science and Mathematics Education).

Driver, R. (1983) *The Pupil as Scientist?*, Bletchley: Open University Press.

Durkheim, E. (1956) *Education and Sociology*, New York: Free Press.

Durkheim, E. (1964) *The Division of Labor in Society*, New York: Free Press of Glencoe.

Durkheim, E. (1977: 1938) *The Evolution of Educational Thought: Lectures on the Formation and Development of Secondary Education in France* (Trans. P. Collins), London: Routledge and Kegan Paul.

Durkheim, E. (1983) *Pragmatism and Sociology* (Trans. J.C. Whitehouse and J.B. Allcock with an Introduction by F. Cuvillier), Cambridge: Cambridge University Press.

Durkheim, E. (1995: 1912) *The Elementary Forms of Religious Life* (Trans. K. Fields), New York: The Free Press.

Durkheim, E. and Mauss, M. (1970) *Primitive Classification*, Chicago: University of Chicago Press.

Eagleton, T. (2005) 'Lend me a Fiver', a review of Jay, M. (2005) *Songs of Experience: Modern American and European Variations on a Universal Theme*, in *London Review of Books*, 23 June.

Engestrom, Y. (1991) *Learning by Expanding*, online. Available at: <http://lchc.ucsd.edu/ MCA/Paper/Engestrom/expanding/toc.htm> (accessed 28 February 2007).

Engestrom, Y. (2004) 'The new generation of expertise: seven theses', in Fuller, A., Munro, A. and Rainbird, H. (eds) *Workplace Learning in Context*, London: Taylor and Francis.

Ensor, P. (2003) 'The national qualifications framework and higher education in South Africa: some epistemological issues', *Journal of Education and Work*, 16 (3): 325–347.

Entwistle, H. (1979) *Antonio Gramsci: Conservative Schooling for Radical Politics*, London: Routledge and Kegan Paul.

Ertl, H. (2002) 'The concept of modularisation in vocational education and training: The debate in Germany and its implications', *Oxford Review of Education*, 28 (1): 53–73.

Evans, K., Hodkinson, P. and Unwin, L. (eds) (2003) *Working to Learn*, London: Kogan Page.

Fay, B. (1996) *Contemporary Philosophy of Social Science*, Oxford: Blackwell.

Finegold, D. and Soskice D. (1988) 'The failure of training in Britiain: analysis and prescription', *Oxford Review of Economic Policy* 4:21–53.

Finegold, D., Keep, E., Miliband, D., Raffe, D., Spours, K. and Young, M. (1990) *A British Baccalaureate: Ending the Division Between Education and Training*, London: Institute of Public Policy Research.

Floud, J., Halsey, A.H. and Martin, F.M. (1956) *Social Class and Educational Opportunity*, London: Heinemann.

Floud, J. and Halsey, A.H. (1958) 'The sociology of education: a trend report and bibliography', *Current Sociology* 3 (3): 66.

Foster, A. (2005) *Realising the Potential: A Review of the Future Role of Further Education Colleges*, London: DfES.

Frankfurt, H.G. (2005) *On Bullshit*, Princeton: Princeton University Press.

Freidson, E. (2001) *Professionalism; The Third Logic*, Cambridge: Polity.

Fuller, A., Munro, A. and Rainbird. H. (eds) (2004) *Workplace Learning in Context*, London: Taylor and Francis.

Gallagher, S. (2006) 'Blurring the boundaries or creating diversity? The contribution of further education to higher education in Scotland', *Journal of Further and Higher Education*, 30 (1): 43–59.

Gamble, J. (2006) 'What kind of knowledge for the vocational curriculum?', in Young, H. and Gamble, J. (eds) *Knowledge, Curriculum and Qualifications for South African Further Education*, Pretoria: HSRC Press.

Gamoran, A. (2002) 'The curriculum', in Levinson, D., Cookson, P.W. and Sadovnik, A. (eds) (2002) *Education and Sociology: An Encyclopedia*, New York/London: Routledge Falmer.

Garnham, N. (2000) *Emancipation, the Media and Modernity*, Oxford: Oxford University Press.

Gay, H. (2000) 'Association and practice: the City and Guilds of London Institute for the Advancement of Technical Education', *Annals of Science* 57: 369–98.

Gellner, E. (1974) 'The new idealism', in Giddens, A. (ed.) *Positivism and Sociology*, London: Heinemann.

Gellner, E. (1992) *Post Modernism, Reason and Religion*, London: Routledge.

Gibbons, M., Nowotny, H. and Scott, P. (2000) *Rethinking Science*, Cambridge: Polity.

Gibbons, M., Limoges, C., Nowotny, H., Schwartzman, S., Scott, P. and Trow, M. (1994) *The New Production of Knowledge*, London: Sage.

Giddens, A. (1979) *Central Problems in Social Theory*, London: Macmillan.

Giddens, A. (1993) *The Giddens Reader*, Basingstoke: MacMillan.

Giroux, H. (1983) *Theory and Resistance in Education: Towards a Pedagogy for the Opposition*, New York: Bergin and Garvey.

Gorbutt, D. (1972) 'Education as the control of knowledge: the new sociology of education', *Education for Teaching* 89: 3–12.

Gould, J. (1977) *The Attack on Higher Education: Marxist and Radical Penetration*, London: Institute for the Study of Conflict.

Gouldner, A. (1968) 'Sociologist as partisan', *The American Sociologist*, 3: 103–116.

Gramsci, A. (1971) *Selections from the Prison Notebooks* (ed. and trans. Q. Hoare and G. Nowell Smith), London: Lawrence and Wishart.

Green, A. (1990) *Education and State Formation*, Basingstoke: Macmillan.

Griffith, R. (2000) *National Curriculum: National Disaster*, London: Falmer.

Griffiths, T. and Guile, D. (2001) 'Learning through work experience', *Journal of Education and Work* 14 (1): 113–131.

Grugulis, I. (2003) *Skill and Qualification: The Contribution of NVQs to Raising Skill Levels*, SKOPE Research Paper 36, Cardiff: University of Cardiff.

Guile, D. (2000) What is distinctive about the knowledge economy? Implications for education, in Lauder, H. *et al.* (2006).

Haack, S. (1998) *Confessions of a Passionate Moderate*, Chicago: Chicago University Press.

Habermas, J. (1990) *The Philosophical Discourse of Modernity*, Cambridge: Polity Press.

Habermas, J. (2001) *The Liberating Power of Symbols: Philosophical Essays* (Trans. P. Dews), Cambridge, MA: MIT Press.

Hacking, I. (2000) *The Social Construction of What?*, Cambridge, MA: Harvard University Press.

Hardt, M. and Negri, A. (2000) *Empire*, Cambridge, MA: Harvard University Press.

Harre, R. and Krausz, M. (1996) *Varieties of Relativism*, Oxford: Blackwell.

Harris, J. (2006) 'Questions of knowledge and the curriculum in the recognition of prior learning', in Andersson, P. and Harris, J. (eds) *Re-theorising the Recognition of Prior Learning*, Leicester, England: NIACE..

Hartley, D. (1997) *Re-Schooling Society*, London: Falmer.

Hatermas, J. (1990) *The Philosophical Discourse of Modernity*, Cambridge: Polity Press.

Hedegaard, M. (1999) 'The influence of societal knowledge traditions on children's thinking and development', in Lompscher, J. and Hedegaard, M. (1999) *Learning Activity and Development*, Aarrhus, Denmark: Aarrhus University Press.

HMSO (1991) *Education and Training for the 21st Century*, London: HMSO.

Hirst, P. (1983) 'The foundations of the National Curriculum: why subjects?' in O'Hear, P. and White, J. (eds) *Assessing the National Curriculum*, London: Paul Chapman.

Hirst, P. and Peters, R. (1970) *The Logic of Education*, London: Routledge and Kegan Paul.

Hodkinson, P. (2000) Review of Young (1998), *Journal of Education and Work* 13 (1): 119–23.

Homans, G. (1964) 'Bringing men back in', *American Sociological Review* 29 (6): 809–818.

Horton, R. (1974) 'Levy-Bruhl, Durkheim and the scientific revolution', in Horton, R. and Finnegan, R. (eds) *Modes of Thought*, London: Faber.

Hoskyns, K. (1993) 'Education and the genesis of disciplinarity', in Messer-Davidow, E., Shumwy, D. and Sylvan, D. (eds) *Knowledges: Historical and Critical Studies in Disciplinarity*, Charlottesville, VA: University of Virginia Press.

Howieson, C., Raffe, D., Spours, K. and Young, M. (1997) 'Unifying academic and vocational learning; the state of the debate in England and Scotland', *Journal of Education and Work*, 10 (1): 5–35.

Jansen, J. and Christie, P. (1999) *Changing Curriculum*, Johannesburg: Juta Academic.

Jenks, C. (ed.) (1977) *Rationality, Education and the Social Organization of Knowledge: Papers for a Reflexive Sociology of Education*, London: Routledge and Kegan Paul.

Jessup, G. (1991) *Outcomes: NVQs and the Emerging Model of Education and Training*, Brighton: Falmer Press.

John-Steiner, V., Scribner, S. Cole, M and Souberman, S. (eds) (1978). *Mind in society: the development of higher psychological processes*. Cambridge, MA: Harvard University Press.

Karabel, J. and Halsey, A.H. (eds) (1977) *Power, Ideology and Education*, Oxford: Oxford University Press.

Keddie, N. (1971) 'Classroom knowledge', in Young, M. (ed.) *Knowledge and Control: New Directions for the Sociology of Education*, London: Collier Macmillan.

Keddie, N. (ed.) (1973) *Tinker, Tailor... The Myth of Cultural Deprivation*, London: Penguin.

Keep, E. (1998) 'Changes in the economy and the labour market: we are all knowledge workers now', in *Work and Education*, London: University of London Institute of Education (Post 16 Education Centre).

Keep, E. (2006) 'State control of the English education and training system – playing with the biggest train set in the world', *Journal of Vocational Education and Training* 58 (1): 47–64.

Knorr-Cetina, K. (1999) *Epistemic Cultures: How the Sciences make Knowledge*, Cambridge, MA: Harvard University Press.

Kraak, A. and Young, M. (2001) (eds) *Education in Retrospect: Education Policy in South Africa 1990–2000*, Pretoria: HSRC Press.

Kuhn, T.S. (1970) *The Structure of Scientific Revolutions* (2nd edn), Chicago: Chicago University Press.

Lasonen, J. (1996) *Strategies for Achieving Parity of Esteem in European Upper Secondary Education*, Finland: Institute of Educational Research, University of Jyvaskyla.

Lather, P. (1991) *Getting Smart: Feminist Research and Pedagogy: With/in the Postmodern*, London: Routledge.

Lauder, H., Brown, P., Dillabough, J-A. and Halsey, A. H. (2006) *Education, Globalisation and Social Change*, Oxford: Oxford University Press.

Lave, J. and Wenger, E. (1991) *Situated Learning: Legitimate Peripheral Participation*, Cambridge: Cambridge University Press.

Layton, D. (1984) *Interpreters of Science: A History of the Association of Science Education*, London: Murray.

Lecourt, D. (1977) *Proleterian Science? The Case of Lysenko*, London: New Left Books.

Leitch, S. (2006) *Prosperity for all in the Global Economy: World Class Skills: Final Report*, London: The Stationery Office.

Loft, S.G. (2000) *A 'Repetition of Modernity'*, New York: State University of New York Press.

Lompscher, J. and Hedegaard, M. (1999) *Learning Activity and Development*, Aarrhus, Denmark: Aarrhus University Press.

Lucas, N. (2004) *Teaching in Further Education*, London: Institute of Education.

Lukes, S. (1972) *Emile Durkheim: His Life and Work*, New York: Harper and Row.

Luria, A.R. and Vygotsky, L.S. (1992) *Ape, Primitive Man and Child*, Hemel Hempstead, England: Harvester Wheatsheaf.

Mansfield, B and Mitchell, L. (1996) *Towards a Competent Workforce*, Aldershot, England: Gower.

Markus, G. (2003) 'The paradoxical unity of culture: the arts and the sciences', *Thesis Eleven* 75: 7–24.

Maton, K. (2000) 'Languages of legitimation: the structuring significance for intellectual fields of strategic knowledge claims', *British Journal of Sociology of Education* 21 (2): 147–167.

Mendick, H. (2006) 'Review Symposium of Moore', *British Journal of Sociology of Education* 27 (1): 117–23.

Merton, R.K. (1957) *Social Theory and Social Structure*, New York: Free Press.

Merton, R.K. (1973) *The Sociology of Science: Theoretical and Empirical Investigations*, Chicago: University of Chicago Press.

Messer-Davidow, E. Shumway, D. and Sylan, D. (1993) *Knowledges: Historical and Critical Studies in Disciplinarity*, Charlottesville: University of Virginia Press.

Michelson, E. (2004) 'On trust, desire and the sacred: a response to Johann Muller's "Reclaiming Knowledge"', *Journal of Education* 32: 7–30.

Mills, C. (1998) 'Alternative epistemologies', in Alcoff, L.A. (ed.) *Epistemology: the Big Questions*, Oxford: Blackwell.

Moll, L. (1990) (ed.) *Vygotsky and Education*, Cambridge: Cambridge University Press.

Moore, A. (2006) (ed.) *Schooling, Society and Curriculum*, London: Routledge.

Moore, R. (2000) 'For knowledge: tradition, progressivism and progress in education – reconstructing the curriculum debate', *Cambridge Journal of Education* 30: 17–36.

Moore, R. (2004) *Education and Society*, London: Polity.

Moore, R. and Muller, J. (1999) 'The discourse of "voice" and the problem of knowledge and identity in the sociology of education', *British Journal of Sociology of Education* 20: 189–206.

Moore, R. and Maton, K. (2001) 'Founding the sociology of knowledge: Basil Bernstein, epistemic fields and the epistemic device', in Morais, A., Neves, I., Davies, B. and Daniels, H. (eds), *Towards a Sociology of Pedagogy*, New York: Peter Lang.

Moore, R. and Young, M. (2001) 'Knowledge and the curriculum in the sociology of education; towards a reconceptualisation', *British Journal of Sociology of Education* 22 (4): 445–61.

Moore, R. and Muller, J. (2002) 'The growth of knowledge and the discursive gap', *British Journal of Sociology of Education* 23 (4).

Muller, J. (2000) *Reclaiming Knowledge: Social Theory, Curriculum and Education Policy*, London: Routledge Falmer.

Muller, J. (2006) 'On the shoulders of giants: verticality of knowledge and the school curriculum', in Moore. R *et al.* (ed.) *Knowledge Power and Reform*, London: Routledge.

Muller, J. (2007) 'On splitting hairs: hierarchy, knowledge and the school curriculum', in Christie, F. and Martin, J.R. (eds) *Language, Knowledge and Pedagogy: Functional and Sociological Perspectives*, Sydney: Continuum Press.

Nash, R. (2005) 'The cognitive habitus: its place in a realist account of inequality/difference', *British Journal of Sociology of Education* 26 (5): 599.

National Committee of Enquiry into Higher Education (1997) *Higher Education in a Learning Society*, London: Stationery Office.

Needham (1970) *Introduction to Durkheim and Mauss*.

Nozaki, Y. (2006) 'Riding the tensions critically: ideology, power/knowledge, and curriculum making, in Weiss, L., McCarthy, C. and Dimitriadis, G. (eds) *Ideology, Curriculum and the New Sociology of Education*, New York and London: Routledge.

O'Halloran, K.L. (2006) 'Mathematical and scientific knowledge: a systematic functional multimodal grammatical approach', in Christie, F. and Martin, J.R. (eds) *Language, Knowledge and Pedagogy: Functional and Sociological Perspectives*, Sydney: Continuum Press.

Ollman, B. (1976) *Alienation: Marx's Conception of Man in Capitalist Society*, Cambridge: Cambridge University Press.

Papineau, D. (ed.) (1996) *The Philosophy of Science*, Oxford: Oxford University Press.

Payne, J. (2000) 'Review of "The Curriculum of the Future"', *British Journal of Sociology of Education* 21 (3): 457–463.

Pelz, D. (1996) 'Ken Mannheim and the sociology of scientific knowledge: towards a new agenda', *Sociological Theory*, 14 (1): 30–48.

Penrose, R. (2005) *The Road To Reality*, London: Vintage Books.

Piore, M. and Sabel, C. (1984) *The Second Industrial Divide*, New York: Basic Books.

Polanyi, M. (1962) *The Republic of Science*, Chicago: Roosevelt University.

Power, S., Aggleton, P., Brannen, J., Brown, A., L Chisholm, L. and Mace J. (eds) (2001) *A Tribute to Basil Bernstein 1924–2000*, London: Institute of Education, University of London.

Pring, R. (1972) 'Knowledge out of control', *Education for Teaching* 89 (2): 19–28.

Qualifications and Curriculum Authority (1999) *Developing Provision for Curriculum 2000*, London: QCA.

Raffe, D. (1992) *Modularisation in Initial Vocational Training: Recent Developments in Six European Countries*, Edinburgh: Centre for Educational Sociology, University of Edinburgh.

Raffe, D., Howieson, C. and Tinklin, T. (2007 forthcoming) 'The impact of a unified curriculum and qualifications system: the Higher Still reform of post-16 Education in Scotland', *British Educational Research Journal* 33 (4).

Raggatt, P. and Williams, S. (1999) *Governments, Markets and Vocational Qualifications: an Anatomy of Policy*, Brighton: Falmer.

Reich, R. (1991) *The Work of Nations*, London: Heinemann.

Rowlands, S. (2000) 'Turning Vygotsky on His Head: Vygotsky' 'Scientifically Based Method' and the Socioculturalist's 'Social Other', *Science and Education* 9 (39): 553 –75.

Royal Society of Arts (1998) *Redefining Work: An RSA Initiative*, London: RSA.

RSA (2003) *Opening Minds: Education for the 21st Century*, London: Royal Society of Arts.

Rytina, J.H. and Loomis, C.P. (1970) 'Marxist dialectic and pragmatism: power as knowledge', *American Sociological Review* 35 (3): 308–318.

Sassoon, A. (1988) *Gramsci's Politics*, Minneapolis: University of Minnesota Press.

Schmaus, W. (1994) *Durkheim's Philosophy of Science and the Sociology of Knowledge*, Chicago: Chicago University Press.

Scott P. (2000) *Higher Education Reformed*, London: Falmer Press.

Scruton, R. (1991) 'The myth of cultural relativism', in Moore, R. and Ozga, J. (eds) *Curriculum Policy*, Oxford: Pergamon/Open University.

Selwyn, N. and Young, M. (2007) 'Rethinking schools and technology', London Knowledge Lab Seminar Series, Occasional Paper 1.

Shapin, S. (1994) *A Social History of Truth: Civility and Science in 17th Century England*, Chicago: University of Chicago Press.

Sokal, A. (2003) *Intellectual Impostures: Postmodern Philosophers' Abuse of Science*, London: Profile Books.

Tomlinson, M. (2004) *14–19 Curriculum and Qualifications Reform*, London: DfES Publications.

Toulmin, S. (1996) 'Knowledge as shared procedures', in Engestrom, Y., Mietennen, R. and Punamaki, R. (ed.) *Perpsectives on Activity Theory*, Cambridge: Cambridge University Press.

Tuomi-Grohn, T. and Engestrom, Y. (2003) *Between School and Work: New Perspectives on Transfer and Boundary-crossing*, Oxford: Pergamon.

Usher, R. and Edwards, R. (1994) *Post Modernism and Education*, London: Routledge.

Valery, P. (1991 Letters to Gide, 72) *Selected Writings of Paul Valery*, Paris: New Directions.

Valery, P. (1941) *Selected Writings of Paul Valery*, Paris: New Directions.

Verene, D.P. (1969) 'Kant, Hegel, and Cassirer: the origins of the philosophy of symbolic forms', *Journal of the History of Ideas* 30 (1): 33–46.

Vygotsky, L.S. (1962) *Thought and Language*, Cambridge, MA: MIT Press.

Vygotsky, L.S. (1987) *The Collected Works of L.S. Vygotsky* (Volume 1), (eds R. Reiber and A.S. Carton), New York and London: Plenum Press.

Walkerdine, V. (1988) *The Mastery of Reason: Cognitive Development and the Production of Rationality*, London: Routledge.

Ward, S. (1996) *Reconfiguring Truth*, Lanham, MD: Rowman and Littlefield.

Ward, S. (1997) 'Being objective about objectivity: the ironies of standpoint epistemological critiques of science', *Sociology* 31: 773–91.

Wardekker, W. (1998) 'Scientific concepts and reflection', *Mind, Culture and Activity*, 5 (2): 143–53.

Weber, M. (1948) 'Science as a vocation' and 'Politics as a vocation', in Gerth, H. and Mills, C.W. (eds) *Max Weber: Essays in Sociology*, London: Routledge and Kegan Paul.

Weelahan, L. (2007 forthcoming) 'How competency-based training locks the working class out of powerful knowledge: a modified Bernsteinian analysis', *British Journal of Sociology of Education*.

Weiner, M.J. (1981) *English Culture and the Decline of the Industrial Spirit*, Cambridge: Cambridge University Press.

Weiss. L. *et al.* (2006) 'Ideology, critique and the new sociology of education: revisiting the work of Michael Apple', London and New York: Routledge.

Wellens, J. (1970) 'The anti-intellectual tradition in the west', in Musgrave, P. (ed.) *Sociology, History and Education*, London: Methuen.

Wertsch, J.V. (1990) 'The voice of rationality in a socio-cultural approach to the mind', in Moll, L. (ed.) *Vygotsky and Education*, Cambridge: Cambridge University Press.

Whitty, G. (1985) *Sociology and School Knowledge: Curriculum Theory, Research and Politics*, London: Methuen.

Whitty, G. and Young, M. (eds) (1976) *Society, State and Schooling*, Brighton: Falmer Press.

Wilkinson, R. (1970) 'The gentleman ideal and the maintenance of a political elite', in Musgrave, P. (ed.) *Sociology, History and Education*, London: Methuen.

Williams, B. (2002) *Truth and Truthfulness: An Essay in Genealogy*, Princeton: Princeton University Press.

Williams, R. (1961) *The Long Revolution*, London: Chatto and Windus.

Williamson, J. (2002) 'Forward by degrees with higher education funding', *Observer*, 6 August.

Willis, P. (1977) *Learning to Labour*, England: Saxon House.

Wolf, A. (1995) *Competence-based Assessment*, London, Open University Press.

Woodhead, C. (2001) 'Cranks, claptrap and cowardice', *Telegraph online*, 1 March. <http://www.telegraph.co.uk/arts/main.jhtml?xml=/arts/2001/03/02/tlwood02.xml> (accessed July 2007)

Woodhead, C. (2002) *Class War*, London: Little, Brown.

Woodhead, C. (2004) *How to Lower School Standards: Mike Tomlinson's Modest Proposal*, London: Politeia.

Worsley, P. (1956) 'Durkheim's social theory of knowledge', *Sociological Review* 4 (1): 47–62.

Young, M. (ed.) (1971) *Knowledge and Control: New Directions for the Sociology of Education*, London: Collier Macmillan.

Young, M. (1998) *The Curriculum of the Future*, London: Falmer Press.

Young, M. (1999) 'Knowledge, learning and the curriculum of the future', *British Educational Research Journal* 25 (4): 463–477.

Young, M. (2000) 'Bringing knowledge back in: a curriculum for lifelong learning', in Hodgson, A. (ed.) *Policies, Politics and the Future of Lifelong Learning*, London: Kogan Page.

Young, M. (2005) *National Qualifications Frameworks: Their Feasibility for Effective Implementation in Developing Countries*, Geneva: International Labour Office.

Young, M. and Whitty, G. (eds) (1977) *Explorations in the Politics of School Knowledge*, Driffield, Yorks: Nafferton Books.

Young, M. and Spours, K. (1998) '14–19 education: legacy, opportunities and challenges', *Oxford Review of Education*, 24 (1): 83–99.

Young, M. and Gamble, J. (eds) (2006) *Knowledge, Curriculum and Qualifications for South African Further Education*, Pretoria: HSRC Press.

Young, M. and Muller, J. (2007) 'Truth and Truthfulness in the sociology of educational knowledge', *Theory and Research in Education* 5 (2): 173–203.

Ziman, J. (2000) *Real Science*, Cambridge: Cambridge University Press.

Original sources of previously published papers

With the exception of the Introduction and Chapters 10, 11 and 15, the chapters of this book are revised versions of previously published papers. Chapter 2 is a revised version of a paper originally written with Rob Moore (see below). Chapter 10 draws on material used in a paper written jointly with John Beck (Beck and Young 2005). Chapter 15 was written jointly with Johann Muller, and appears here in its original form.

I am most grateful to my three original co-authors, and to the editors and publishers of the books and journals for permission to draw on material in previously published papers. The original papers on which the chapters draw, or of which they are revised versions, appeared in the following journals and books:

Chapter 1: *British Journal of Sociology of Education* 21 (2000).
Chapter 2: Revised version of Moore, R. and Young, M. (2001) 'Knowledge and the curriculum in the sociology of education; towards a reconceptualisation', *British Journal of Sociology of Education* 22 (4).
Chapter 3: *London Education Review* 1 (2) (2003).
Chapter 4: *Critical Education Studies* 1 (1) (2007).
Chapter 5: Lauder, H., Brown. P., Dillabough, J-A. and Halsey, A.H. (eds) *Education, Globalization and Social Change*, Oxford: Oxford University Press.
Chapter 6: Moore, Alex (ed.), *Schooling, Society and Curriculum*, London: Routledge.
Chapter 7: *International Studies in Sociology of Education* 14 (1) (2004).
Chapter 8: Evans, K., Hodkinson, P. and Unwin, L. (eds) *Working to Learn*, London: Kogan Page.
Chapter 9: Fuller, A., Rainbird, H. and Munro, A. (eds) *Workplace Learning in Context*, London: Taylor and Francis.
Chapter 10: Not previously published, but draws on some material used in Beck and Young (2005).
Chapter 11: Not previously published in English. The chapter is based on a keynote address to the Netherlands Conference of Sociologists of Education, November 2005.
Chapter 12: *Perspectives in Education*, 24 (3) (2006).

Chapter 13: Andersson, P. and Harris, J. (eds) (2006) *Retheorising the Recognition of Prior Experiential Learning*, Leicester: NIACE.

Chapter 14: Journal of Education, 36 (September 2005).

Chapter 15: (with Johann Muller) Theory and Research in Education, 4 (2) (2007).

Chapter 16: Power, S. (ed.) (2001) *A Tribute to Basil Bernstein 1924–2000*, London: University of London (Institute of Education).

Index

242 *Index*